The
Haunted
Reader
AND SYLVIA PLATH

The
Haunted
Reader

AND *SYLVIA PLATH*

GAIL CROWTHER

FONTHILL

Fonthill Media Language Policy

Fonthill Media publishes in the international English language market. One language edition is published worldwide. As there are minor differences in spelling and presentation, especially with regard to American English and British English, a policy is necessary to define which form of English to use. The Fonthill Policy is to use the form of English native to the author. Gail Crowther was born and educated in the United Kingdom; therefore British English has been adopted in this publication.

Fonthill Media Limited
Fonthill Media LLC
www.fonthillmedia.com
office@fonthillmedia.com

First published in the United Kingdom and the United States of America 2017

British Library Cataloguing in Publication Data:
A catalogue record for this book is available from the British Library

ISBN 978-1-78155-547-7

Typeset in 10pt on 13pt Sabon
Printed and bound by CPI Group (UK) Ltd, Croydon, CR0 4YY

'Your Blue Hour—For Sylvia Plath, Fitzroy Road, 1963'

In your blue hour, before the world awoke,
You were pristine, shining white, sharp and straight as an arrow.
You wrote like never before
Like pen and paper were invented just for you
Just for these hours.
You wrote like never before.
Oh yes these poems will make your name.
Forged in fierce flames, furious, fighting, frightened genius.
Giving birth to immortal verse
In that blue hour.

In your blue hour, driven by freezing fever,
You turned inside-out, spewing your ghosts across the pages.
Creating a new art.
Never before. Never since. Never never again.
The moon hid behind a cloud, awed and afraid, watching you
Creating a new art.
Oh yes you have it in you.
Sitting alone, abandoned, adrift in an abyss apart.
Giving birth to immortal verse
In that blue hour.

In your blue hour, the colour soothed you,
Moved you to say the unsayable, write the unwriteable.
Red would have hurt you.
Ghostly, he places a red tulip beside you.
But the tulip turns to dust. You are too powerful for it.
Red would have hurt you.
Oh yes you are writing the best poems of your life.
In the worst winter weeks when weather wounds without warmth.
Giving birth to immortal verse
In that blue hour.

But later:

In your blue hour, you paced and paced.
Right on the edge, did you mean to do it?
Making your kitchen your Auschwitz.
You did it too exceptionally well this time.
You gambled your life and you lost—or did you win?
Making your kitchen your Auschwitz.
Oh yes you did it so it felt real. It was real.
Betrayed, bereft, beaten black blue, burnt to the bare bones.
Giving birth to immortal verse
Wasn't enough to keep you from dying
In that blue hour.

I have read your daughter's poem "Readers,"
And I have felt ashamed.
I have read your husband's poem "The Dogs Are Eating Your Mother,"
And I have felt ashamed.
Empathy, connections, dreams, love, aching pain for you.
All of this I feel and yet: what of it?
Strip it bare and all that remains is this:
I am a reader. I am a dog.

But still
I will
Still I will sing this song:

In your blue hour, when pain shrank you to nothing
You created your most terrifying art ever: your death.
No Lady Lazarus you, no rising from the ashes this time.
But I fancy your blue hour held its arms out to you –
Held you close, calmed you, soothed you, made you safe.
I see it cradling you and carrying you to a beautiful place.
Not lying in your chamber, your head in the oven –
But riding Ariel bareback.
Free, joyful, tossing your mane, your jewel eyes glittering.

This is what I sing for you
In that blue hour.

Morney Wilson

Sylvia Plath's grave in Heptonstall, West Yorkshire. (*Gail Crowther*)

Acknowledgements

Thank you to my respondents for trusting me with their narratives: Peter, Sonia, Florian, Anna, Kiki, Megan, and Morney. I would like to add a special mention for Morney, who is no longer with us, but left behind beautiful poems, one of which opens this book. Sincere thanks to Carolyn Brown for her permission to reproduce Morney's work.

A special thanks goes to Peter K. Steinberg, on a professional and personal level, especially for his enthusiasm for this research, our discussion of ideas, his feedback, proof reading, and his generosity in sharing information.

Thanks also go to Carole and Ces Crowther, Joanne and Peter Whiteside, Rob Sanders, and Elizabeth and William Sigmund. Additionally, Lynne Pearce and Yoke Sum Wong for supervising this research in its PhD incarnation and Hilary Hinds, Catherine Spooner and Danielle Fuller for further academic support. Thanks also to Richard Larschan for permission to reproduce Plath's caduceus, and Tony Cockayne for permission to reproduce *For Sivvy*; to Jay Slater at Fonthill Media for encouragement and efficiency, and Jamie Hardwick for editing. Special thanks to Kate McNicholas Smith, Kevin Cummins, and George.

All photographs © to the author Gail Crowther except: the images of Plath's caduceus wood carvings © Richard Larschan; Sonia's hands and potholder © Sonia Flur; Plath's hair © Peter K Steinberg; 'For Sivvie' © Anthony Cockayne.

CONTENTS

Introduction

Prologue

The last time I visited the grave of Sylvia Plath, there was snow on the ground. My footprints left a ghostly trail across the churchyard, in the shadow of the bell tower and the trees. Plath's grave was covered with pebbles and pennies, tangerines, avocados, mangoes, beads, candles, and small daffodils. People had come here to lay tributes to a writer, perhaps the writer who made a significant difference in their lives. As I lay my red tulips among the snow, I wondered: why was I paying this visit? I did not know this person; she had died years before I was born. I wondered why people had left tributes and messages to a person that they also perhaps had never known. What was I doing offering tulips in the snow?

Who is 'Sylvia Plath'? Soap opera, blame, and legacy

> The passion between reader and writer is born from writing, conducted through writing, sustained by writing.[1]

This books aims to explore the role of Sylvia Plath in the life of her readers. As such, what follows is really only indirectly about Plath. She is a spectral figure that seeps from the pages of her texts and imbues places, images, objects, and things with her presence. For some readers, this presence enters their lives and stays there, captured and haunted as they are by this figure of Plath. This the first piece of primary research to be carried out on reader-fans of Plath. A plethora of books exist dealing with the biography of Plath and the textual analysis of Plath; however, no studies until now have attempted to explore what Plath means to her readers or how they use this relationship in their day-to-day lives.[2] Why do certain readers love Plath so? What is it about her that creates such a strong attachment between reader and writer? What are the stories that people tell about the role that Plath plays in their lives? It is these stories that interest me the most—how and why this spectral figure of 'Sylvia Plath' becomes so important.

A seminal work discussing the figure of a ghostly Plath present in our culture is *The Haunting of Sylvia Plath* by Jacqueline Rose. This book formed the starting point for my own research as Rose states in her first sentence: 'Sylvia Plath haunts our culture'.[3] Rose works from the assumption that whenever she speaks about Plath (and her husband, Ted Hughes), 'I am never talking of real people, but of textual entities (Y and X) whose more than real reality, I will be arguing, goes beyond them to encirculate us all'.[4] In other words, Rose is not claiming access to any 'authentic' historical figures and this viewpoint will be adopted within this book. For Rose, it is not Plath herself that is the spectral presence:

> What we are dealing with is, obviously enough, not Plath herself but her representations, her own writing together with all the other utterances that have come to crowd it—joining in the conversation, as one might say. It is this effigy that haunts the culture.[5]

Rose continues with the claim that this haunting effigy is true of any writer who is no longer alive, but in the case of Plath and her legacy, the quarrels have been so bitter 'it is hardly surprising that at moments it seems as if the effigy, like the earthenware head of her poem, haunts her'.[6] This adds a new level to the haunting—namely, the spectre haunting the spectre. These different levels of haunting are discussed in particular in the first chapter.

Rose 'starts from the assumption that Sylvia Plath is a fantasy' and then proceeds to explore the ways in which this fantasy is created by the writings and utterances, not only of Plath, but of others writing about her.[7] She recounts various texts that comprise Plath's writing, asking 'what is the body of Plath's writing?[8] That is, what is the body that Plath writes?' and begins to examine journals, poems, correspondence, and the editing and presentation of Plath's work.[9]

This led to Rose's now (in)famous dispute with Ted Hughes, which she recounts in her chapter 'The Archive'.[10] She discusses the 'fragility' of the 'literary remains and legacy of Sylvia Plath' and the 'impossibility of reading Plath independently of the frame, the surrounding discourses, through which her writing is presented'.[11, 12] By this, Rose presumably means the wealth of biographical literature and literary criticism that exists around Plath, but also, 'the logic of blame'.[13] Although this book is not about Plath *per se*, what we will see is how this legacy of blame infiltrates my respondents' accounts. Rose calls this the 'soap opera' of Plath's life and one in which those closest to her become entangled.[14] It is therefore important to bear in mind Rose's claim:

> The story of Sylvia Plath seems to have the power to draw everybody who approaches it into its orbit, to make you feel that you somehow belong. The Plath story at once involves you and asks for judgement. It asks you to apportion blame, to parcel out innocence and guilt.[15]

Rose believes it is the anxiety created by this conflict that can be 'productive', for if we 'stay with this anxiety', it will allow us to explore just how uncertain truth can be.[16, 17] Rose describes her book as 'one reading of the work of Sylvia Plath, one part of a story that has clearly not come to an end'.[18] It is at this point where my own research steps in and hopefully continues Rose's story. Once this haunting figure of Sylvia Plath is in circulation, what becomes of her? What do people do with her, and how does she manifest herself in people's lives?

I began with two main questions. First, how and in what ways can the dead return and haunt our culture? Second, once a spectral presence captures our imagination, how does it impact upon our identity formation? I decided to approach these questions by engaging with a number of Plath readers to find out what sort of stories they had to tell about Plath.

Instantly, the term 'reader' seemed inadequate. Some people seemed to be more than readers. There seemed to be something else going on. I wondered whether a more accurate term might be 'fan'. Despite some of the cultural aesthetics used to dismiss words like fandom as somehow being low culture, this was not the reason why I shied away from this term. Likewise, the association with scholarship and solitary practice of reading did not quite seem to explain what was occurring. In fact, it seemed an odd hybrid of the two, therefore throughout this book, my respondents are referred to as 'reader-fans'. This seems to embody both the active engagement of reading a text and the subsequent relationship that develops with the writer from this.

In what ways do reader-fans narrate Plath into their lives? If Plath is a ghost-like figure in our culture, how do people encounter her? Certainly, Rose establishes Plath as a spectral presence, but this research aims to extend Rose's thinking into what happens to this spectral presence when it comes into contact with other people. In Chapter One, the particular focus is on the role and impact of Plath's own texts. What happened the first time our reader-fans encountered Plath? Why was it such a life-changing moment for them? In Chapter Two, I explore the notion of doubling, asking why some reader-fans feel they are just like Plath and why this might be. Chapter Three looks in some detail at places relating to Plath that have become sites of pilgrimage, such as her old homes, her grave, and places that she wrote about. The impact of photographs that exist of Plath is explored in Chapter Four. Finally, in Chapter Five, I discuss what happens when reader-fans come into contact with objects that belonged to, or are associated with, Plath. All of these chapters begin with theory which is then followed by the reader-fans' stories. If ghosts are some sort of social negotiator between the past and present, in what ways does Plath's haunting manifest itself? Boundaries leak and seep, and ghosts are present everywhere—in texts, in places, in books and spaces.

I was faced with the problem of how to collect and analyse these sorts of narratives. There were ethical issues, not to mention practical ones. The obvious method to gather information seemed to be unstructured interviews, in which I could talk at length to respondents about their relationship and attachment to Sylvia Plath. However, this method felt too prescriptively directed by the researcher. I decided I wanted a method that would involve the least amount of interference from me in the creation of the data. This would hopefully ensure that respondents could narrate their own sense of self without too much exterior influence. Obviously, what happened to the data afterwards would involve my direct intervention, but it seemed important to me that respondents were allowed as much freedom as possible to decide how to narrate their attachments and desires. This approach, however, is not without its challenges.

Bearing this in mind, I settled upon a method which I have called 'creative autobiography' which requires a minimum amount of interference from the researcher. While I was keen to draw on personal experience suggested by the genre of autobiography, I was less convinced by the accuracy or reliability of self-narration. The 'creative' aspect of autobiography, both in the construction of the self and the medium in which it can present itself (writing, art, music, etc.), needed to be acknowledged somewhere in my method choice, hence the 'creative' autobiography. However, what did emerge, despite my requests for any medium of autobiography from respondents, was the predominance of writing as the main form of expression. This could be linked to my respondents' own set of expectations suggested by the genre of autobiography, but it may also be related to their level of comfort within a particular medium. The nature of their attachment is to a writer, thereby suggesting a medium which they enjoy, and are involved in on some level.

Having made these decisions regarding methodology, I then requested from my respondents a piece (or pieces) of autobiography detailing their thoughts and feelings about their relationship with Sylvia Plath (more later on actually finding my respondents). I did not prescribe any categories or subjects to be discussed, but aimed to allow any potential respondent to engage in a free flow of thoughts and ideas. By approaching the data as autobiography, it was already assumed that a certain level of fictionalisation would have occurred along with the choices and selections that accompany any autobiographical production. I do not refer to my respondents' work, then, as some sort of empirical data, but as stories—stories of their lives that they have chosen to tell and share.

> We all tell stories about our lives, both to ourselves and others; and it is through such stories we make sense of our selves, of the world, and of our relationship to others. Stories, or narratives, are a means by which people make sense of, understand, and live their lives.[19]

Since Sylvia Plath plays such a pivotal role in many of her reader-fans' lives, it made sense to explore how they narrated this attachment.

Some of the material is sensitive and requires delicate handling, while some is contradictory and complex. Faced with these issues, I decided being as open and transparently self-reflexive as possible may at least help reduce my role as the 'interfering' researcher. Each time I probe beneath the surface to question a respondent's account, I highlight that this is what I am doing, and that what I am offering is simply one of a number of readings. Perhaps by being as explicit as possible about my own assumptions, I can start to unravel some of the complex interplay of power shifts between researcher and respondent. Whether I have succeeded in doing justice to these stories can best be judged by how the reader feels when reading the following chapters.

Access is another issue. Locating Plath reader-fans is perhaps not so difficult, especially when you are one yourself, and numerous online forums, blogs, and websites were my starting point for making contact with people. The main source initially for this was The Sylvia Plath Forum established and maintained by Elaine Connell. Elaine sadly died in 2007, but her legacy of ten years of archives on her website became my starting point for locating Plath reader-fans. There were many false starts to this process, but finally, I managed to identify four committed reader-fans willing to share their feelings about Plath and who made it very clear to me that this was an important story to tell. Luckily, a timely conference, the Sylvia Plath 75th Year Symposium held at Oxford University, led to more meetings with people who either knew Plath or were dedicated reader-fans of her work and provided me with three more respondents.

It was precisely the degree of commitment to Plath that distinguished all these respondents; although I believe that this reduced the sample size, it was the nature of the longer narratives of the pivotal role Plath played in readers' lives that seemed the more suitable method to use for my research. This allowed me to focus in more depth upon those reader-fans who were, and remained, especially attached to Plath to a much higher degree than the more transitory relationships to her. I received 577 emails from my respondents in total. Some of these were fragmented, simply one or two lines; others had attachments to documents, the largest of which was eighteen pages long. Almost all of this data was in written form and included accounts or poems and journal extracts.

Prior to the collection of data, I had felt a need to inform my respondents that I was not only a Plath reader-fan, but that I would be including my own stories in the book. For Henry Jenkins, any identification between researcher and participants can ease the levels of potential mistrust; in *Textual Poachers*, his study of television fans, Jenkins describes himself as both an 'academic' and 'a fan (who has access to the particular traditions and knowledge of that community)'.[20, 21] While he argues writing as a fan can improve access and trust, it does not excuse the researcher from issues of power, representation, or accountability. In fact, becoming less detached and identifying yourself as a fan surely increases the issues of accountability in the researcher, since there is greater potential for misrepresentation and feelings of betrayal by the respondents. Locating my own data involved exploring old journals, pieces of writing, and letters, then subjecting these to the same selection process as above. Within academia, this emotional engagement can be frowned upon. There is a school of thought that believes the researcher should stay as objective as possible, should not 'embarrass' themselves with personal revelations. I, on the other hand, come from a firm feminist background that not only believes in, but actively promotes, the use of 'I' in academic writing. I believe that, as feminists, we should write about our own lives because that is truly how we come to learn about the lived experiences of a wide range of people.

I strongly believe that the text of people's life stories are not to be tampered with and, beyond the inevitable selection process, I have not changed the materials that have been sent to me. Any grammatical inconsistencies or awkward turns of phrase have been left to keep the voices of their authors intact, with the exception of two respondents who asked me to correct their English (since this was not their first language).

Over the years, and across a range of media and genres, Plath reader-fans have been given a rough time. If not 'ranting feminists' or 'loonies', they have typically been seen as 'depressive maniacs' who all want to kill themselves. Plath has even been referred to colloquially as 'The Patron Saint of Women Who Wear Black'. Readers of Plath who became interested in her life, or scholars wishing to write about her, were referred to by Olwyn Hughes as 'cultists'.[22] These depictions are as insulting to Sylvia Plath as they are to her reader-fans. Perhaps Plath's story and the discourses surrounding it—as we have seen in Rose, what she called the 'soap opera' of Plath's life—have encouraged such polarised depictions, but this does not mean that they are fair or accurate.[23] This book aims to reinstate the voice of those reader-fans who have every right to read and comment on what Plath means to them in their day-to-day lives.

Introducing the participants

The first drafts of this research began by using the respondents' full names. I shifted to using surnames before finally settling upon first names. Some respondents chose to change their names for publication given the personal nature of their disclosures. It is hoped that you, as a reader, will grow familiar with their names and voices as you read through the chapters that ensue. However, as an initial introduction, these are the people whose stories you are about to read:

Peter. 40s. Male. American. Prolific Plath scholar. Runs and maintains a website and a blog and has published many articles and a biography of Plath. Works as a digital archivist.
Anna. 30s. Female. Swedish. Discovered Sylvia Plath in her early twenties. Doctoral student.
Morney. 40s. Female. British. Published poet and writer.
Megan. 20s-30s. Female. British. Graduate student.
Kiki. 40s. Female. American. Lives in Detroit, occupation unknown, but travels much with work.
Sonia. 40s. Female. Swedish. Writer. Has one son, partner of Florian.
Florian. 40s. Male. Swedish. Writer and works in Swedish television. Has four children, partner of Sonia.

Reading Clusters

The interdisciplinary nature of this project could be mapped out by the use of library spaces, authors, and the disciplines employed. I found myself reading books from sociology, women's studies, literature, literary criticism, psychology, cultural studies, tourism, mobilities, German, French, art, photography, religion, and philosophy. The reading for this project can be mostly clustered into scholarship on psychoanalysis, haunting, fandom scholarship, and theories of authorship and reception. These areas of scholarship helped me to formulate a theoretical framework with which to approach my data. The first two chapters focus heavily on Freud and psychoanalysis. The following three chapters use theory that deals with place, photographs and the special nature of the object. As with Rose, I offer this as one possible reading of the relationship between a reader and a writer; other theories would almost certainly offer a different emphasis.

However, to refer to these reading areas as 'clusters' perhaps gives the mistaken view that they did not inform each other. Indeed, the entanglements between these different theoretical approaches were fascinating and necessary;

a complex web of connectivities and echoes. Trying to extricate them in order to discuss them seems to mistakenly simplify the process and it is hoped that as a reader you will see the complexities that unfurl throughout the chapters to come.

This book, then, began with a poem by Morney Wilson called 'Your Blue Hour'. Morney describes this poem as her 'long tribute to Sylvia that in the end captured everything I wanted to say'. She speculates about the beautiful place that Plath was carried to in that blue hour. But, as this book aims to show, 'Sylvia Plath' did not really go anywhere at all. She has been with us all the time.

Plath graffiti in Hebden Bridge, West Yorkshire. (*Gail Crowther*)

1

Encounter

One of the key questions for this book is how and in what ways can the dead return? We may well ask who or what are the dead? Helene Cixous says, 'I like the dead, they are the door keepers who while closing one side give way to the other'.[1] I like the dead too. Cixous is right; the dead do open doors, but they are doors that can swing either way. The dead can come back to us just as we, eventually, pass into being the dead.

Sylvia Plath discusses this two-way door between the dead and the living in her poem 'All the Dead Dears'.

> *All the long gone darlings: they*
> *Get back, though, soon,*
> *Soon: be it by wakes, weddings,*
> *Childbirths or a family barbeque:*
> *Any touch, taste, tang's*
> *Fit for those outlaws to ride home on,*
>
> *And to sanctuary: usurping the armchair*
> *Between tick*
> *And tack of the clock, until we go,*
> *Each skull-and-crossboned Gulliver*
> *Riddled with ghosts, to lie*
> *Deadlocked with them, taking root as cradles rock.*[2]

There is a sensuality about the return of the dead here, 'any touch, taste, tang', and the implication is that ghosts can return quite easily—almost any excuse is enough for them to materialise. Then, they stay with us, 'usurping the armchair' until we ourselves join them, 'lie' with them, 'Riddled with ghosts'. There is no barrier here, but rather a blurry intricacy in which the living and the dead become 'Deadlocked' in a sort of two-way intersection between life and death.

This blurriness is a complicated idea and is explored further by Derrida, who claims that in mourning, 'we weep precisely over what happens to us when everything is entrusted to the sole memory that is "in me" or "in us"'.[3] In other words, what Derrida appears to be suggesting here is that the dead are only 'with us' in so much as they are 'in us'. This, he argues, is how they return. Perhaps, it is no surprise that when faced with loss, we internalise the person in some way via memories, thoughts or daydreaming. In this sense, the lost person does return to us, both as part of our own sense of self, but curiously as something exterior to us as well.

Derrida sees this relationship as pretty much one-way: 'it is only "in us" that the dead may speak ... it is only by speaking of or as the dead that we can keep them alive'.[4] For Derrida, the dead only have a voice if we give them one, if we care to remember them. I also wonder if this odd relationship that occurs between the living and the dead allows room for a quite different type of haunting. In addition to the haunted interiority of remembrance, there appears to be some kind of haunted exteriority of production. This, I believe, is when ghosts are not merely alive through remembrance, but alive through their very presence as a transformative potential within our lives; we do not simply remember ghosts and choose to give them a voice, but rather they impact directly on our lives, transforming the sort of person we may be, guiding our choices, bringing about positive changes and influencing decisions that we may make.[5] This transformative potential implies that the play between the living and dead may not be quite such the one-way occurrence described by Derrida. Certainly, this appears to be the case in the stories that you are about to read.

In fact, this whole book aims to demonstrate that the nature of communication taking place between the living and the dead is neither one-way nor restricted to an interiority. The dead, it appears, can return to us in many ways via imagination, places, texts, images, and objects. Certainly, ghosts require a space to return. Castricano argues haunting requires an 'inside' and it is therefore no coincidence that the word 'haunting' is etymologically bound to that of the word house.[6] She word-plays with this interiority since, for her, haunting is always the haunting of either a house or a space 'since space is understood as that which houses'.[7] The creation then of an inside, a place for haunting, is essential. What then we appear to be creating is a space for something that is neither quite dead nor fully alive.

Lynne Pearce discusses this not-quite-dead state in *Romance Writing*. Rather than seeing death as defined by a moment of freezing, it is defined by 'a moment of infinite deferral'.[8] In her discussion of nineteenth-century literature and culture, Pearce argues that Victorian sensibilities became invested in keeping the dead alive for as long as possible. This initially involved the belief in an afterlife and rituals surrounding the 'body' of the corpse and the *memento mori* taken.

Elizabeth Hallam and Jenny Hockey argue that 'material objects evoke the dead'; indeed, Victorian culture drew on a number of beliefs and rituals to evoke and, I would argue, invoke the dead.[9] The removal of hair from the corpse to be plaited into rings and pieces of jewellery worn by mourners was a way of retaining something physical. But, Pearce argues, as the century progressed, this belief in an afterlife became internalised, a 'move towards an acknowledgement that what is haunted is not the world but the human consciousness', that haunted interiority that Derrida describes. But what of this space created for haunting?[10] Could it be that there is a spectral return both in the mind and in the world? This book will argue that certainly the haunting of the human consciousness is a powerful event, but that ghosts do not stay contained. They seep out and they seep into wherever there is space for them.

> *Is my life so intriguing?*
> *Is it for this you widen your eye-rings?*[11]

I've had author obsessions before. But I keep returning to Plath. (Anna)

Plath is everywhere I've been and everywhere I go. (Peter)

As previously discussed, Rose argues that Sylvia Plath haunts our culture, a spectral figure who refuses to die. I will explore the notion that Plath is not an unwelcome ghost, but actively evoked by her reader-fans via the complex play and dynamics of the reader-author relationship.

An early question that we must ask is why Plath? This is a pertinent question, and one which is hopefully addressed throughout this book in direct relation to the respondents. We could equally ask if any other person would fascinate us so; why, for my respondents, Sylvia Plath and not Anne Sexton or Virginia Woolf? What is it about a particular presence or personality that captures our imagination?

I will begin in this first chapter then, by highlighting how readers may initially establish a relationship with different types of text, and then explore how this relationship moves from the text, to the narrator, to the author.

I am a ghost and as far as I know I haven't even died[12]

Let us return to the space we discussed at the beginning of this chapter, to the space between the living and the dead. If the dead can come back, then what might they have to say to us and why would we be drawn to their message?

For the reader-fans of Plath, it is initially the text that draws them in, and with Plath, there are many differing types of text: poems, novel, stories, journals, drawings, and letters. The speaker within these texts changes; Wayne Booth refers to this as the 'implied author', for 'the author can to some extent choose his [*sic.*] disguises but he can never choose to disappear'.[13] In other words, for Booth, the 'real' author is represented by this substitute, implied author, often 'designated as the author's second self'.[14] According to Booth, when we read a poem by Sylvia Plath, we are not reading the voice of the historical Sylvia Plath, but the implied authorial voice she has chosen to adopt. He refers to the relationship between these two voices as 'psychologically complex' and in need of more research, but at the very least he says it is fair to claim that the 'real' author and the implied author need not be, and often are not, identical.[15]

While accepting Booth's distinction, I am nevertheless wary of his terminology. 'Real' author suggests some claim to authenticity—a fixed, stable figure that can be accessed. Even if we were able to unravel the psychologically complex relationship between the historical figure of the author and the implied author, we are still unlikely to be able to make any great or certain claims about this so called 'real' author. For this reason, this book will use the term 'historical' figure or author to indicate that figure of Plath who stands 'outside' of the narrative text.

We see, from Booth's comment, another space emerging between the historical figure of the author and the 'second self' that they choose to present (the 'implied author'). For Plath, this voice differs from poem to poem. In her novel, *The Bell Jar*, the implied author lets her character Esther Greenwood direct the narration; although as Booth informs us, the presence of an author becomes obvious every time they slip in and out of a character's mind.[16] The notion of the role of the author is more complex than this, especially when asking the pertinent question of what exactly the author is, but these are issues and arguments that will be revisited in Chapter Two.

For the meantime, we have to be aware that the readers of Plath are seemingly initially captured by the voice(s) of the text, not Plath herself. In some cases, the voices of the poems may be mistaken for the figure of the historical Plath, yet it appears to be the words, the fictionalisation of personal events, and the appeal to the reader's understanding and empathy that creates part of the attraction for the reader. If Plath simply wrote self-indulgent poetry that spoke to no one but herself, then we as readers would in some way feel shut out, isolated from the reading experience.

My first encounter with Plath was accidental, dramatic and quite frankly, astonishing. Age 13, for an English lesson at school, we were put into the library for an hour and told to "read a book":

I turn, pondering the books nearest me, which luckily happened to be poetry. Randomly I run my finger along the spines. Sylvia Plath. I pull the book out and open a page. Chance. Luck. Visually this memory is very strong and very cinematic. The library shrinks to the page quickly and suddenly, like an extra fast zoom lens. Tunnel vision. "I am silver and exact". I think these are the words I first read but it could be any of Sylvia's words that jumped out in that straightforward, bold and unflinching voice. I felt that she was talking to me. Who was she? Who was Sylvia Plath? I immediately wanted to know who wrote these words.

This striking sense of a direct relationship with an author had never happened to me before and has never happened to me since. One enduring question is why might this have happened in this way, at this time? Was it something about me or Plath, or was it the way in which her narrator addressed her readers? Certainly, there was an immediate fascination—a reader response that leapt instantly from the poem to the historical figure. What had reading Plath done to me?

Christopher Lasch argues there is a difference between manipulating personal events and simple self-disclosure.[17] For Lasch, the notion of the author straightforwardly unburdening themselves on the reader is a cheap shot which 'appeals not to his [*sic*.] understanding but to his salacious curiosity about the private lives of famous people'.[18] The danger of this sort of 'unburdening' by a writer runs the risk of destroying any mystique about them. If we suddenly know everything, will we continue to care? Possibly, in order for us to remain captured and fascinated readers, the enigma of the author has to remain intact. Perhaps then, Plath was especially adept at creating this enigma around herself—that deceptively open, yet mysterious voice. Surely if an author remains an enigma, then reader-fans are more likely to retain their fascination with her.

This movement that occurs, for the reader, from the text to the historical author is interesting and something we shall explore in more depth as we meet our respondents. It is perhaps no surprise to find that Plath herself was already aware of this distinction—the fine line between the historical author and text and the use of personal material within writing. She explained in a 1962 interview:

I think my poems immediately come out of the sensuous and emotional experiences I have, but I must say, I cannot sympathise with these cries from the heart that are informed by nothing except a needle or a knife or whatever it is. I believe that one should be able to control and manipulate experiences, even the most terrifying like madness, being tortured, this sort of experience, and one should be able to manipulate these experiences with an informed and intelligent mind. I think that personal experience is very important, but certainly it shouldn't be a kind of shut-box and mirror-looking narcissistic experience. I believe it should be relevant and relevant to the larger things, the bigger things such as Hiroshima and Dachau and so on.[19]

It is this 'shut-box experience' that Plath dislikes—the open use of personal material relevant only to the narcissist who writes it. This type of writing is 'mirror-looking', and quite simply 'cries from the heart'. For Plath, it is perfectly acceptable to use personal material ('I think my poems immediately come out of the sensuous and emotional experiences I have'), but it has to be manipulated and made relevant to other things—'larger things'. Could it be this space for the 'larger things' that Plath creates for the reader, which encourages them to be captivated by the text, and then by the historical writer herself?

In *The Rhetorics of Feminism*, Lynne Pearce quotes Adrienne Rich, whose comments eerily echo Plath's own; Rich does use the 'I' persona, but she deplores what Hume George refers to as its 'descent into a mere personal whine'.[20] Rich is clear that what is essential is that 'the reader has a very full sense of the 'I' who is both the subject and the narrator of the text'.[21] This means that, in some form, readers have to be able to connect with the narrator constructed by the implied author. Surely then, becoming aware of the distinction between the 'subject' and the narrator of the text, it is not so great a leap to becoming aware of the historical authorial figure themselves. The shift from text–implied author–narrator (for example, Plath's poetic voice or Esther Greenwood) to the historical figure (Plath) makes sense if we regard it in light of the enigmatic author—that shimmering figure behind the text, concealed and yet almost, but not quite, visible. As we shall see, readers encountering Plath for the first time immediately want to know who the writer actually is, which seems to challenge Barthes and his 'death' of the author.[22]

These distinctions are important to understand why we, as readers, may vault from the voice on the page to the person in the real world, who may or may not still exist. For Wilson, this leap occurs because we become captivated readers, seduced by the words on a page and then seduced by the writer herself.[23] In this leap, we indulge in 'the exchange of books for bodies', despite knowing paradoxically that 'the physical presence of a writer is not necessary in order for a seduction to take place'.[24, 25] How can this be?

It begins to make more sense if we consider the possibility of exchanging books for spectral bodies. Reader-fans of Plath make the leap from her writing to her (non-existent) ghostly body. It is this ghostly nature of the communication between reader and writer that makes me reluctant to use Wilson's word 'seduced', with all of its sexualised connotations. Is this because of the absence of a physical body? I do not think so; as Pearce informs us, many nineteenth-century ghosts, such as those conjured up by Christina Rossetti and Emily Brontë, are highly sexualised.[26] Furthermore, Elisabeth Bronfen discusses how death can freeze a moment: the beautiful and youthful corpse that will never decay, the female corpse that through 'her inaccessibility and impenetrability again poses an insoluble enigma'.[27]

With Plath, her body is seemingly frozen in that moment of death—young, beautiful, talented. It is perhaps her very 'inaccessibility' that creates the fascination—the 'insoluble enigma'; the less we can know, the more we want to know.

Many years after encountering Plath for the first time, I wrote:

> We place dead people in our personal histories, sometimes so closely that it feels as though we merge and suddenly there is a blurring between absence and presence. Sylvia seemed to me to grow in power with the passing of time. I felt so close to her textually that it seemed impossible that she had already been forty years dead.

So perhaps, if we reflect on this type of presence, it is not Plath's body frozen in time that readers are reviving. It is more likely to be the ghostly figure of Plath—the enigma of Plath—that they discover through her work.

This is Wilson's 'literary seduction' in which often 'the reader's love of the writing tends to become indistinguishable from his [*sic.*] love of the writer'.[28] The temptation to mistake the writerly voice for the actual writer is, in some cases, overwhelming and almost all readers cross this, admittedly blurry, boundary at some point. However, this is not the only confusion that seemingly takes place:

> Reading erodes time, not only is it impossible to tell for how long we have been reading, but also it is an effort to recall who we are when we stop. We all indulge in the psychic dissolution of space when we read, the experience of being neither '*here* or *there*', as Michel de Certeau says of the reader straddled between the inside of the book and the outside of the other world, 'one or the other simultaneously inside and outside, dissolving both by mixing them together.[29]

So, curiously, something like time becomes undermined as readers find themselves both here and there. It is in a very real sense that feeling of being lost in a book, of losing track of time. Here, with the act of reading, we can see that not only does time become muddled, but space as well (being both inside and outside a book at the same time). This confusion creates a new category: 'dissolving both by mixing them together'.[30] What we have is an odd melding of categories where it seems something can be more than one thing at the same time, and our tidy predictability swirls into a mix of the familiar and unfamiliar. Meaning is neither fixed nor transparent, and, as we shall see, it is the reader who appears to be the active creator of meaning in any given text.

Up to this point, we have focussed mainly on the possibility of the haunting author. As we discussed at the beginning of this chapter, the dead open doorways that give place to this 'other'; if this other is some form of space in which we can communicate with the dead, then we ourselves as readers become ghostly also. Pearce raises this issue when she discusses where the reader is placed within the text: 'the reader-ghost is destined to continue her wanderings long after the actor ghosts have gone'.[31] This depicts the ghostly reader as the remaining presence in the text. Julian Wolfreys, aware of this spectrality, emphasises the solidness of books and texts: 'Books appear to have a material presence, without which anchoring that such materiality provides, our lives would assume a ghostly condition of impermanence'.[32] It seems that too much spectrality—a ghostly author, the haunted reader—will lead to 'impermanence', a curious choice of word in this discussion of the dead who do not, and are not allowed to, die. There seems little fading away in this whole story. For us, Plath has left her traces; it is only on the surface that she has seemingly gone.

As readers haunting her texts, is it true that we do not allow her departure to happen? Do we willingly conjure up the ghost of Plath and bring her back? For Wolfreys, this amounts to a 'reanimation' of the text by substituting the name of the author as though the 'text were merely a conduit, a spirit medium by which the author communicates'.[33, 34] In many ways, this disputes Derrida's notion that the dead can only speak through us. Wolfreys' view seems to focus much more on the agency of the author and ultimately the presence of the dead:

> The return of the author appears a little ghostly but in speaking of a voice we implicitly assume some presence, form or identity which was once present and which was once the origin of any given text.[35]

The words 'return' and 'presence' appear to indicate that, for Wolfreys, the dead can be uncannily revivified. Is this what reader-fans of Plath are engaging in? Hauntings—they appear to be everywhere.

According to Wilson, writers write because they themselves have 'succumbed to the seductive allure of language'.[36] In fact, she goes as far as to say 'they are driven to write and will risk—or forfeit—their lives for their vocation'.[37] Wilson makes writing sound like a risky business and her choice of the word 'forfeit' is interesting with its connotations of surrender and sacrifice. It becomes even more significant when we consider how, with Plath, we are dealing with a writer who committed suicide. Certainly, Plath found writing an essential part of life:

> ORR: But basically this thing, the writing of poetry, is something which has been a great satisfaction to you in your life is it?

PLATH: Oh, satisfaction! I don't think I could live without it. It's like water or bread, or something absolutely essential to me.[38]

If writing can be some form of sustenance to the author, we might argue the same for the reader, complicating the two way relationship between reader and writer even further. Cixous neatly captures this symbiotic movement and agency of both the reader and the writer:

> When choosing a certain text I am called: I obey the call of certain texts or I am rejected by others. The texts that call me have different voices. But they all have one voice in common, they all have with their differences, a certain music I am attuned to, and that's the secret.[39]

The idea of 'choosing' a text, while at the same time being 'called', illustrates that moment of captivation. What is a particularly delightful thought is that there is something secretive about this process. It is not transparent and open to scrutiny but a little bit mysterious. What Cixous does offer us is the notion that different voices can call us—think of the multiplicity of Plath's voices in poems, novel, journals, and letters—but within this difference there is commonality, the historical figure of Plath herself. The voices this figure adopts appear to have their own (metaphorical) pitch and one which is especially pleasing to our ears.[40] We tune in, just as we tune out of those texts that 'reject' us, that are off pitch and have nothing to say to us.

I am the story which happens to me[41]

Moving from the text to the author does not seem such an irrational step to take when we consider the level of fascination that can occur between a reader-fan and an author; the one can seemingly fold in upon the other in a dynamic interchange. Reasons why a reader may be drawn from a text to a particular author may, to a certain extent, best be explored by drawing upon the models offered to us by psychoanalytic theory, such as the Freudian concepts of identification, mourning, melancholia, and narcissism. Although these psychoanalytic models provide useful frameworks, they have their limitations. Mourning and identification may appear to be linked, but do they necessarily have to be? These models will allow us to start unpacking the complexities of identity formation and address that crucial question: why Plath?

The following pages are necessarily theory heavy. Much time was spent considering how the presentation of these theoretical frameworks could best be presented to the reader in the most accessible way; presenting them via the respondent stories seemed too messy. I felt the theory needed to be in place before the respondents' voices. Since the theories underpin all aspects of the following chapters—doubles, places, images, objects—it felt important to present the theory in its 'original' form, which would allow the reader to understand the context in which the theory was developed and its subsequent use by me in this book. The following sections begin to draw together the complex strands of psychoanalytic theories dealing with identification, loss, mourning, melancholia, and narcissism. Simultaneously, as we work through the theory, we need to keep the same questions at the back of our minds: why are certain readers so fascinated with Plath? What is it about her?

Identity formation and identification

Identity is a slippery subject. Identity formation, by definition, implies an unstable or undeveloped sense of self; thus we necessarily have to see identity formation as an ongoing process, an area of change and flux that is influenced by people and things around us. In particular, our relationships with other people can have a profound effect upon our identity formation. Freud refers to this relationship with others in certain contexts as the process of identification.

For Freud, identification is the 'expression of an emotional tie with another', an 'other' that we wish to be like, whom we idealise and love.[42] However, identification is more than simply feeling some sort of emotional bond with another person; it is a process that can have profound effects upon the subject's sense of self. Identification can manifest itself in the form of wanting to be like another and wanting to have another. Moreover, a common feature of identification is taking the characteristics of, and copying, the idealised love object. The earliest example of identification is manifested, according to Freud, in childhood between father and son:

> A little boy will exhibit a special interest in his father; he would like to grow like him and be like him, and take his place everywhere. We may simply say that he takes his father as his ideal.[43]

We can see how the 'ideal' the child has taken influences the type of person he develops into—'he would like to grow like him and be like him'. In other words, his sense of self will be shaped by the very person he aspires to be.

If, at its most basic level, identification is an emotional tie with another person, then there seems to be no reason why the identificatory figure could not be anyone who has a 'special interest' taken in them. In fact, Freud suggests that 'we can only see that identification endeavours to mould a person's own ego after the fashion of the one that has been taken as a model'.[44]

If this is the case, then it seems possible for reader-fans of Plath to be identifying with the one person they have begun to take a special interest in, namely Plath herself. If Plath is taken as the 'ideal', then we have to consider the ways in which her reader-fans may aspire to be like her or fashion their own ego in light of hers. But, why her? It seems reasonable to suppose that part of this idealisation of (and special interest in) Plath is based on the feeling of some kind of connection or empathy. Remember earlier in my personal account, I felt that Plath was talking directly to me.

This is one important area which Freud mentions only briefly, the role of empathy, *Einfuhlung*, in the choice of the loved object.[45] On one level, this introduces us to the notion of yearning, wanting to be like or have another, but also the yearning for some form of connection via an empathetic relationship. This desire for empathy can be found in some of Plath's own letters and journals. Plath wrote to her mother on 21 October 1962, in light of the breakdown of her marriage:

> Don't talk to me about the world needing cheerful stuff! What the person out of Belsen—physical or psychological—wants is nobody saying the birdies still go tweet-tweet, but the full knowledge that somebody else has been there and knows the *worst*, just what it is like. It is much more help for me, for example, to know that people are divorced and go through hell, than to hear about happy marriages. Let the *Ladies Home Journal* blither about those.[46]

What Plath appears to be claiming is that the most fruitful, or most 'helpful' relationships, are those based upon the recognition of some kind of shared experience. It is this desire for empathy that, frustratingly, Freud does not allow himself in 'Identification' to elaborate on, but I shall consider the significance here based on what Freud has offered us.

Empathy is described in the Collins Dictionary as 'the ability to sense and understand someone else's feelings as if they were one's own'.[47] We could argue that perhaps readers retroactively sense Plath's feelings, knowing as they often do, much about her life. It could even be that the enigma of Plath herself inspires a desire for some form of empathetic connection. Enigmatic figures surely inspire many sorts of desires, but if there is a wish to 'know' the enigma, then there must certainly be a wish to understand as well.

It is undoubtedly the sense that Plath apparently understands her reader-fans' feelings that is the significant point. As with haunting, there is a two-way traffic, with empathy seemingly occurring both ways between the reader and writer. The fact that neither the reader nor the writer actually knew each other is of little importance, since the role of fantasy and imagination can fill that gap. Moreover, if the figure of Plath necessarily remains an enigma in order to sustain the subject's fascination, then fantasy and imagination may be the only tools that can be applied to fill these gaps. Since our imaginative life can be especially vivid, the revivification of Plath could well be more colourful because of these empty spaces. It brings to mind an observation from Antonio Porchia, that Don Paterson uses as a forward to one of his poems: 'I would rather grieve over your absence than over you.'[48]

This notion that the actual loss can in some cases usurp the figure themselves now needs to be explored within the context of the mourning process. If we identify strongly with, or create an emotional tie with, an 'other', then what happens when that loved other, as in the case of Plath, is lost?

Love, Loss, Mourning, and Melancholia

It seems that, when thinking of Plath, we cannot escape the emerging themes of loss and death. Plath haunts the reader, and the reader themself is ghostly, possibly yearning for an enigmatic loved object she can never have. It is the very loss of this loved object that lies at the heart of Freudian theory.

In 'Mourning and Melancholia', Freud explores the impact of the loss of this loved object.[49] His exploration involves not only how loss may make a person feel or behave, but more directly how it may impact upon their self-identity. For Freud, the loss of the loved object can bring about two responses; either the process of mourning, or the condition of melancholia. It is essential to establish that, although these two conditions of mourning and melancholia are triggered by the same event—namely loss—they differ in quite subtle ways.

First, mourning occurs after the death of a loved one or the loss of a loved object: 'he has suffered a loss in regard to an object' and the mourner must work through dealing with this loss.[50] The significant point here is that the lost object—for example, Plath—remains the 'other', outside of the person who is mourning—the reader-fan.

In contrast, melancholia can have far reaching effects on the subject's own sense of self. In an attempt to hold on to that which has gone, the lost object no longer remains 'outside', but is consumed by the ego of the subject; although maybe feeling that something is lost, they cannot access what it is. The consequences of consuming another into the self in this fashion causes problems such as anger, sleeplessness, and self-hatred. The lost object is not truly dead for it has become part of the subject's own ego and melancholia becomes about returning the dead through the self.

> Melancholia resembles a ghost story in which the ghosts of the dead past actually invade the self. In Freud's theories loss may be rampant, but those who are lost often return to haunt their survivors.[51]

Thurschwell's quote applies to the agency we have been exploring between both reader-fans of Plath and the author herself. However, Thurschwell's use of the word 'invade' seems a little harsh for our purposes as it implies an invasion against one's will, whereas Plath is often a welcome ghost; 'possession' may be a more appropriate word for our context with both its connotations of the joy of being possessed by a loved object and the possessive nature of any close relationship. The further implication of the word 'invade' is that melancholia is always associated with negative qualities, which as we shall see in due course, is not necessarily the case.

To secure the difference then, mourning is about a painful but justifiable and recognisable loss. Melancholia, on the other hand, is a little more puzzling and damaging to the ego. For the melancholic, the loss adopted by their own ego becomes the focus of anger and resentment; these feelings are turned inwards to the self. One result of both mourning and melancholia is to prolong, at least psychically, the existence of the lost object. As we discussed earlier in relation to haunting, keeping the dead alive or evoking them from the dead to return is clearly a way of denying, or rejecting, their loss.

Could it be that readers of Plath potentially fall into two categories? The reader-fans who mourn the loss of Plath as another, someone outside of themselves and the melancholic who consumes the lost object of Plath until she is indistinguishable from their own sense of self? Either way for Freud, this 'work of mourning' is a painful process that needs to be worked through before it can pass.[52]

If we reintroduce the notion of identification here, for those reader-fans who do identify with Plath, mourning seems to be the more likely model. Upon identification with their ideal, they could simultaneously experience pain and loss. As soon as they find a person they feel an emotional tie to, that person is simultaneously lost to them. For Pearce, the pain of mourning has a certain double edge to it, in that 'this long goodbye is intensely pleasurable as it is painful'.[53, 54] If we think about that moment of captivation, that second when we suddenly fall for the writer, that loved object, we are equally overwhelmed by the pleasure and possibility of pain. For Roland Barthes, this significant moment that signals the start of a romance is called *ravissement*; 'for love at first sight requires the very sign of its suddenness (what makes me irresponsible, subject to fatality, swept away, ravished)'.[55] It is overwhelming, giddily terrifying, and horribly pleasurable. This, argues Pearce, is the direct mirror image to mourning:

> There are striking parallels between the landscape of *ravissement* and mourning insomuch as the lover's intense focus on his/her 'lost object' fills everything around him or her with surreal brightness and significance.[56]

The parallels of falling in love and the loss of the loved object share many characteristics: the overwhelming fascination; the 'intense focus; and the lack of room for anything or anyone else.

In a cruel twist for Plath reader-fans, presumably the moment of *ravissement* is very short lived. For no sooner do they discover and fall in love with their beloved writer and her work, they equally as swiftly encounter the distressing knowledge that their loved object has already gone; the loss is immediate. In some cases, where readers already know of Plath's death, the *ravissement* and loss could even be simultaneous, creating a powerful and overwhelming pleasure–pain scenario.

Both falling in love and losing that love create, in their own ways, yearning. This does not necessarily have to be a negative emotion. As Pearce stated earlier, a prolonged goodbye can be pleasurable—that 'infinite deferral of death' not only prolongs the presence of the lost object, but prolongs their journey towards immortality so that 'the journey towards immortality becomes indistinguishable from the state itself—and it is intensely pleasurable because it replicates the period when s/he was first discovered and first lost'.[57, 58]

Perhaps it is this merging of the journey to immortality, and the state itself that we can see echoed in the subjects of mourning. It appears that in some cases, the yearning itself becomes more significant than the perceived loss; this

An image of Plath's grave. (*Gail Crowther*)

may be especially relevant for those reader-fans of Plath who never met her or who were born many years after her death.[59] Any yearning for her could become indistinguishable from Plath herself, and the enigmatic traces that she left behind.

In a short written piece and a painting called *For Sivvy*, the artist Anthony Cockayne captures this Freudian notion of mourning. Having become interested in Plath via her drawings that were on display at The Mayor Gallery in London in 2011, what followed for Cockayne was 'a deep immersion in her life and her work.'[60] On 5 February 2012, he took a single red rose to 23 Fitzroy Road, the house where Plath died in 1963. As during the last weeks of Plath's life, snow was heavy on the ground. As Cockayne placed the red rose on the doorstep, he remarked how producing a painting was far from his mind:

> The desire to take the rose, to her last home, was an uprush, a sort of confluence of emotion, time, place, the weather and my deep engagement, at that time with *The Journals*, *Letters Home* and her poetry, of course. It was snowing here. As I knelt on the steps, the door opened and a young man emerged and for a brief time, I saw into the hallway, where Plath kept the pram. The young man seemed to be perfectly understanding of my action.[61]

What Cockayne seems to be demonstrating here is this notion of mourning—a deep 'uprush' of emotions resulted in an action that somehow remembered and paid homage to the lost loved object of Plath. There is a hint of sadness and yearning as Cockayne briefly looks into and imagines the hallway containing the memories of Plath's pram for her children. He is engaging with and encountering the traces that Plath has left behind. What these emotions resulted in five days later, was a painting called *For Sivvy*. This features a rose in the snow, and would eventually be displayed for a short time in The French House where Plath signed the contract for her first volume of poems *The Colossus*.

This type of engagement with the past, the staring into a passageway of a house that once contained objects belonging to Plath, is all about residue, about what gets left behind. For Freud in 'A Note Upon the "Mystic Writing Pad"', once something has occurred, it leaves permanent traces. Like the writing imprint on the wax paper of a magic writing pad, even when something is erased from the surface, it is still visible under certain conditions—'thus the pad provides not only a receptive surface that can be used over and over again, like a slate, but also permanent traces of what has been'.[62] Plath is perhaps the thing that existed, that has been lost and is used over and over again, each time differently but at the same time leaving those very traces and remains that inform the readings of her.

This positivity is not limited solely to mourning either. Up to this point, we have focussed on the more puzzling and negative aspects of melancholia. Recent theorists, however, have started to reclaim the seemingly self-

For Sivvy by Anthony Cockayne. (*Anthony Cockayne*)

destructive aspects of this condition. Writers such as Ranjanna Khanna, David Eng, and Suzette Min have all attempted to highlight the 'moments of production' that loss can bring about.[63, 64, 65, 66] In fact, Eng concentrates not only on the productivity of loss, but how it can be a collective process that brings people together. While, he argues, we may have a better understanding of the process of mourning, what we now need is an equally full understanding of melancholia so that it may be 'depathologized'.[67]

Judith Butler also explores the more positive aspects of melancholia, seeing it as a form of 'becoming' and how 'it probably remains true that it is only because we can know its stasis that we can trace its motion, and that we want to'.[68, 69] If, as we stated at the start of this chapter, the dead can return not just in the form of remembrance but as an exterior transformative presence, then Eng and Butler's view of the active melancholic appears to support this notion.

It would seem for Eng and Butler that the potential for loss and melancholia to have transformative power—perhaps we can even say redemptive power— is immense and a new area of theoretical development that I will apply to my respondents' voices. Even Freud, in a way, implicitly refers to the movement within melancholia, although he does not acknowledge the transformative potential of it—'the fact that it passes off after a certain time has elapsed without leaving traces of any gross changes is a feature it shares with mourning'.[70] However, the fact that it does not leave 'gross changes' could be the first hint that it does not have to be negative changes that occur. This opens the space for a fuller and more productive reading of melancholia.

Narcissism

What we love, according to Plato, is part of us or someone like ourselves; this is where the narcissistic elements of loss and love emerge. We have to consider the possibility that when we love and lose those who are like a 'part of us', we may, in fact, be mourning the loss of part of our own sense of self. This means that the mourning process, the condition of melancholia, and our identification with a beloved other could all stem from narcissistic traits within ourselves.

Could Plath reader-fans feel such levels of empathy and connection to her that she appears to be their 'other half'? If this is the case, then narcissistic traits within the reader-fan cannot be ignored.

In general, Freud describes narcissism as denoting 'the attitude of a person who treats his own body in the same way in which a sexual object is ordinarily treated'.[71] A cruder description of narcissism has tended to be self-love, yet this term restricts the far-reaching implications of the condition. Its impact upon our identity formation and how we relate to other people is crucial to understanding how narcissism may work. Freud claims that all narcissism stems from that first love object 'the woman who nurses him'—i.e. the mother.[72] In most, but not all, cases of psycho-sexual development as the child progresses, this love attaches itself to an 'object-ideal', or loved object outside both the self and the mother. In cases where this does not occur, the attachment becomes internalised. For Freud, this signifies two types of narcissism—primary and secondary. The distinctions between the two are important.

For a primary narcissist, this transition of love from the self or the mother to the other does not occur—all possibility of loving another is lost, and the attachment is turned back upon the self. This results in a desire for self-aggrandisement; the world becomes a mirror to reflect back adulation—the very thing the ego needs to survive. As Christopher Lasch puts it, 'the primary narcissist depends on others to validate his [sic.] self-esteem. For the narcissist the world is a mirror'.[73] For Freud, this type of primary narcissist is unusually attractive to others:

> For it seems very evident that another person's narcissism has a great attraction for those who have renounced part of their own narcissism and are in search of a love-object. The charm of a child lies to a great extent in his narcissism, his self-containment and inaccessibility, just as does the charm of certain animals which seem not to concern themselves about us,

such as cats and large beasts of prey.[74]

According to Freud, often those types who are attractive have some kind of self-contained, inward looking certainty about them, like the 'charm of a child'. Perhaps for those with an uncertain sense of self, the narcissist's lack of self-consciousness is precisely that which becomes attractive; they appear to be inaccessible and impenetrable. Freud argues that this enigmatic personality then becomes desirable.

The fact that these figures are 'enigmatic' relates to their spectral nature; the more we try to pin them down, the more they slip away from us. There is, in other words, something essentially unknowable about them and this, paradoxically, is perhaps what compels us to want to know more. If we consider the elusivity of Plath, the conflicting discourses surrounding her, and the enigmatic historical figure behind her authorial voice, then we are dealing with a very seductive type.

> *Out of the ash I rise*
> *With my red hair*
> *And I eat men like air.*[75]

Who or what can be more self-contained, more outwardly assured than the voice of Lady Lazarus?

Who could sound more self-reliant and autonomous than the speaker in 'Daddy'? 'Daddy, Daddy, you bastard, I'm through.'[76] Who could be self-sufficient enough to taunt and reject even God?

> *O God, I am not like you*
> *In your vacuous black,*
> *Stars stuck all over, bright stupid confetti.*
> *Eternity bores me,*
> *I never wanted it.*[77]

Is it any wonder that another person's narcissistic declarations can hold a great attraction for us?

For the secondary narcissist, the transition to a love object does take place, and an 'outside' other becomes the object of their attraction. They are able to identify with an idealised person, and subsequently love them. In many cases, this object of love may well be the highly attractive primary narcissist; of course, there is a complex relationship here. The primary narcissist wants to be adored and is not required to contribute anything to the relationship; the secondary narcissist is happy to be a mirror reflecting back the adoring vision a primary narcissist needs to sustain their ego. But, and here is the interesting part, the secondary narcissist relies on the object of their affection to remain truly amazing in order for themselves to sustain a stable sense of self; in other words, the secondary narcissist can only be content if the object of their affection stays dazzling for them.

Let us pause for a moment to consider the implications for this book. Through the subtle relationship between the primary narcissist, who needs adulation, and the secondary narcissist, who provides it, we can see a possible model emerging. Plath could well play the primary narcissist role and her reader-fans the secondary. However, the interdependence goes even further than this; although the primary narcissist is dependent upon adoration, the secondary narcissist is equally dependent upon the undiminished ego of their love object in order to guarantee their own stability.

For ourselves, we must question whether reader-fans are somehow sustained by their idealised Plath. This would explain why some people choose certain love objects over others (e.g. Plath instead of Sexton) and model themselves on—or, in relation to—that person's identity. The primary narcissist needs people to feed their ego. The secondary narcissist chooses an idealised and distanced other just enough like themselves for certain traits to be recognised, but just different and idealised enough to create desire and yearning. It could be that Plath is just enough like her reader-fans to create identification, and just different enough for them to idealise. Therefore, it could be something specific about Plath that her reader-fans see reflected in themselves, and it could be something specific about Plath that they aspire to and yearn for.

The impact of narcissism on the ego can be linked to the process of mourning and melancholia very explicitly in the case of Plath. As we have already established, the secondary narcissist, who idealises a love object outside of themselves, may be more prone to mourning; in fact, the degree of adoration directed towards the loved object may be expected to increase were that love object ever to be lost. So, a reader-fan may well both love and mourn a lost loved object outside of themselves—i.e. Plath.

For the primary narcissist, however, all attachment is directed towards the ego; there is no recognition of a love object beyond themselves and, following Freud, this personality-type is more likely to succumb to melancholia. Could it be that it is Plath herself who is most properly thought of in these terms? Certainly, in her journals, Plath discusses her discovery of Freud's essay 'Mourning and Melancholia' stating she feels it perfectly describes her own condition—the death of her father at a young age, the loss turned in on her own ego resulting in self-loathing, and a desire to be loved:

> Read Freud's 'Mourning and Melancholia' this morning after Ted left for the library. An almost exact description of my feelings and reasons for suicide.[78]

If Plath can identify elements of the melancholic in her ego, she perhaps addresses the issue of narcissism even more bluntly in her claim that, 'I do not love; I do not love anybody except myself. That is a rather shocking thing to admit.'[79] If Freud is correct, it could be precisely Plath's ability to make this statement that makes her personality so attractive to her reader-fans. It is the lack of inhibition, the 'shocking' nature of it that draws others to her.

Although she is aware of this 'self-love', Plath's insight goes further; she is equally aware this only comes from comparing herself to others, not out of interest, but out of competitiveness, or as she puts it, 'against being found wanting'.[80]

> My interest in other people is too often one of comparison, not of pure intrigue with the unique otherness of identity. Here, ideally, I should forget the outer world of appearances, publishing, checks, success. And be true to an inner heart. Yet I fight against a simple-mindedness, a narcissism, a protective shell against competing, against being found wanting.[81]

Displaying Freud's classic features of the primary narcissist, Plath appears to use other people as mirrors to, or comparisons of, herself. In contrast, we could say for the secondary narcissist, Plath herself becomes both the object of intrigue and the point of comparison or idealisation.

The final area we need to explore in relation to identification, mourning, melancholia, and narcissism is emotional ambivalence. We have already seen above, with melancholia, how love can quickly turn into anger. For Freud, 'identification, in fact, is ambivalent from the very first; it can turn into an expression of tenderness as easily as into a wish for someone's removal'.[82] If we have idealised an exterior love object, then it is likely that close to our feelings of adoration are feelings of envy; perhaps there is even the threat that this love object holds all the power within the relationship.

Love can easily turn to hate; this is perhaps a particular risk if the love object has been idealised and then 'falls from grace'. This becomes increasingly interesting when we consider that the love object may already be dead, as in the case of Plath. Does this make her a safer option for her reader-fans, in that she is less likely to disappoint or betray them? If we are attached to a living love object, they surely run the risk of disillusioning us at some point in the future.

The connections between death, haunting, identity formation, narcissism, mourning, and melancholia are undeniable. What is interesting is the way in which they appear to bleed into each other. Following one inevitably means dealing with the others in a labyrinth of death, ghosts and loss. Each model offers its strengths and limitations. Certainly, it would seem Freud's notion of identification and mourning may well describe the process occurring between reader-fans and Plath. Yet, as we are about to discover, it seems that some reader-fans identify but do not mourn, while others mourn but do not identify. Furthermore, since we have linked identification to narcissism, what of those reader-fans who identify with Plath's emotions but not herself as a subject? Finally, what of those reader-fans who on the surface appear to be suffering from the condition of melancholia?

What we now need to explore in detail are the ways in which these questions 'play out' in the reader-fan relationships that develop with Plath. It is time to hand the chapter over to the voices that will speak throughout this book and for them to tell us about the very first time that they encountered Sylvia Plath.

Peter

> My introduction to Plath came in 1994, as a college junior, in a course titled 'Introduction to Poetry'. I took this course for two primary reasons: recently I declared my major to be English and my girlfriend, and first love, dumped me. So going the poetry route seemed the right way. In this poetry course we covered many different poetic movements, and we touched eventually, those poets labelled "confessionals".

Our first respondent, Peter, immediately connects two important areas of his life: the loss of his first love and the discovery of another lost, loved object, Sylvia Plath. As a major in English, it is perhaps unsurprising that it is Plath's words—the 'implied author'—that initially strike Peter. In this case, it is the speaker of one of Plath's poems:

> Assigned to read 'Lady Lazarus' for class, the language gripped me. For days I read and reread the poem, engrossed particularly with the lines, "out of the ash/I rise with my red hair…"

We see Peter becoming a captivated reader, by the re-reading of the poem, the same lines. There is a hint of *ravissement*—that moment when he is gripped, initially involuntarily, until he allows himself to be become 'engrossed' and suddenly the loved object 'fills everything around him'.[83] Despite this initial attraction being with the words, the spectral figure of Plath had already started to seep from the page:

> In the next class, I asked my professor for more information, particularly intrigued with the brief biography given in our text book and in class … died by suicide; compared a penis to a "turkey neck and turkey gizzards" in her novel *The Bell Jar*, etc. In response to my query, he told me basically that he did not much care for Plath and could not recommend anything further. Thankfully the library was well-stocked with books.

This highlights the way in which some writers draw people in and leave others unmoved—it seems fair to assume Peter's professor did not especially like

Plath. For Peter, the enigmatic Plath is already creating intrigue. He wants more information; his fascination has moved from the implied author to the historical figure by mentioning the word 'biography'. This shift is important for all of the reasons that we have mentioned above. Over the years there has been no shortage of biographies written about Plath; perhaps the wonderfully ironic point here is that Peter eventually ended up writing his own biography of Plath.

It seems that Peter was not discouraged by his professor's lack of encouragement and 'over the next couple of years I bought and read everything by Plath in print'. It could be that this obstacle offered by his professor actually increased his interest in the same way that Pearce discusses how obstacles placed in the way of reaching the loved other only increases their enigma and status.[84] This was just the start of a prolific relationship between Peter and Plath that would culminate in extensive scholarship and textual production.

Initially, this curiosity about Plath resulted in Peter's own writing being influenced by her, 'culminating in two poems written for Plath'. The literature around fandom shows that often an admired other can generate much productivity. In his essay 'The Cultural Economy of Fandom', John Fiske argues that one type of this productivity is textual:

> Fans produce and circulate among themselves texts which are often crafted with production values as high as any in the official culture.[85]

Fiske argues that one reason for the writing of texts is to minimise the distance between the writer and the object of desire. This is relevant to the writing of Peter's poems. Along with this, we see how the actions of Peter's everyday life come into play. In 'Sodium Pentothal' (1996), Peter's narrator is experiencing an uncomfortable visit to the dentist:

> *I do not wear a gas mask. Nothing of that sort.*
> *The oral surgeon ties a rubber band around my forearm*
> *And asks what I study to distract me.*
> *I tell him I am completely addicted to Sylvia Plath–*
> *Like a bad habit, like nicotine.*

The newfound interest in Plath is regarded by the speaker of the poem as something negative, 'a bad habit' with a hint of destructiveness 'like nicotine', something that ultimately will not be healthy or good. The use of language is interesting, as we see that an addiction to Plath implies some sort of dependency, some kind of devotion without which the addict would be a lesser person. Perhaps at this stage, we are seeing Peter's writerly voice expressing the lack he feels without Plath, the loss of the loved object, even if yearning for that loss is ultimately 'bad' or unhealthy.

This brings to mind Freud's notion of mourning—the 'known lack that exists in the world'; something is missing and the natural reaction is grief.[86] It also echoes Eng, who argues that loss can be a positive thing and can involve productivity.[87] There is something incomplete—lacking—about Peter's sense of identity that is further implied by the following line: 'He has broken the solidarity of my skin'. For the writer, even a unified embodiment has come under threat; the skin can no longer contain the self and it seems it is this uncertainty that creates the 'addiction' to Plath. Ultimately, this fascination appears to bring about the unfulfillable yearning; as a lost, loved object, Plath can never be regained. Peter experiences dissatisfaction as 'reading her works and reading about her life did not fulfil me'. Perhaps writing poems for her that helps to lessen this distance.

It seems that Freud's model works—the mourning 'is fully accounted for'.[88] We can understand the lack in the world that creates the longing. Plath remains 'other' to Peter which brings about both pain of loss, and pleasure of prolonging that loss and this also ensures that Plath remains an object of desire. However, Peter's mourning does not resolve itself in identification or the complex process of consuming the other associated with melancholia. His sense of longing, of self may be under threat—unstable—but this does not lead him to form a sort of identity merged with Plath. She is a separate entity, an object of longing, and he is the mourner.

Anna

> I 'discovered' Sylvia Plath when I was about 22–23 years old. I picked up *The Bell Jar* with some other stuff, it was a book that was familiar to me only by name—the year before I had had a roommate who had read it and liked it, and I had a feeling it was one of those books you should have read.

Anna's initial meeting with Plath, like Peter's, was with a book and not a person. Whereas Peter encountered the fierce and fiery persona of 'Lady Lazarus', Anna encounters the highly dramatic persona of Esther Greenwood in *The Bell Jar*. It may be useful to consider whether there is any relevance in these differing voices; I think that there is. The novel falls into that tricky category of fictionalised autobiography, a term I always struggle with since I assume all autobiography is fictional. However, there are recognisable episodes from the novel that feature in Plath's biography, so it seems fair to assume this is one occasion when Plath is manipulating her personal experiences for the sake of her writing.[89]

It was the book that was familiar to Anna and the reputation of the text itself as 'one of those books you should have read'. In an uncanny echo of

Peter's first introduction to Plath, Anna writes:

> Then as it happened, I broke up with a short-term boyfriend and was feeling
> really crappy, so I basically just stayed at home and did nothing but lie on the
> couch reading and writing for about two weeks (I've heard of other people
> getting stuck on SP while they, too, were broken-hearted!). And then I picked
> up *The Bell Jar*. I can't remember exactly what made me want to read it at
> that exact time—maybe I read the back-cover, and the idea of reading about
> a young woman's breakdown seemed tempting at the time. Not that I was
> Esther Greenwood-ing in any way. Just feeling a bit crappy.

The connection between Peter and Anna becoming fascinated by Plath during
periods of anguish is probably no coincidence. In *A Lover's Discourse*, Barthes
describes the empty space that can often precede the start of a romance, a
captivation, or—as Barthes says—a *ravissement*. He claims, 'the hypnotic
episode, it is said, is ordinarily preceded by a twilight state: the subject is in a
sense empty'.[90]

Barthes suggests we have to be in the right frame of mind to be receptive
to a *ravissement*. Equally if we are drawn to those who we feel are like us,
as Freud suggests, then subject matter that seems to speak to our own lives
will instantly be interesting, or as Anna claims, 'tempting'. What is tempting
is to introduce the notion of an identificatory relationship. Anna's self-worth
is low due to the breakdown of her romantic relationship. Then, suddenly,
there is Plath, dazzling with her assured writing and streetwise narrator Esther
Greenwood. However, Anna does deny specific identification with the main
protagonist of the novel—'Not that I was Esther Greenwood-ing in any way'.
In spite of this, some empathy between the character and herself may be seen
to be taking place—'Just feeling a bit crappy'. Like Peter, Anna finds herself
inspired to read and reread:

> I do remember being sucked into the book immediately; I just couldn't put it
> down. I stayed up all night reading it, and then the next day, I reread it.

It is this account of extreme consumption—both the speed and repetition—
that is striking about Peter and Anna's accounts. If Peter describes himself as
a Plath addict, then there is certainly something of the addiction in Anna's
claim that she 'just couldn't put the book down'; something about the words
on the page are compulsive. In *The Rhetorics of Feminism*, Pearce discusses
this process as being slightly more complicated. Referring to her own
earlier work, she claims that 'there is no such thing as a straightforwardly
"identificatory" reading of a text: both readers and texts are too fractured
for this'.[91] We can see this almost filtered and 'fractured' identification taking

place with Anna in the way she creates meaning for herself from Plath's words:

> This was in May, and I left in June for the summer, which I spent alternating between my family's summer cabin, my parents' house and a friend's apartment. Over the summer, I reread *The Bell Jar* several times. I read Plath's journals, the collected poems, *Letters Home*, and Anne Stevenson's *Bitter Fame*. I underlined everywhere in everything, and found so many passages especially in the journals, that spoke to me personally. I actually often find her quite inspiring. And also, when I'm feeling low or insecure or suffer from writer's block, there are days when I just want to crawl up and read her journals where she expresses moods and feelings that are very similar to mine.

In this passage, Anna begins to identify with Plath. In fact, although superficially she appears to be discussing Plath's work, a closer reading reveals this comment is just as much about Plath herself; the Plath of the journals 'spoke to me personally' and Plath 'expresses moods and feelings that are very similar to mine'. This is a fine example of what we may term the empathetic reflex, but in fact goes beyond empathy and into some form of potential healing and rejuvenation. For Freud, identification in its simplest form is 'the expression of an emotional tie with another person'.[92] Here, Anna demonstrates not only this emotional tie, but how this relationship can become both an active and a positive one. In other words, it is not simply the reader absorbing Plath, but relating to Plath in such a way as to bring about a change or process: 'I actually often find her quite inspiring'.

We could also account for this in terms of narcissism. Anna sees in Plath a 'sameness', but a sameness that still allows distance—'she expresses moods and feelings that are very similar to mine'. Freud's theory that we are drawn to people like us, but still sufficiently different to us, appears to apply in this case. There does not appear to be any evidence of mourning. Certainly, there is an 'obsession' as Anna describes it, but this obsession seems to be centred on the encounter with Plath, not the loss of her.

As with Peter, despite the fact the initial 'encounter' was with Plath's writing, the fascination soon moves from the literary outputs to the person herself. There is an argument here that in the case of encountering *The Bell Jar*, this fascination could have been simultaneous, particularly given the packaging of the novel.[93] However, we see in Anna's prior statement how she herself regards this fascination with the historical figure of Plath occurring after she had read all the letters, journals, and biographies:

> After having read Plath's work over and over, I then started to read about

her obsessively. This was perhaps one or two years after having started Plathing about. Since then, it has been kind of a double interest for me—both an interest specifically in Plath and her texts, and an interest in her as a phenomenon and a subject for study. I've learnt so much about literature and literary theory in general from this extensive reading, and have the bad habit (just ask my boyfriend) of basically connecting the most various topics to something I've read about SP. "As Plath once wrote…"; "I think Plath's said something about this…."

Anna's use of language is revealing. If as we claimed earlier, her relationship with Plath is an active one, there is even more evidence for this, as Plath becomes an activity—'Plathing about.' We already know from Freud that identification is not a 'passive' process and here Anna appears to be making a conscious choice.[94]

We have seen, through the discussion of David Eng on loss, mourning, and melancholia, how loss can actually lead to productivity and animation. As with Peter, Anna refers to her relationship with Plath as a 'bad habit', an addiction she cannot give up. In fact, Plath appears to imbue all sorts of unexpected areas of Anna's life with meaning—'the most various topics'; to Anna, these links appear to be a source of enjoyment, even if they may become a pain for those around her. We also see that Anna is able to categorise her 'obsession' with Plath into two areas: the woman and the work. However, Anna is aware that the Plath she relates to is no reproduction of a 'real' or 'authentic' Plath, but a 'phenomenon'.

Ultimately, Anna displays her fascination with Plath and her empathy with the woman and the work. There are even hints of a narcissistic identification. But as with Peter, although Plath is clearly important to Anna's own identity formation, a space is still maintained between herself and the idealised other. Plath may be a lost, loved object for Peter and a point of identification for Anna, but their relationship with her depends upon a recognition of her unconditional 'otherness'.

Megan

I cannot remember being familiar with Plath, the person or her work, whilst I was growing up. There were definitely no copies of her collections of poetry or her novel in the house, so I would never have been introduced to her in my home environment.

In direct contrast to Peter and Anna, Megan recognises a much larger space between herself and Plath. Interestingly, Megan immediately draws distinctions between the subject of Sylvia Plath and the body of her work. Although looking back, Megan cannot remember any of Plath's books in her home, she does state that 'even in my early teens all I seem to recall her representing to me was some vague notion of importance and tragedy'. For Jenson in 'Fandom as Pathology: The Consequences of Characterisation', this creation of a mythic persona, particularly with well-known people, is one of the ways in which fans are drawn in. Rather than being familiar with Plath's own writing, Megan is aware of Plath's reputation created by what Jensen calls the 'structures and strategies of celebrity public relations', noting how they function to create what they call the celebrity 'persona'.[95] This is, as Anna described it, the 'phenomenon' of Plath.

Megan's 'real' introduction to Plath—by this, Megan appears to mean the work, not the reputation or life—came about through reading *The Bell Jar* as a teenager. It is important to note that even with this quasi-autobiographical text, the distinction between life and art is still maintained: 'when I read *The Bell Jar* I still knew relatively little about Plath and her body of work, or her personal life'. What does begin to occur, as with Peter and Anna, is some initial identification with the language and message of the text:

> My real introduction to Plath therefore came when I read *The Bell Jar* at sixth-form College. I can't remember exactly why I chose to read the book, but I would guess that it had probably been mentioned in class and it caught my eye whilst I browsed in a book shop. I clearly remember that the book provoked a very strong response in me. I immensely enjoyed it and felt that it spoke for and about something in me at that time. Plath became for me a voice that I recognised, an echo of some of things I was experiencing and feeling.

The significant point to note is that, for Megan, there is still a clear boundary between the woman and the work. Unlike Peter and Anna, who were both drawn to the writer herself, for Megan it is the text *qua* text which provokes a response—it is a disembodied voice that echoes familiar feelings. Megan appears to identify with abstracted emotions that have nothing exclusively to do with Plath or her life:

> [I] realised even at the time that this was a portrayal of a somewhat typical young woman and that many people would relate to those feelings whilst imagining they had a special relationship and similarity to the character.

Unlike Peter and Anna, who experienced a sort of revelatory meeting or *ravissement* with Plath, Megan's association with the work of Plath went through various false starts and sporadic contact as she travelled to Tanzania and worked as a volunteer in an orphanage for two months. She notes that 'during my stay at the orphanage I was extremely lonely and anxious at times'; it was during her journey home, in the city of Dar Es Salaam, when she bought a copy of the *Collected Poems* of Sylvia Plath from a bookshop in the marina:

> When I came to read the book I just flicked aimlessly through the pages, finding the number of poems all crammed together in one volume difficult to penetrate as I so often do with large collections of poetry.

The lack of interest is striking—no bold voice jumps from the page, no life changing experience. Nothing beyond what almost resembles boredom. If Freud's model of mourning helps explain the nature of Peter's fascination with Plath, and the Freudian notions of identification help to account for Anna's, neither of these models are suitable for Megan. Far from identifying with Plath, we could argue that at this point, Megan had become disconnected from Plath. This is possibly because she found the poetry disappointingly cerebral after *The Bell Jar* which, as a work of fiction with a strong central character, facilitated identification. Although Freud's model allows room for ambivalence within identification, it seems with Megan, identification failed to occur at all with the poems of Plath.

Consequently, although *Collected Poems* remained in the background of Megan's first two years at university, lying unread on a shelf, she nevertheless 'carried it back and forth every term with me'. It was not until she had to choose a dissertation topic in the final year of her studies that Megan decided to tackle Sylvia Plath:

> I knew that I liked Plath's style from reading *The Bell Jar*, but I also chose to use her because I was aware that I still had a huge amount to find out about Plath and her work, which would keep me focused and motivated, and maintain a sense of newness in the research.

We see Megan showing the first signs of interest in the actual person of Sylvia Plath as she explains wanting to find out more about Plath and her work:

> ...the little wider reading I had encountered seemed to indicate that Sylvia Plath the writer and the woman had a fascinating draw on many women and readers in general ... I sensed a powerful (sometimes even hysterical?!) bond between some Plath readers and their icon, and wanted to discover why this poet seemed to speak for these women today.

Megan hints at the pathology of fandom, as presented by the cultural theorist Joli Jenson, who describes the slightly unhinged, hysterical and unstable fan. However, Megan is aware that readers are using Plath and her writing in their own lives. Freudian theories of identification do not cover this reading process *per se*, therefore it will be useful to extend our discussion into fandom scholarship and explore other ways in which reader fans may use texts in identity formation.

In his essay 'Is there a Fan in the House?: The Affective Sensibility of Fandom', Lawrence Grossberg discusses several ways in which the relationship between a text and its audience is an active and productive one; he explores the notion that a text does not carry its own meaning or politics but that people actively struggle to connect it to their lives and own desires—'a text can only mean something in the context of the experience and situation of its particular audience'.[96] This idea is useful, in that up to this point, our use of Freudian theory has had a certain ahistoricity about it. Grossberg offers an account of how identity formation necessarily has to be rooted in a cultural and historical context; he claims readers are not 'cultural dopes' and neither are they homogenous, but what they do engage in is creating their own cultural environment from the resources available to them. For Grossberg, 'audiences and texts are continuously remade—their identity and effectiveness reconstructed—by relocating their place within different contexts'.[97] This seems to coincide with Megan's claim that Plath 'speaks for women today' and that readers interpret their own 'Sylvia' and use her for their own purposes.

However, Grossberg argues that what binds the audience to the text is a sensibility and an apparatus, a particular cultural context, both of which define the 'possible relationships between texts and audiences located within its spaces'.[98] Within these spaces, presumably different apparatuses produce different sensibilities and it is the sensibility of the reader that produces the structures of pleasure and enjoyment. The reader's relation to the text operates in the domain of affect—mood, feeling of life—and the same object or text is very different as our affective relationship to it changes. This mechanism could help to explain Megan's own haphazard introduction to Plath. There were times when Plath meant nothing to her and when the poems were meaningless. It was a change in cultural context, the experience of isolation and anxiety in Tanzania that brought about a shift in Megan's approach to Plath.

Grossberg's theory further supports this notion since he claims that readers invest in ways which enable them to gain a certain amount of control over their affective lives; this allows them to further invest in texts in order to cope with new forms of pain, alienation, or terror. This positive use of textual interaction shows, for Grossberg, that 'fandom potentially, at least, is the site of optimism, invigoration and passion'; this notion is echoed in Anna's own statement that she actually finds Plath inspiring.[99] For Megan, writing her dissertation allowed her to explore the cultural and historical significance of Plath within her own social context as well as 'my own initial reaction to Plath and why I have been drawn to her as a young woman'.

With Megan's account, we begin to see the limits of Freudian theory precisely because her relationship with Plath is more self-conscious and intellectual, drawing a more careful distinction between the biographical phenomenon and the texts.

Morney

> There was a very definite point in my life where I felt like she saved my life. I had a breakdown and attempted suicide just over 3 years ago and for a long time afterwards I couldn't read or do anything that I normally could do. I'm not sure what would have got me through that stage if it hadn't had what feels like a special connection to her.

Although Morney does not directly address the first time she encountered Plath, she does address the first time Plath became essential to her survival ('I felt like she saved my life'). Like many previous respondents, Morney was experiencing an especially distressing time and found her empathetic relationship with Plath helped her through this. We do not know what created the suicide impulse in Morney, but what we can see is that during this period of distress, Plath becomes a loved object to cling to. Despite Morney's torpor, 'I couldn't read or do anything I normally could', the one active dimension in her life was Plath, not merely reading her writing, but what Morney refers to as maintaining 'a special connection'.

It is here that we see *Einfuhlung*—the empathy that was discussed earlier in relation to Freud; Morney felt as though the empathy was coming 'from' Plath, who understood what Morney was experiencing in the same way that she was able to relate to the subjects Plath was writing about. Plath becomes the idealised object and a person to turn to in crisis. The identificatory relationship with Plath provides not only a source of comfort, but a certain level of what can only be described as redemption. Interestingly, Morney does not specify exactly what Plath she was reading at this time, and this would certainly be significant in terms of who, or what, she was empathising with, since we have already seen the differing impacts of differing texts.

The most striking feature of Morney's story is this figure of Plath as a saviour—as someone throwing a lifeline and offering support. In *Imagining the Divine*, Lloyd Baugh explores the notion of the redemptive Christ-like figure within film. Some of his observations seem particularly pertinent for the figure of Plath:

> The Christ-like figure is ... embodied in a variety of guises or models, some traditional and others more original, some representing the totality of the Christ-event and others of a more limited scope, only some of its aspects.[100]

Baugh seems to be suggesting that any figure offering redemption can not only adopt a number of different guises, but does not necessarily have to be the traditional Christ-like figure we may normally envisage. This is convenient in relation to Plath's gender, but when we look at Baugh's list of Christ-like dimensions, it becomes a little uncanny just how many we can relate to Plath.[101] It is worth taking some time to examine these points and relate them directly to certain interpretations of Plath's life and work.

The first possible dimension, for Baugh, is that the Christ-like figure may have mysterious origins—consider Plath and the enigma of the historical figure. Second, the figure must possibly be capable of attracting a group of followers—see, for one example, the respondents in this book. Third, the figure may have the potential to be committed to justice and, in particular, to free people from injustice—consider Plath's posthumous role in second-wave feminism. Fourth, potentially there has to be some sort of conflict between the protagonist and some authority figure(s)—consider representations of Ted Hughes. Fifth, the Christ-like figure may end up a sacrificial victim or scapegoat—consider certain interpretations of Plath's suicide. Finally, there may be metaphorical representations of the resurrection—consider the spectral Plath, the haunting presence. We can relate Morney to the second dimension discussed here, as being a 'follower' of Plath, but considering the number of Christ-like dimensions Plath can potentially fill, perhaps the surprise is that more people do not regard her a redemptive figure.

Within Morney's work, there is a sense of sadness for the idealised object of Plath; as much as Morney identifies with her, she is also aware that Plath has gone. It is the attempt to recapture, to resurrect the lost Plath that creates the sense of mourning. This is vividly captured in one of Morney's own poems, 'Your Blue Hour':

> *I have read your daughter's poem "Readers",*
> *And I have felt ashamed.*
> *I have read your husband's poem "The Dogs Are Eating Your Mother"*
> *And I have felt ashamed.*
> *Empathy, connections, dreams, love, aching pain for you.*
> *All of this I feel and yet: what of it?*
> *Strip it bare and all that remains is this:*
> *I am a reader. I am a dog.*

> *But still*
> *I will,*
> *Still I will sing this song*

The speaker raises the thorny issue of both private and public mourning.

For Plath's family, the actions of her reader-fans can sometimes feel intrusive and unwelcome.[102] Morney's speaker, while acknowledging this difficulty, reclaims her right to her own Sylvia Plath. She states boldly, 'I am a reader'; this resistance in the face of criticism is exhilarating. Morney's speaker has claimed her Sylvia, the one she credits with saving her life, the one she feels an attachment to and who offered her redemption.

At the same time, Morney is also puzzled by this 'special connection' to Plath. She acknowledges, 'I have plenty to say about Sylvia's influence on my life' and adds, 'not to mention the hours I've lain awake at night thinking about different aspects of it'. It appears that Morney employs her mourning in an especially active manner, for while there may be sleeplessness and 'aching pain', this actually results in a positive—her own survival. Morney certainly finds her identification with Plath painful, but also liberating.

The obvious difference between Morney and the other respondents seems not to be based in the Plath writings she was reading and accessing, but the way in which she employed Plath as her Christ-like redemptive figure. The figure of Plath becomes a sort of safety net, or an emotional crutch, in which she is able to anchor her own sense of identity and gain some comfort.

Kiki

There is an immediate difference between Kiki and the previous respondents. For the first time, a reader-fan raises the issue of image and appearance:

> Like many or most female teenage readers of Sylvia Plath, I was a card carrying member of the Goth Girls club, Doc Martens, dressed in black, skull ring, partially-shaved head.

Within this book, this is the only time a respondent acknowledges that she embodies the 'stereotypical' Plath reader. Before Kiki relates her first meeting with Plath, we are aware of her characteristics and physical appearance. We do not have dates for Kiki's first encounter with Plath, although by her account of Gothic fashion I would place it at some stage in the 1980s. Should this be important? Yes. As we have seen in our previous discussion, and as Grossberg suggests, our interpretation of texts is directly based on our cultural and historical surroundings; we are dealing with different cultural moments and contexts occurring between our respondents and Plath.

Another reason why appearance is important is because certain respondents pursue their identification with Plath through emulating her or trying to look like her. For John Fiske, this would be a fine example of 'enunciative productivity' —fans putting certain meanings into social circulation via hair, clothes and appearance as 'ways of constructing a social identity and therefore of asserting one's membership of a particular fan community.[103, 104] In other words, this is what a Plath reader looks like; you can know who I am from the clothes that I wear. Ironically, for Kiki, her self-image is about as far removed from Plath the historical figure as she can possibly get:

> I never wanted to be the kind of girl or woman that she seemed so desperately trying to be. Quite the opposite. Perhaps it was just a matter of growing up in a different family and in a different time. I never felt I had to prove myself the way she did. And I never wanted to look like anyone else, or dress like anyone else around me.

In light of Freud's notion of identification, we could argue that Kiki is totally confident and self-assured; she did not want to be like anyone else around her, Plath included. However, it is interesting that what Kiki has picked up on is the ambivalence of Plath's conformity; her desire to both conform to 1950s notions of femininity while at the same time trying to 'prove herself'. For all of Kiki's seeming confidence, when it comes to her relationship with Plath, there is an element of possessiveness:

> I have the feeling (and I think others have it, too) of being a little jealous of sharing my 'special' relationship with SP with other 'worshippers'—a sort of adolescent angst I think many of us feel when we realize that SP is not just our 'best friend', she's 'best friends' with a lot of other people!

Choosing to describe certain Plath readers as 'worshippers' affords Plath a Messianic quality, which we discussed earlier in relation to Morney—the charismatic leader collecting a group of followers who hang onto their every word. While this may seem a little melodramatic, we have already considered how Plath fulfils many of the potential criteria for the Christ-like figure, including her ability to attract a group of followers who she may teach, form, or save. Equally important is the resurrection of Plath by her readers, and the ways in which they form 'special relationships' with her. Part of the idealisation process certainly may be seen to involve projecting Christ-like dimensions onto Plath—conflict, sacrifice, and resurrection—in which the ghostly figure of Plath is seen as fully deserving of all our beliefs and desires.

For Kiki, however exclusivist her own relationship with Plath feels, she is aware that it is not unique and that some people take their identification to the ultimate stage:

> Esp. with SP I feel like people have a proprietary relationship with her, to the

extent that there are always several people who write that they feel like they are the reincarnation of SP!

In a similar fashion to Anna, Kiki appears to partially identify with Plath while at the same time keeping her distance. The Freudian model of identification seems to work here to a certain extent, certainly if we extend it with the notions of Christ-like dimensions discussed by Baugh. The identification may well be predicated on Plath's enigmatic nature, and mysterious origins, along with her 'sacrifice'—or suicide—which inspires followers. However, there are limitations to how far identification does work in this case, as Kiki openly states, 'I never wanted to be the kind of girl or woman that she seemed so desperately trying to be'. We can see that in some ways, Kiki already feels as though she 'owns' Plath within a special relationship and therefore this sense of ownership appears to absorb any feelings of mourning. If 'Plath' is already owned, and therefore in many ways, not lost, there is no loved object to mourn. Furthermore, Kiki lacks any sense of idealisation, but rather Kiki actively rejects the personality adopted by Plath, neither wishing to aspire to it, nor to desire it.

Sonia & Florian

> I had never heard of Sylvia Plath or read her poems until a day in 2004. A friend who has psychic talents claimed that I was a reincarnation of Sylvia Plath. I was of course very sceptical. I believe in reincarnation, but the possibility that I should have been famous had never occurred to me. (Sonia)

The shock of this was not for Sonia alone, since her partner Florian also had to deal with this information:

> It was 2004, we had been together for about two years. It all began when Sonia showed me a book with lots of pictures of a person that had a strong resemblance to her. It took some time to really see it. Since we both believed in reincarnation we asked ourselves if it was possible that Sonia had been this Sylvia Plath in her previous life.

What Florian does not make clear in this statement is what 'took some time to really see', whether he is referring to Sonia's physical resemblance to Plath, or the possibility of her being the reincarnated Plath. Either way, what Sonia and Florian both appear to be experiencing here is what Freud refers to as the uncanny, or *unheimlich*. The uncanny, explored by Freud in his 1919 paper, is something that can incite fear and dread; in general, its curious combination of making something familiar to us, in this case Sonia herself, equally unfamiliar at the same time, so herself as another person—Sylvia Plath. While Freud gives examples of the uncanny as being the fear that dolls or automata may suddenly come alive, he also cites the example of the return of the dead: dead bodies, spirits, ghosts, and haunted houses. Although Freud does not discuss reincarnation in his essay, it seems reasonable to assert that reincarnation is quite simply, the return of the dead, or that which will not die, but reanimates itself and returns to haunt again and again.[105] In fact, Freud argues that in relation to the uncanny and the double, 'the subject identifies himself with someone else, so that he is in doubt as to which his self is, or substitutes the extraneous self for his own'.[106]

If we apply psychoanalytic theory to Sonia's belief, it is possible to argue that she has identified with Plath to the extent that she has become Plath. This is quite puzzling; while it is tempting to claim that Sonia's ego has utterly consumed the lost, loved object and taken the characteristics as its own, a symptom of melancholia, the idea of her being the reincarnated Plath came before she even knew who Plath was. Sonia was directed to Plath by an outside source (her psychic friend) so Sonia could not mourn a love object that she neither knew or had lost. Despite this puzzle, let us continue a little more, for Freud's theory of mourning becomes useful when we analyse Florian's next statement:

> It took some time for me to digest, but at the same time my love and appreciation deepened. Because I got a better understanding why Sonia was like she was, why she was bound by her pessimism and her fears. Not only that they had so many physical and mental similarities, Sylvia's destiny explained all the mental characteristics of Sonia.

In this sense, the 'shadow of the object has fallen upon the ego'.[107] Sonia's sense of self has divided and become interchangeable with that of Plath and events from Plath's life are used to make sense of Sonia's current situation.

It was during Sonia's realisation that another similarity also struck her:

> Then I saw a photo of Otto Plath [Sylvia's father] and he looked scarily like Florian. I saw so many connections and many strange things started to happen in my life.

In an uncanny doubling of Sonia's own experience, of being directed to her reincarnated self by an outside source, she repeats this with her own partner by likening him to Plath's father. For Florian, the 'strange things' that began to permeate Sonia's life also permeated the uncanniness of Otto's image and the implications for his relationship with Sonia:

Sonia also showed me a photo of Otto with a big smile. She wanted to see my reaction. She had seen the resemblance immediately, especially in the eyes of Otto. To me it was also kind of spooky, but I did not dare to believe it from the start, but I had to admit, the body, the shape of the skull, the ears, the hair quality, the eyes, the silly smile … yup, those were just like mine alright. Of course it felt kind of strange that I might have been her father as well, but still, it made sense.

Aside from the obvious connotations to the Freudian Electra Complex at play here, it is interesting to note that for both Sonia and Florian, the uncanny or 'spooky' resemblance between themselves and the Plaths is important, as if physical continuity is a significant feature of reincarnation. [108]

If we employ psychoanalytic theory, we could explain this in light of extreme identification in which the subject takes in all aspects of the idealised other. As we shall see in Chapter Two, this extends itself to doubling with the loved other and becoming each other's alter-ego. Rather than the writing creating the Sylvia and Otto they know, the identification comes from the photographic representation of the historical figures themselves; whereas Anna, Megan, and Morney recognise part of themselves in the writing of Sylvia Plath, Sonia recognises herself actually as Sylvia Plath. Whereas all the other respondents' first encounter Plath through a number of differing texts with differing impacts, here for the first time the implied author, the narrator of the texts, is meaningless—for at the moment of encounter, Sonia and Florian had never heard her voice(s).

Not only do Sonia and Florian 'recognise' themselves in Sylvia and Otto Plath, both physically and emotionally, they actually become them. There is no distance or gap, simply an utter consumption. Any mourning that takes place appears to be not for a lost loved object but for their own sense of self, with Sonia and Florian being the same as Sylvia and Otto in their perception. With Sonia and Florian, the egos and figures of Sylvia and Otto Plath become somehow conjoined; they believe that the Plath father and daughter figures are their identities. Sonia and Florian blame their current state on previous experiences; Plath and Otto Plath become responsible for their present situation. Could this be the first instance of melancholia being more appropriate vocabulary than 'mourning' to explain what is going on with two of Plath's reader-fans? Certainly, key elements seem to be present— the ego assimilation and apparent lack of space between object and subject. While on the one hand there appears to be an utter ego assimilation, on the other, Sonia's narrative occasionally slips into referring to Sylvia as the other, outside of herself. We see evidence of this in later chapters with Florian also. Total consumption of Plath, it seems, cannot be maintained. This is why we can see evidence of mourning, but not melancholia.

There is an implicit accusation in these narratives too, that previous actions should be held accountable. This hints at Freud's insistence that 'identification, in fact, is ambivalent from the very first; it can turn into an expression of tenderness as easily as into a wish for someone's removal'.[109] While Sonia may implicitly blame Plath for her current situation, most of her feelings towards her are of tenderness and gratitude:

> I have had great gain from going into the story and life of Sylvia, and it is a kind of healing process that has been taking place. I have come to understand myself on a deeper level after reading about Sylvia, and reading her diaries and poems.

Conclusion

This chapter has gone some way to demonstrating the uses and limitations of psychoanalytic theory in an understanding of the special relationship my reader-fans have formed with Sylvia Plath. By exploring the first encounter between Plath and my respondents, I have been able to interrogate the extent to which loss, mourning and narcissism play a part in the process of identification. We can see how some reader-fans engage with the poetic voice, some with the historical figure, and others with photographic images of Plath. First encounters are powerful moments, and each of these stories are unique. As a reader, you may want to consider your own first discovery of Plath—how and where that occurred and what sort of impact that made on your life.

What my exploration of these first encounters with Plath has revealed is that for my respondents, Plath is an immensely influential and powerful presence in their lives. In light of the unstable and insecure processes of all identity-formation, Plath offers her readers 'the one solid the spaces lean on'.[110] She nevertheless means different things to people in different contexts. I have attempted to explore the subtle variations that occur during these processes of identification. In this flux of maddening paradoxes and this swirl of ghosts, hauntings, loss, and mourning—despite seemingly being irretrievably lost—the spectral figure of Plath is still always present.

2

Doubling

I shall never get out of this!
There are two of me now.[1]

Identification, as we have discussed in the previous chapter, can take subtly differing forms. The most extreme end of the spectrum is when the narcissistic self literally consumes the lost loved object, so the two become indistinguishable. But whatever form it takes, Freud tells us that identification is about a tie with an 'other'; often this other can appear to share some of our characteristics and traits. In some cases it could be said, it feels as though we 'have a double'. In Greek mythology, Narcissus falls in love with his own image and dies as a consequence of the longing for this seemingly unobtainable other. The above quotation from Plath's poem 'In Plaster' reveals how doubling can result in being pursued by an inescapable other. Both of these examples highlight the mythology and folklore surrounding the notion of the double—a notion which itself is multifaceted and contradictory.

To frame the chapter within the context of our two main questions involves considering: how does the concept of the double help to explain the return of the dead? Furthermore, if a double does appear, in what way might it impact upon a subject's sense of self?

We have already briefly discussed Freud's notion of the doppelgänger as it appears in his work on the uncanny—something which is either both strange and familiar or something which repeats itself can become troubling and unnerving to us. Dolls may spring to life, wax works models may suddenly move, or the dead may return in demonic form to pursue us. For Freud, the doppelgänger is the perfect of example of the *unheimlich*, as it is something which is both familiar and yet strange—another that looks, or seems, just like us. Freud argues that the purpose of the doppelgänger has changed over time from being a protective spirit to a menacing demon or a harbinger of death.

Otto Rank carried out a psychoanalytic study into the double, covering its anthropological, historical, and folkloric significance. He also examined the role that the double plays in literature, and the characteristics of authors who write about the double. For Rank, at any stage in history or any place in culture, the existence of the double pointed to one thing, 'a universal human problem, that of the relation of the self to the self'.[2] Also implicit in Rank's study is the curious doubleness of the double itself, as it appears on many levels to stand for opposing yet interrelated issues; it is this duplicity of the double that we will explore at the beginning of this chapter.

Within anthropology and folklore, the double appears to take on a number of forms. The stories are full of mystery and swirling mists, superstition, and apprehensive beliefs. The dead can return, or are never truly dead. Mirrors become the reflection of what is, or what might be. Mirror or water reflections are believed to be directly linked to the soul; on certain days upon midnight, one might see a real true love or a menacing demon over one's shoulder in a mirror. The souls of dead people are supposed to be present in the mirror and can become visible under certain circumstances. When there is a corpse in the house the mirrors must be veiled for whoever sees their mirror reflection at this time will surely die. If there are thirteen people sitting at a dinner table, the one sitting opposite a mirror will die. A broken mirror can result in bad luck; viewing one's own image in a broken mirror can bring about that person's death. The mirror has magic properties and inexplicable powers.[3]

It is not just mirror reflections that hold such powers though. A water reflection, or even lack of one can cause dread and terror. We have already discussed the fate of Narcissus, but Rank also informs us that anthropological studies reveal that Zulus will not look into a dirty or murky swamp because it casts no reflection.[4] Their belief is that a monster dwelling there has taken away their reflections which means they shall die.

Rank also discusses how models or images of people can cause alarm and horror. Folklore dealing with the dread of one's own portrait or photograph is found all over the world; he claims that, according to anthropological studies, in certain parts of Africa, people became so disturbed by plastic representations of themselves that they had to be destroyed.

Shadows too become significant. Whoever casts no shadow risks death, whoever sees their shadow during Epiphany faces death, stepping on one's own shadow is a sign of death, to lose your shadow is to lose your soul. Any headless shadow person will certainly die within a year. Rank informs us that inhabitants of Amboyna and Uliate will not leave their houses at noon for fear of casting no shadow. There is an explicit link made to death here for 'since the souls of the deceased are shadows, they themselves cast no shadows'.[5] However, a lack of a shadow not only implies impending death, but also impotence and castration—a loss of power. Conversely, shadows can also be protective spirits, signs of fertility, and a misty embodiment of the human soul. Spirits, elves, and ghosts have no shadows, as they are already shadows themselves. Rank concludes that 'what the folkloric representations and several of the literary ones directly reveal is a tremendous thanatophobia' (fear of death).[6]

The link to death, and fear of death, leads to our second paradox regarding the double; not only can it be regarded as a bringer of death, but it can also act as a protective spirit and provide immortality. In Oscar Wilde's novel *The Picture of Dorian Gray*, it is the doppelgänger in the portrait that ages, while the narcissistic Gray himself remains young and handsome. For Rank, the creation of a double is inexplicably linked to the ego and the fear of death. Here lies a crucial area—namely, in what way does the double impact upon our reader-fans? Indeed, does the double have any relevance at all?

Looking back over my own relationship with Plath, I became aware there was a time when I felt I was engaged in quite a menacing exchange with her:

> It seems almost for as long as I can remember Plath has been with me in some shape or form and I have nearly always been really happy about that. I can't think of a better companion. However, there was time when I was completing my MA when I somehow felt absolutely 'hounded' by this thing I had started. I was writing my thesis about her and had shut myself up for days to work on it and suddenly I spent all my days thinking about her and dreaming about her and in my diary I talk about being suffocated by her, almost as if I am breathing her in. There was a definite feeling of scary pursuit and I was convinced I wouldn't escape.

Here, we see almost a physical description of consumption, 'breathing Plath in', but what is more interesting for us in terms of the theory of the double is the notion that Plath appears as a slightly menacing, pursuing figure. I wrote about wishing to escape, about feeling 'suffocated'. Rank's *The Double* is full of literature and folklore dealing with this kind of pursuit—never being able to escape the one thing that hounds you until you either come to terms with it, or it drives you mad and destroys you. Certainly, it would seem that a positive resolution was, thankfully, reached:

> After I finished my thesis, I went away for three months and lived in Greece. I worked on the beaches protecting turtles, very physical work, walking eight miles a day and digging nests and watching over hatchlings in the early hours. I had my Plath *Collected Poems* with me, of course, but she became less of a suffocating presence and returned once more to being like a friend. As I watched the Mediterranean I was able to read her lines 'where it pours bean green over blue.' I felt in so many ways so close and as ever her words returned to being the comforting words of a good friend.

In this narrative, Plath switches from being the pursuing tormentor to the protective figure, thus somehow managing to encompass both aspects of Rank's notion of the double.

According to Rank, this protective aspect of the double can be taken even further; he argues belief in a double can save us from an overwhelming fear of our own impending death. That unbearable destruction of the ego at the moment of death can be denied by the belief in a double. Insomuch as mirror and water reflections or shadows may be menacing demons in pursuit of the self, the substitution of our self by the double enables them to undergo the impending death on our behalf; thus it is possible to free oneself from thanatophobia:

> The most primitive concept of the soul is an image as closely similar as possible to the physical self, hence a true double. The idea of death, therefore, is denied by a duplication of the self-incorporated in the shadow or in the reflected image.[7]

It is this idea, the notion of protection from death which we will explore in relation to the respondents in this study who feel they double with Sylvia Plath. Certainly, my own feelings of being pursued by Plath did eventually fade and turn into something much more positive once I was less immersed in writing about her.

This also raises the question of the different types of doubling that may occur. The double can either take the form of a physical doppelgänger—i.e. an 'other' who closely resembles the outward appearance of the self—or an ego-double. As we have already discussed, a physical double may be one way to afford protection against death. But a double, while having to be similar in some way, does not necessarily have to be a physical likeness. Doubles can take differing forms and it may be perfectly possible for us to discover a double that does not look like us, but appears to mirror us in our beliefs, feelings or emotions—an ego-double, if you will.

> The uncanny double is clearly an independent and visible cleavage of the ego (shadow, reflection)—and different from those actual figures of the double who confront each other on real and physical persons of unusual external similarity and whose paths cross.[8]

For Rank, an ego-double would fulfil a similar role to a physical double. Formed from fear ('fear shapes from the ego-complex the terrifying phantom of the double'), the existence of an ego-double allows us to shift instincts, desires, fear, and responsibility onto another.[9] Our ego-double can be held accountable for all those things we cannot face ourselves.

It is this role of substitution that interests me, both in a physical and an ego sense, in that there is a feeling that an 'other' can become an alternative or surrogate self. If by destroying a double, we can either protect ourselves against death, or allow our double to die on our behalf, then what we see occurring here—beyond protection from our own thanatophobia—is in effect a symbolic, surrogate death. While I do not want to labour the notion of Christ-like dimensions discussed by Lloyd Baugh in the first chapter, there is nevertheless a Christ-like resonance when talking about somebody dying on behalf of another. Does this mean that reader-fans who double with Plath could be able to ward off their own thanatophobia, because she has died for, or before, them?

In *Beyond the Pleasure Principle*, Freud introduces the notion of a death drive within us all. While this initially seems to dispute our argument so far regarding thanatophobia, if we analyse this in a little more depth we can see some uncanny connections occurring. Freud sees the human death drive—*Todestrieb*—as a counter force to *eros*. He argues that we have within us all a compulsion to repeat things, especially events which are traumatic or cause upset; this occurred to him while watching a small child repeat a game in order to cope with the absence of his mother. Freud argues that repetition gives the impression of some demonic force at work and that this 'compulsion to repeat', to cause displeasure to the ego, is actually a desire to return to what he refers to as an inorganic state.[10]

Drawing upon literature, in particular *Hamlet*, Freud discusses the possibility that Hamlet's ultimate desire is for a blissful ending to life's difficulties, which for Freud amounts to a desire for regression back to what we once were. 'It seems, then, that an instinct is an urge inherent in organic life to restore an earlier state of things'.[11] We are left with two opposing instincts: *eros*, the drive for life—which I would link to feelings of thanatophobia—and *Todestrieb*, the desire for death—to return to an inanimate state.

Doubling with another may allow us to simultaneously appease these two conflicting instincts of Freud's. On the one hand, we can use our physical or ego-double to assuage our sense of fear over death and substitute their death instead of our own. At the same time, through killing them, we are satisfying our own death instincts by returning what we believe to be part of ourselves back to that inorganic state of blissful nothingness. In this sense, it becomes clearer why some reader-fans may possibly identify and double with someone who is already dead; they may have substituted this double's death for their own. This, in turn, puts an ironic twist on most fandom scholarship, (Jenson 1992, Dyer 1998, Rojek 2001, Reece 2006, Doss 2008) which deals with identification between icon and fan as being fuelled by sexual desire.[12, 13, 14, 15, 16] In fact, between those reader-fans who double with Sylvia Plath, it could be that their very identification with her is fuelled by death.

To recap, we have the doubleness of the double, which can be both a protective spirit and a menacing torment. We have the possibility of a physical, fleshy double or a psychological ego-double. While on the one hand, a double can be a harbinger of death, it can also offer immortality. While it can also be about loss and fear of loss, it is at the same time about creating another.

> *You are not I—but I am You.*
> *And you—it's you—you mirror'd domino,*
> *Wherein the hues, like ocean's tints, do reel*
> *You face without a mask: the seal me show,*
> *That, of your thoughts, the sources will reveal:*
> *Is't you yourself? A sign—you nod to me:*
> *Archaic seal and mask—do me I see?*
>
> 'Masks' by Richard Dehmel[17]

Dehmel's speculation on the flow of identity between the self and a mirror image is by no means unique in literature. For Rank, this is a crucial point because the existence of the double in literature points to a particular sort of mind set that is attracted enough to write about it. If, as we have seen above, readers may be both dealing with their own death drives and doing away with their thanatophobia, what exactly is the psychic structure of authors who write about it? Rank identifies a certain number of features related to those authors who write about doubles and doppelgängers. He argues they tend to be 'pathological' personalities who often suffer from psychic disturbances or mental illness. Often they can be depressed, neurotic, have phobias, and engage in compulsive brooding. More often than not, they have tragic lives, inner enemies, flashes of anger, and suicidal impulses and attempts.

However seductive Rank's description may be in drawing together a neat and tidy theory, there are problems attached to this. First, Rank was writing about a particular set of writers: all male, all white, all European. Second, he drew rather far-reaching generalisations from this fairly isolated sample. Therefore, we must take care when attempting to apply his theory. The writers whom Rank studied—E. T. A. Hoffman, Jean Paul, Oscar Wilde—did fit his psychological profile, so much so that Rank concluded, 'we must take into account the striking fact that so many of the writers whom we consider here met their wretched ends from severe neurological or mental illnesses'.[18] Rank is talking here about the historical figure of the writer, not the implied author of the texts.

There are problems with this approach. If we take Sylvia Plath as an example, there are many instances of doubling within her work. The poem 'The Lady and the Earthenware Head' tells the story of the fear of a clay model. 'The Other Two' deals with two duplicate couples living each others' lives in a Spanish villa. 'Mirror' discusses the power of not only the mirrored reflection, but also the water reflection. 'Contusion' explores death and the reflection in a house where the mirrors are sheeted. 'In Plaster' focuses on a menacing, tormenting double that needs to be destroyed. 'Sculptor' is about the uncanniness of wooden bodies lying around an artist's studio. 'By Candlelight' examines the power of the shadow image. What we have to question is whether, within these poems, we are hearing the voice of the historical Sylvia Plath, or the writerly voice Plath chooses to perform, that 'implied author'.[19] This is a thorny issue that cannot be avoided because if we have readers doubling with the voice of Sylvia Plath, we have to ask exactly who or what they are doubling with.

In the first chapter, we opened this discussion by exploring possible relationships between the historical author and the implied author, and laid the groundwork for considering the possibility that the two do not have to be—and frequently are not—the same; what we need to explore now in a little more detail is the actual nature of this author.

The discussion dealing with the relationship between a text and its author is a well voiced and ongoing debate. Foucault denies the presence of the author once a text has been produced; he asks whether it matters who is speaking in his lecture, 'What is an Author?' Author-function, for Foucault, springs from using the author's name, for it can act as a descriptor. When the name Sylvia Plath is mentioned, a reader may form a certain set of assumptions. Often author's names can become adjectives—such as certain writing being described as 'Proustian.'

Roland Barthes had already examined this relationship between author and text in 'The Death of the Author', claiming that the explanation for a piece of work is always sought in the person who produced it. Yet for Barthes, the meaning of a text is not so transparent, for it is the reader who produces the meaning at the cost of the author—i.e. the death of the author.

This pondering on the role of author function is highly pertinent, in particular, for this chapter. If Foucault and Barthes are correct, then it is impossible for Plath readers to identify or double with the 'historical' Plath herself; they are merely responding to an author performance. In *Rhetoric of Fiction*, Wayne Booth questions Barthes' claim of the death of the author; he suggests, 'the author can to some extent choose his [*sic*.] disguises, but he can never choose to disappear'.[20] These disguises can be very effective and open to interpretation by the reader.

In *The Rhetorics of Feminism*, Lynne Pearce describes an incident in which she herself, as an implied author, became subject to this sort of misreading:

Here, I am inevitably reminded of one of the reviews to my own, first single-authored text in which I was compared to a fighter pilot (!) and how superbly at odds the reviewer's image of his 'implied author' was to the shy, retiring, marginal, twenty something persona I inhabited at the time![21]

This echoes conversations I held with Plath's old friends in which they recounted with glee how both Plath's reading voice and persona in her poems made them laugh—'Er, exactly where did you get that plummy voice from, Syl?' (Marcia Brown), and 'She was nothing like the fierce woman of her poems' (Jillian Becker).[22, 23] For Pearce, the reader needs to be offered enough of the writer to even want to make meaning from the text. This does not mean that a historical Plath is accessible from her texts; Pearce claims that the very act of writing, like the self, has a fragmented nature about it. Writings can be 'one-off performances that take their "meaning" only from the re-iteration of other performances'.[24] Acknowledging this discontinuity, for Pearce, is the only way to proceed. Julian Wolfreys approaches the problem a little differently, by claiming that we cannot help but see the text as some form of author communication; even if the author appears a little ghostly, there is nevertheless 'some presence, form or identity which was once present and which was once the origin of the text'.[25]

In answer to Foucault's question—does it matter who is speaking?—I would argue, yes it does. Although it is important for us to remember that for most of our respondents, their first line of identification was with Plath's 'implied author', they did make the leap from this to what Wolfreys calls 'the origin of the text'.[26]

There undoubtedly existed a historical Sylvia Plath, the 'real' Sylvia Plath—real in the sense of *a priori*, not authentic. This *a priori* figure was historicised, had a life, a history. This 'real' Sylvia Plath was also an author figure who transformed *a priori* events from her history into fictionalised pieces of work spoken via either her 'implied author' or narrator. This manifested itself via the poems—the written word. It does not matter that this figure cannot be accessed directly. The fact that the figure is there at all, as some sort of spectral presence behind the text, is enough. It is perhaps this that creates an active relationship with the reader, for the reader affects the poems, and the poems affect the reader, thus creating a circuit of productivity that in turn creates the text.

However fictionalised or inaccessible this *a priori* Plath may be, the poems do produce a subject with both a history and a story. The 'implied author' creates a speaker which results in the reader-fans having, what Adrienne Rich calls, 'a very full sense of the "I" who is both the subject and the narrator of the text'.[27] Barthes would argue it is this authorial voice that has died and yet, for some Plath reader-fans, it seems they are reluctant to relinquish the very figure that produced this authorial voice. It is almost as though readers somehow interfere at that meeting point between the *a priori* Plath and the 'implied author' Plath, as if they want to be co-authors or voyeurs at what happens during this transformation of biography into fiction. Perhaps this is the site which could become a space for readers to identify with the person behind the text. This may explain not only how identification occurs upon reading Plath, but how there is enough sense of the writer herself to allow ego-doubling to take place.

It is important to establish that I am not claiming that an 'authentic' Plath can be accessed. Whether dead or alive, this seems unlikely in light of our previous discussion in Chapter One about the enigmatic role of the author. Equally, I am not arguing that readers have some sort of entirely fictional understanding of Plath. What I am trying to demonstrate is that the author can be reinstated in such a way that a meeting point can occur for the reader between the impossibility of an authentic Plath and the seemingly endless versions that could exist of a fictional Plath. As Pearce suggests, there has to be some notion of the person behind the text.[28]

For some reader-fans, Plath's presence is strongly felt both behind and in the text, enough for them to recognise certain characteristics and enough for them to want to identify with her. In his discussion of writers dealing with the double, Rank confirms as much when he claims that texts do not become intelligible from the writer's individual personality, 'in the writer as in the reader a super individual factor seems to be unconsciously vibrating here, lending to these motifs a mysterious, psychic resonance'.[29] If the figure of the double is depicted as slightly magical and half hidden behind swirling mists, then the process by which we actually create a double is even more so.

In the context of this book, we need to ask the question: why is it that some reader-fans 'double' with Sylvia Plath and some do not? In dealing with this typically slippery subject, we could argue it is uncanny when they do and uncanny when they do not. Moreover, at what point exactly does identification tip over into doubling? In the previous chapter, we have seen the extreme end of the identification spectrum with Sonia, who claims that she is Sylvia Plath. Does this amount to doubling? What interests us in relation to Sylvia Plath and her reader-fans is the fact that doubling does not have to involve a physical likeness—although this can be relevant too—but is equally content with an ego likeness. This allows for a potentially broad range of doubling with Plath for we can include not only people who believe they are her physical double, but also her mental double.

As we shall see in the later chapters dealing with place, images, and objects, time also plays a significant role. The crumbling of a linear chronology allows us to link the double to shifting time, for it seems that the double's very self is based upon the past, present, and future. In terms of the past, Rank states that often the double will symbolically represent our own past:

The basic idea is supposed to be that a person's past inescapably clings to him [*sic*] and that it becomes his fate as soon as he tried to get rid of it.[30]

In this sense, the double is some sort of spectral embodiment of past deeds. However, at the same time it can capture the present via the form it takes in influencing the relationship between the subject and the double. Is it a protective spirit? A menacing torment? Does it need to be destroyed? The future then is also often captured in how the double manifests itself. *The Picture of Dorian Gray* depicts what he will become. In folklore, the reflections in the mirror at midnight can reveal future events and true loves. Time once again becomes playful, neatly captured in a quote from Rank:

> Then I saw you and I wanted to become you—but that won't work for I cannot go back; but you can go ahead, one of these days you will become myself.[31]

In what ways do reader-fans of Sylvia Plath 'become' her or allow her to 'become' themselves?

Sonia

> In the very beginning I was riding the subway to work one day (Feb 2004) when I saw an old black and white photo in the paper. The picture was about 2×3-cm and my eyes were instantly drawn to this picture. "Me!" was my first thought. It was like looking at a photo of myself, looking into my eyes. And then I read the text, saying something about a poet I had never heard of, Sylvia Plath, who had committed suicide.

Sonia's first encounter with Sylvia Plath was not linguistic, but visual; the notion of physical doubling was very strong for Sonia from the start. Wondering why a picture of herself was in the newspaper, she initially came to the realisation that it was not her, but an 'other'.

> The facial features, the body, it's all there. She was just as tall as me. ... The hands, the look in her eyes, some form of stiffness that I have, insecurity maybe. ... I recognise myself in some way in almost all the photos I have seen of her. I'm thinking "Ah, that's exactly what I used to look like when I was younger".

This attention to detail is not unusual, and Rank himself suggests that often upon finding a double 'we always find a likeness which resembles the main character down to the smallest particulars such as name, voice and clothing'.[32]

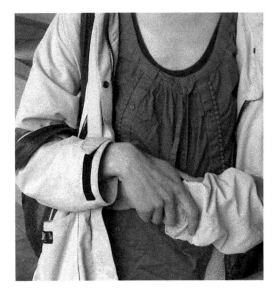

Comparative images of Sonia's and Sylvia's hands. (*Sonia Flur*)

The doubling that Sonia experiences with Plath does not stop there; as well as seeing physical similarities, upon reading Plath, Sonia discovers similar psychological characteristics:

> Next thing I did was to buy Sylvia's diary. I read and it felt so familiar. It was like reading my own confused thoughts, going from extreme happiness one day to opposite pessimism the next day. Since I became curious of this Sylvia, I started to read about her. There were even more things that we had in common: her psyche seemed to be just like mine. I have since early childhood been struggling with mental problems of different kinds, and the thought of suicide came early as well.

We see a connection to Freud's notion of *Todestrieb*. Sonia's death instincts were present from a very young age, while at the same time countered by a fear of death. While wanting to die, it was also something that terrified her. She worried about leaving traces, and the fear of death actually prevented her from writing a diary in case someone found it after she had died. If, as we have argued the double is connected to the death drive, then Sonia's next comment makes sense:

> I never liked myself in my childhood and as long as I can remember I have had the feeling that I was worthless. Even though I acted like a cheerful child, I was very unhappy on the inside. My first suicidal thoughts came to me when I was eight years old. I didn't want to live. These thoughts then became my faithful companions throughout my whole youth and adult life.

It was as if I had a deep feeling of guilt of something that I had done in the past, and in this lifetime I had a longing for making things better.

There are a number of issues to unravel in this statement. Sonia's sense of *Todestrieb* is overwhelming; the 'compulsion to repeat', which Freud states as being evidence of this death drive, seems to occur to Sonia repeatedly throughout her childhood and adulthood, to the extent that she describes these death urges as 'faithful companions.' Interestingly, the sense of guilt links to Rank's claim that we tend to find an ego-double when we feel guilty about something and want to shift responsibility from ourselves onto another; guilt may force the self to displace blame upon another ego. Time again reveals its playfulness as Sonia merges past, present and future—feeling guilty in the present about something that happened in the past and wanting to make things better in the future. In fact, Rank describes the creation of a double as being about a sense of self-preservation—a longing to escape death or the submergence into nothingness and the hope of waking to a new life.[33] Sonia's conflicting drives of *eros* and *Todestrieb* appear evident in both her desire to die and her longing for things to become better in the future.

Beneath all of this identification, doubling, and uncanny similarities, there is something more at play between life and death and the use of an 'other'. For Diana Fuss in *Identification Papers,* the act of identification is about invoking phantoms, it is 'the detour through the other that defines a self'.[34]

By incorporating the spectral remains of the dearly departed love-object, the subject vampiristically comes to life. To be open to identification is to be open to a death encounter, open to the very possibility of communing with the dead.[35]

For Sonia, this communing with the dead takes place in a more literal sense, for rather than simply being like Plath, she believes that she is Sylvia Plath, reincarnated:

Still, with scepticism, I googled her name and I saw image after image looking like me! She even seemed to have the same hands and tall body like I have. I had to catch my breath. What was this? It felt so unreal. And at the same time so familiar. Could it actually be me? Could I have lived about forty years ago in another body? Sylvia died when she was thirty and I was born in 1972, the same year that she would have turned forty.

Furthermore, while psychoanalytic theory seems to provide a fairly tidy framework for Sonia, this does not coincide with her beliefs. She talks about her own scepticism and a feeling of unreality, but at the same time she expresses a belief in the 'soul'; this belief that, according to Rank, plays a significant role in the belief in a double. A problem occurs here though between a usable psychoanalytic study (like Rank's) that appears to explain Sonia's situation, and her own beliefs which are somewhat different. How might we respond?

First, the fact that psychoanalytic theory is relevant for Sonia is in no way intended to undermine her own belief structure, which is equally valid and equally explanatory. While Rank and Freud deal with the relation of the self to the self, Sonia's beliefs—still involving the self—involve a wider and perhaps more spiritual view:

> After Sylvia killed herself she got stuck in a zone between the spirit and physical world. That is what happens when spirits become ghosts. They are drawn to something in the physical world and are unable to go to the spirit world. Being in this zone is often very painful, since we aren't able to let go of things or people. In Sylvia's case she was very concerned about her children, and regretted deeply that she had left them and also felt a lot of guilt. But she couldn't undo what had happened. She wanted to comfort them and reach them but wasn't able to.

Sonia's explanation of the possibility of reincarnation raises some familiar issues—hauntings, inability to let go of things we love, mourning, guilt, a desire for something better. The fact cannot be avoided that Sonia connects these issues to her own difficulties as a mother. In an honest account of her experiences after giving birth, she writes:

> I hadn't been able to sleep more than an hour a day during a whole week, and once Nimbus [her son] came, the production of breast milk didn't get started and he was very unhappy, and just cried and cried all night, and it was just horrible and hard in every way. So I had a bad start. I was completely worn out. And that, I guess, got in the way for me and Nimbus to really connect to each other in the beginning. All this made it difficult for me to become a mother.

For Rank, the creation of a double is a way to satisfy desires and instincts indirectly. Therefore, working with his theory, it is possible to see that Sonia's emotions of guilt, in this case her feelings of inadequacy as a mother towards her son, were displaced onto another—her double in a previous life, who 'left' her children by committing suicide.

While elements of Sonia's story are sad, she nevertheless views 'finding' Sylvia as a positive aspect of her life. As we saw in the first chapter, sometimes there is slippage in her references to Sylvia Plath and, rather than the blurring of Sonia and Sylvia's identities, we see an acknowledgement of distance. In explaining her relationship to Plath, Sonia says:

I have come to understand myself on a deeper level after reading about Sylvia, and reading her diaries and poems. I am not in any way sure that I have been Sylvia. And it doesn't really matter. The main thing to me is that I have learned so much by investigating Sylvia's life. And if I should write something for your work I would write about the psychological gain that her story has given me.

Morney

We have argued that doubling may be a way to somehow confront both the life and death drives. Rank explicitly links the notion to death when he claims that the double 'almost regularly leads to suicide, which is so frequently linked with pursuit by the double, the self'.[36] As we discussed earlier though, the double can also be about a guardian or protective spirit, and Morney credits Plath with saving her life after suffering a breakdown and suicide attempt. However, this identification with Plath came after the suicide attempt, so to blame a belief in the double as the precipitating factor seems inaccurate in this case:

> Although my interest in her has been intense for about twenty-two years now, there was very definitely a point in my life where I felt like she 'saved my life' in the same way that I felt it about Morrissey. I had a breakdown and attempted suicide just over three years ago and for a long time afterwards I couldn't read or do anything that I normally could do. I found the only thing I could do was listen to my tapes of her reading her poems. Gradually I started to re-read the books I had about her, then gradually I started to write poetry myself again.

It is interesting to note that at this point no doubling is occurring, either in a physical or ego sense. In fact, Morney is very clear that her relationship with Plath is not about obsession (a term that she finds offensive), but about a special empathy. It is perhaps this empathy that we first see leading to a hint of ego-doubling, particularly when it comes to writing her own poetry. While Morney has received many awards for her writing, it is interesting that ego-doubling occurs at this meeting point mentioned earlier between the *a priori* person and the writerly voice; Morney writes poems in the voice of Plath, or in her words 'on behalf of Plath'. She discusses how this first occurred:

> 'The Truth' is one [poem] I wrote after I had read an article by Eilat Negev, an Israeli journalist, with Assia Wevill's sister.[37] The article contained long quotes from Ted Hughes which honestly so infuriated me at the time that I couldn't sleep until I had written the poem! Anyway, I was so infuriated by

several of TH's descriptions of SP that I wrote the poem, then found that halfway through, it began to be SP writing on behalf of her and Assia, which I really hadn't expected. I finished that poem very late at night and I was quite disturbed by it—especially when my bedroom door slammed shut violently in the middle of the night despite there being no breeze.

What is interesting to note here is not only the projection of Morney onto Plath, speaking on her behalf, but the slightly mysterious nature of writing in this manner. Speaking in someone else's voice, which is still at the same time your own, amounts to some sort of doubling performance, but projecting what it is your speaker would have liked the person to say.

> *But I was there, darling,*
> *when you wrote those letters.*
> *I stood behind you and watched*
> *your pen leak excuses,*
> *ink made from our blood.*
> *Weaving your pages of myths.*
>
> *I, your first wife, I.*
> *I inevitably died.*
> *Written in the stars from the day I was born.*
> *Mad thing that I was.*
> *How else could it end?*
>
> 'The Truth'

This appears to be an example of Fiske's argument that within the productivity and production of fandom, textual productivity plays a large role.[38] Fans may draw features from the original subject, rephrase lines, speak in their voice, mainly (as far as Fiske is concerned) in order to reduce the distance between themselves and their love object.

For Morney, writing these poems appeared to be more about a sense of justice, and, inspired by anger, she seemingly displaces these emotions onto another. Later, reflecting on the process she claimed:

I'm just very aware that I wrote them (especially 'The Truth') when I was in an absolute *fury* after reading some things that Ted Hughes had written about Sylvia. Writing 'The Truth' and 'If You Only Had A Heart' were both attempts really to give her her power back. I think I find it interesting that I felt so strongly on her behalf about these things, that I actually felt I *had* to write the poems, in her voice, before I could relax. I don't often (ever, probably) feel 'inside someone's head' enough to be driven to write something from their point of view to exorcise a feeling that I'm having really strongly about something that happened to them. I didn't write them because I wanted to write them, as such, I wrote them because I had to write them—they were 'shouting' at me to write them. And the truth is that in each case, after the poem was written, the feeling was exorcised. I remember a very strong feeling after writing 'The Truth' in particular, that the air around me had changed. Ok, now I sound like I'm trying to say I'm channelling her spirit!

As we shall see in the following chapter on place, the sense of invoking Plath is not uncommon; however, in this instance the need to exorcise a torment links with Rank's notion of doubles somehow being something that must be destroyed in order to move on. For Morney, the actual exorcism of the voice of Plath allows her to feel released in a physical sense—'the air around me had changed.' Equally there is a psychical element taking place as Morney claims she had to 'feel inside some one's head' to write these poems. Once they were written, she was able to relax. But like Sonia, there is an otherworldly element to this story; although Morney jokes about 'channelling' Plath's spirit, she nevertheless finishes her account with this claim.

Another similarity between the narratives of Morney and Sonia is the role of *eros* and *Todestrieb*. For both respondents, the conflicting life and death forces appear to be at work. Both have felt suicidal at points in their lives and both have been 'saved' by Plath in differing ways, either from death, an alienated life, or both. This form of redemption appears to emerge from either a physical doubling with Plath for Sonia or an ego-doubling for Morney.

Kiki

Why do so many people (mostly women) feel the need to merge with SP to the extent that they declare that they 'are' her? Obviously, they identify with her words and the emotions they evoke to an enormous extent. This to me refutes the criticism that her work is merely personal and all about her, but instead it transcends the self that is SP and is universal.

On the surface, Kiki appears puzzled and somewhat bemused by the notion of doubling; she does not appear to understand why people 'merge' with Plath, or consume her ego to the point of assimilation. In this first statement, Kiki appears to be a direct contrast to the physical and ego-doubling of Sonia and Morney.[39]

Kiki draws a distinction between the historical Plath and her textual work left behind. Kiki's belief is that the work creates the identification, so that the text transcends the writer and becomes 'universal.' As we saw earlier, this supports Foucault's claim about the nature of the author; a text should not be limited by the figure of the person who produced it, but rather exist in 'an absolutely free state'.[40]

However, Foucault's argument only works so far in the case of Kiki; while he argues that in addressing a text we 'would hardly hear anything but the stirring of an indifference: What difference does it make who is speaking?', Kiki does find it necessary in some sense to have a notion of the writer behind the work.[41]

> It's almost as if the text is not enough. There is a deep physical desire to possess or to at least handle her diaries, her books, to see the places she visited, etc.

Not only does this directly challenge Foucault's analysis of the text-reader relationship, but also reveals conflicting impulses in Kiki. As a researcher I am struck that on the one hand, she claims Plath transcends the text, yet on the other, she fully reinstates the figure of Plath behind the work because 'the text is not enough'. This is one of those moments when however much I want the narrative to speak for itself, I cannot help but highlight the inconsistencies.

We can draw on our earlier discussion of Lynne Pearce who, quoting Adrienne Rich, claimed that 'there has to be a person behind the text'.[42] For Kiki, while the text does stand alone and speak for itself, she seemingly cannot separate her relationship between the text and the author; the two are inextricably linked. We see this confusion of voices reflected also in Morney's account, in which she explains that 'Plath'—historical figure and voice of the poems—saved her from a difficult time.

In terms of doubling, Kiki's account offers a paradoxical view of her own positioning. She appears to be aware that reader-fans identify with Plath's 'words and emotions to an enormous extent', but this does not appear to amount to ego-doubling on her part. Neither in Kiki's case does she experience physical doubling:

> Perhaps it was just a matter of growing up in a different family and in a different time. I never felt I had to prove myself the way she did. And I never wanted to look like anyone else, or dress like anyone else around me.

Kiki acknowledges the role of historical and cultural context here, despite her earlier claim for the universality of Plath. As we saw in Chapter One, Kiki does appear to have a curious relationship with Plath, in that she appears on some level to identify with her and have a slightly proprietary relationship— she is unhappy about having to 'share' her with other people—yet neither does a more intimate identification or doubling take place. We have to ask why this is so.

In fact, Kiki openly rejects the idea of doubling with either Plath or anyone else—'I never wanted to look like anyone else'—and she does not necessarily approve of the way historical and cultural conventions pressured Plath into appearing a certain way: 'I never had to prove myself the way she did'. Kiki's sense of self seems both secure and confident, happy to be different, happy to differentiate herself from others. What is striking, however, is a certain wistfulness in Kiki's account of herself in relation to Plath; however secure her sense of self may be, she nevertheless appears to have an acknowledged yearning for some sort of merging between herself and Plath.

In speaking about a photograph taken of Plath on a beach with her then-current boyfriend, Gordon Lameyer, Kiki claims, 'In that one photo, I think I saw a little of what I wanted to see—a little of myself in Sylvia.' With this comment, we can challenge elements of Rank's notions of the double, for he speculates that on the whole, the creation of a double is an unconscious process. He even goes so far as to quote the idea from Ralph Tymms that the double could be seen as an allegorical representation, or a projection, of the second self of the unconscious.[43] This does not seem to allow room for Kiki's conscious willing of a doubling with Plath and her confession that she wants to see part of herself in an 'other'.

In her discussion on the nature of fandom, Jenson argues that there is perhaps something a little dishonourable about trying to categorise attachments that people make to others since 'little is known about the variety of ways people make meaning in everyday ways'; actually, the nature and varieties of affections and attachments that people form can manifest itself in unexpected and complex ways.[44] Jenson claims that people should not be defined as 'a collection of preferences', but rather social researchers should be willing to partake in 'respectful engagement' that illuminates the experiences of others in their own terms.[45] Jenson's argument is a timely reminder that all theory should be handled with care, and that people do not always neatly slot into a well-honed model. However, rather than being an issue, this is what makes researching the relationships between Plath and her readers endlessly fascinating. Kiki's story may have loose ends and unanswered aspects, but if we acknowledge and stay with these unresolved areas, the scope for further exploration opens up.

Peter

So far with our respondents, we have seen very different notions of doubling. For Sonia, this was both physical and psychical; for Morney, ego-doubling; and for Kiki, a sort of wistful and resistant—but not enacted—physical doubling. Peter is the first respondent who does not reveal any form or signs of doubling with Plath at all. This is interesting. As we saw in the previous chapter, he does nevertheless mourn and, to a certain extent, identify with the lost Plath. Here we have an anomaly: why would somebody identify but not double?

On a physical level, gender is an obvious reason why there would be no doubling between Plath and Peter. However, we could argue this would be less of a problem in terms of ego-doubling. Upon speculating whether he encounters any gender barriers between himself and reading Plath's work, he initially denies this is an issue: 'I don't think I do. In fact, most of the poets I like very much are women.' He does qualify this statement with the possibility that 'there is a good chance I don't "get" some of the poems, but for the most part I read poetry for the enjoyment of reading poetry, nothing more nothing less.' I would argue Peter gets much more from Plath, both for himself and other people, through reading Plath's poetry, although, of course, the aspect of pleasure should never be overlooked.

Can we perhaps link Peter's lack of doubling to something else? If with Sonia and Morney there is some relationship between Plath and death, is this lacking with Peter? He does see Plath's suicide as a stumbling block, as creating a silence and an inescapable void in his knowledge: 'I know I won't find Plath, literally (but I know where she lies). I know I won't find the reason for her suicide.' However, with regard to his own views on death, we can see hints of thanatophobia, although nowhere near as overwhelming as in other respondents:

> I've thought about death a bit, I don't know if I'm afraid of dying. ... I'd prefer to say I'm interested to see what happens in my lifetime. ... Of course not knowing what's on the other side. I guess, though, I am a little afraid.

We could argue that Peter's thanatophobia is not so overwhelming that he needs to create a double in order to cope with this fear, especially since he is only a 'little afraid'. If we compare this to Sonia, who had strong death urges from the age of eight that have stayed with her throughout her life, we see how these unused death instincts—as Freud calls them—need to be applied externally, beyond the subject, in order to protect the ego. For Peter, the wish to die has never been so literal; in fact, he seems to speak more of some sort of transformation occurring to him in this lifetime:

> I know that when I was first interested in Plath I was in quite a dark place having just lost my first love. I took that quite badly and I suppose I did want to die (but I'm glad I didn't); and in my poetry class, when I read and learned and memorized and took to heart 'the message' of 'Lady Lazarus', I suppose I began to resurface. When I say 'the message' of 'Lady Lazarus' I do mean the whole re-birth thing, but I didn't consider it necessary to actually die; getting

dumped like that and getting over it for me was more of a metaphorical death. Coming back to life but not through actual death. I think rising out of whatever ash I rose from was like Wordsworth says, 'I cannot paint what then I was.' You come back, different, and in a way that you have a history, but it's not something to which you can revert.

In this statement, Peter's sense of *Todestrieb* seems curiously allegorical rather than literal. His desire to die, the death urge, is countered by his desire to 'resurface', the life urge. Coming back to life for Peter does not mean having to actually physically die. Perhaps this is the key point to consider here; Peter is killing off what he once was and never wants to be again, or more precisely, never can be again.

If our other respondents have doubled with Plath in order to satisfy their own death and survival urges, it seems Peter has formed another tactic. His identification with Plath, discussed in the previous chapter, does not need to go any further; it does not need to tip into doubling because he can appease his instincts from Plath's words alone. He directly links what he calls his 'whole re-birth thing' with the message of the poem 'Lady Lazarus', that in order to live one has to die first.

There are hints of Freud's 'compulsion to repeat'.[46] The fact that Peter not only read and memorised the words to the poem, but relived the 'dark place' he was in through the poem, shows that his *Todestrieb*—on at least, a metaphorical level—brought about a 'death', followed by a 'rebirth'. The work of mourning is taking place on a number of levels. We have already discussed how Peter mourns the loss of Plath, but there is also the loss of a more literal love-object: his first love. It seems that the Freudian description of mourning, a phase that has to be endured and which then passes, applies to Peter; he suffers the 'death' and moves into a new life. However, it is worth speculating whether the recovery from the mourning for his lost first love, is in any way connected with his transferral of feelings onto the figure of Sylvia Plath.

The main difference with Peter is that, whereas the mourning and identificatory processes seem to explain the relationship occurring between himself and Plath, this does not extend into doubling. In this regard, gender difference presents an obvious obstacle. As we shall see shortly in relation to our other male respondent, Florian, doubling is more likely to take place vis-à-vis a male figure—in his case, Plath's father. Identification across gender, while not impossible, is less likely.

Peter also shows much less need to rely on Plath in times of distress, although he does use her as a form of comfort to deal with the loss of his first love. Whereas Sonia and Morney credit Plath with rescuing them on some level, Peter appears to be less afflicted by the contradictory impulses of *eros* and *Todestrieb*. In fact, even at the most distressing time of his life, when he feels as though he 'wants' to die, Peter is able to read his impulse as largely metaphorical: the necessary 'casting off' of an old self. This is in direct contrast to Morney, who actually acted on her suicidal impulses. For Peter, the resurrection took place by 'coming back to life but not through actual death.'

Anna and Megan

As noted in the first chapter, the responses of Anna and Megan to Plath were remarkably similar. Although they both identified with the emotions in Plath's work, they did not fully identify with the person herself. As we shall see in later chapters, although Anna's interest in Plath does eventually extend beyond the text, for Megan it remains strictly a relationship with the words-on-the-page. The reason I have decided to analyse these two respondents together is that although these subtle differences occur, they are the only two female respondents in this study who do not 'double' in some respect with Plath. We find ourselves faced with Anna, who has some sort of identification with Plath but no doubling, and Megan, who has neither identification nor doubling.

For Anna, one main stumbling block in her relationship with Plath is her inability to understand why she committed suicide:

> Anyway, as I remember it, I kept looking at the picture [on *The Bell Jar*] and feeling very uncomfortable about the fact that she killed herself and had such small babies. I still have trouble grasping that sometimes, although now I think I understand it better. At the time it struck me as the greatest tragedy, well it still does. It's unbelievably tragic.

This seems to demonstrate that Anna is not forming any sort of ego-doubling with Plath; they are not alike and, in some ways, she 'has trouble' understanding some of Plath's actions. Rather than Freud's belief that we all desire a sinking into a blissful nothingness—compare Morney's poem 'Your Blue Hour'—Anna perceives the horror of suicide. It is certainly not desirable, but rather 'unbelievably tragic'. However, it is interesting to consider our earlier claim that reader-fans of Plath are drawn to her not by desire, but by death. Here speculating on the tragic suicide of a young woman, Anna may also be seen to be drawn towards Plath by the horror of Plath's story.

For Megan, it was her encounter with *The Bell Jar* that leads her to consider similarities between her own life and the text. It is important to note that Megan does talk about the text and the fictional character within the text and she does not blur this voice with that of the *a priori* Plath:

> It [*The Bell Jar*] also captured how I sometimes felt directionless and lost, and like I was a failure waiting to happen, particularly with academic pressures

and the need to perform to my own perfectionist standards. Although I never even contemplated suicide and I was a successful and happy teenager, the book captured the sense of fear, inertia and isolation that used to creep up in that time of newness and sometimes daunting uncertainty.

Notice the contrast here between Sonia and Morney's stories. All three were actively unhappy. Sonia suffered emotional disturbances from a young age, yet Megan was a 'successful and happy teenager.' Her only moments of anxiety came about through the process of adolescence; she 'never contemplated suicide'. For Anna, suicide equated with tragedy. Therefore, we have to consider whether a self-conscious aversion to self-inflicted destruction causes some Plath readers to actively resist doubling and identification. In fact, the closest Megan gets to some form of connection is with the fictional character Esther Greenwood, the main protagonist in *The Bell Jar*:

> I suppose it was easy to draw a comparison between Esther Greenwood and myself simply because we were both experiencing the same transitional phase into adulthood.

The boundaries are clearly drawn here and not blurred. Furthermore, it is a 'comparison', not a doubling—a key difference. This did not prevent Megan becoming fascinated about the strong bonds other reader-fans of Plath formed. In fact, it was this interest that resulted in her studying the iconicity of Plath for her final-year dissertation:

> The little wider reading I had encountered seemed to indicate that Sylvia Plath the writer and the woman had a fascinating draw on many women and readers in general. I already felt that Plath had a remarkable cultural value today. My original intentions were simply to question this cultural iconicity, and ask if my reaction to Plath as a young female reader was symptomatic of a wider cultural trend. Furthermore, I sensed a powerful (and sometimes even hysterical?!) bond between some Plath readers and their icon, and wanted to discover why this poet seemed to speak for these women today.

Already, Megan shows awareness that seepage of identity, or even doubling, does occur with some readers; however, she places herself firmly outside this process herself, choosing instead to study it within the context of academia.

However, for Anna, one form of doubling does occur, for later on in the text she writes:

> It has been kind of a double interest for me both an interest specifically in Plath and her texts, and an interest in her as a phenomenon and a subject

for study.... The more I read of and about SP, the more interesting I think it gets. I've always felt that anything is more interesting when you know more about it, when you get down to detail-level. So reading more now just makes everything else even more interesting.

Florian

As discussed in Chapter One, Florian—Sonia's partner—also experiences an element of identification in his relationship with Plath, but indirectly, via the figure of Plath's father. While Florian believes Sonia to be a reincarnation of Sylvia Plath, he believes himself to be a reincarnation of Otto Plath. His experience of doubling takes a similar form to Sonia and involves both physical and ego-doubling. In fact, it was Sonia who first made him aware of an uncanny physical resemblance between himself and Otto Plath, and subsequently he became aware of other character similarities. In Chapter One, we were introduced to Florian's first reaction on seeing photographs of Otto Plath. He goes on to explain:

> Later when I saw a photo of Otto as young man in *Letters Home*, the resemblance really struck me. The eyes... wow! So as we learned more and more about the Plaths, the more convincing it all became. It was so exciting to read Aurelia's own words, their whole story.[47] It felt familiar and explained a lot regarding my personality as well.

We have, as with Sonia, the doppelgänger effect of Florian–Otto and the beginning of a cleavage of ego:

> I mentioned my physical similarities with Otto earlier. I can't help it but when I see the pictures it really feel like he has my body. Even the hair seems to have the same thickness. I have also always preferred very short hair on the sides which you can see on photos of Otto from the thirties.

This brings to mind Rank's claim that in finding doubles, we tend to find those that resemble us down to the last detail: features, hair, and clothes.[48] Florian finds direct physical similarities, but he also finds intricate personality traits that cause the two men to resemble each other:

> I have been interested in nature as long as I remember. Unlike most others I was especially fascinated by insects. Not that I liked to bee with them (Freudian miss-spelling), but I felt some kind of empathy with them. I use to rescue bumblebees from my parents swimming pool each day.[49] I always tried to avoid killing insects. There was one detail I discovered just the other

day that made me cry, because sometimes I still doubt in all this. But this small detail was like a validation. Aurelia writes that Otto "felt regret when he accidentally stepped on an ant". As I said I have always felt empathy towards insects… and I have rarely met someone with that same view on insects, so it feels like more than a coincidence.

We see early in the narrative that Florian still has doubts about his doubling, or reincarnation, with Otto Plath, and finding stories that highlight their similarities help him to accept what he believes has occurred. While at this stage in the story, Florian still refers to Otto Plath as a separate entity, this soon changes and there is a true merging of identities:

It is both flattering and embarrassing that we believe we are the incarnations of Otto and Sylvia. Even worse is that I might have become my former daughter's lover! I hope that's excused if there is an incarnation between. It is absolutely mind blowing when I look at pictures of Aurelia, Sylvia, and Warren, to imagine that they have been my wife and children. It feels incredible that this story maybe is for real.

For Florian, having a double serves a number of the purposes raised by Rank in his study. The notion of a reincarnated soul acts as both a protector against death, and an assurance of immortality. We have already seen elements of this in the accounts of Morney and Sonia. We could argue this is a direct result of Florian's thanatophobia; by shifting his belief onto reincarnation and evidence of this reincarnation, he does not have to face the prospect of the destruction of the ego. Unlike Peter, who appears to have a much weaker *Todestrieb*, Florian is more concerned with the cycle of life and death. In fact, Florian links his previous two lives together in a similar way to Sonia; what is occurring for him now in this life is a direct result of what happened in the last. Time flows between the two, creating a direct correlation. He describes an incident walking in a university park in Oxford:

I was walking by myself that time and thought it was absolutely beautiful surroundings. Then I got a strong longing for studying abroad, I realized how many opportunities I must have missed in this life, that I hadn't been independent enough. I decided in my mind that I would study abroad in my next life. As I was walking in the university park of Oxford that feeling came back to me, and I realized that it maybe wasn't about what I wanted to do in the future—it was what I had done in the past. Maybe I was feeling nostalgia from my life as Otto. He must have been in surroundings like these a lot. Whatever it came from, my feeling was there. I had a strong, spontaneous reaction. I felt sad, happy and humble towards life.

Florian ponders on missed opportunities within his life, and his inner turmoil becomes unburdened on the figure of Otto Plath; it is actions from a previous life that create the inadequacies and dissatisfactions in this one. For Florian, this helps to make sense of an upsetting situation that seems unfair. The belief in reincarnation and karma makes life seem much 'fairer' to Florian; seeing one's life not as an isolated incident full of triumphs and disasters but as part of a much larger network of lives—including many doubles along the way— affords an explanation that allows Florian to live a more peaceful life. It also helps him to understand his partner, Sonia:

> All things that have been revealed to us has helped us a great deal to understand our inner conflicts and to work with ourselves. If S didn't discover Sylvia, I think she would still have been confused today. Some people say that it is better to focus on what you have in front of you. I think that is partly right. I think it is also important to get a deeper understanding, why things happen, what connections there are, etc. It makes it easier to confront the problems you have. It is much easier to overcome problems when you have the key and the background.

For Florian, confronting one's double is like confronting one's own past and future self. This is best explained to him by the belief in reincarnation, although he does not discount that others, such as this study, will attempt alternative explanations:

> Well if someone's interested in proving the opposite, or explain it from a materialistic point of view, then you might analyse it using conventional psychological theories. But to me, those are too limited theories ... And I am quite confident in my beliefs so it doesn't bother me to read alternative thoughts about it.

It seems appropriate to end Florian's story by highlighting, once again, the seeming contradictions inherent in the notion of doubling—it seems that having a doppelgänger is very much about 'physical matters'; yet, for Florian, the connection he feels with Otto Plath is beyond this, beyond the material body, and beyond psychological explanations.

Conclusion

This chapter began by exploring Rank's notion of the double and how the 'doubleness of the double' itself means that often the figure can stand for opposing traits. The figure of the double can return the dead by acting as a protective spirit, or a menacing demon. While a double may offer immortality, it can also be a harbinger of death; it may be a physical double or an ego-double. It is the means by which the dead may return in both a physical and a psychical sense. It is about loss at the same time that it is also about creating an 'other'. Moreover, it was these contradictions inherent in the figure that suggests a connection between the notion of the double and Freud's theories of *eros* and *Todestrieb*, the conflicting life and death instincts that he claimed are at work in all of us.

These first two chapters have dealt with the interiority of the subject and its relationship to the phantom-like author, together with the ways in which the dead can return and haunt the human consciousness and have a direct impact upon identity formation. The final three chapters will explore what happens when the ghost leaks from the page and from the mind and haunts the world at large.

3

Place

Finisterre

Our Lady of the Shipwrecked is striding towards the horizon,
Her marble skirts blown back in two pink wings.
A marble sailor kneels at her foot distractedly…

Our Lady of the Shipwrecked is three times life size,
Her lips sweet with divinity.
She does not hear what the sailor or the peasant is saying –
She is in love with the beautiful formlessness of the sea.[1]

In the previous chapters, we have explored the issues of identification and doubling—the ways in which one person psychically, and sometimes physically, identifies a connection with another. While psychoanalytic theory has provided a framework to begin this type of discussion, via theories on mourning and identificatory processes, we can also investigate other types of attachments. In light of our two main questions, we also need to consider that there may be other ways in which the dead can return and haunt us. If the relation of the self to another—particularly when that other self is rather phantom-like—seems an elusive and enigmatic relationship, perhaps focusing on something more substantial, something that appears to be simply there, may open a new path of investigation for us.

This chapter explores how the mourning and identificatory processes connect with space via sites of memory and memorialisation. If the dead can return to us through places and spaces, then how might this affect our sense of self? Why do reader-fans of Plath make pilgrimages to places where she once lived, and sites of which she wrote? Why is Plath's grave so significant? I shall discuss whether reader-fans of Plath attempt to 'find' her in the places that

Our Lady of the Shipwrecked, Finisterre, France. (*Gail Crowther*)

they visit, and explore other possibilities that may be occurring. In particular, Plath's home in Devon where she wrote the *Ariel* poems features heavily in pilgrimages, as does the house in which she died. What do people hope to gain by visiting these places, and why are houses so important?

One clue might lie in the claim of Gaston Bachelard that imagination can seize upon and inhabit place using day-dreams and desires. In *The Poetics of Space*, Bachelard explores how the house is a 'privileged study' of 'intimate space'.[2]

> I must show that the house is one of the greatest powers of integration for the thoughts, memories and dreams of mankind [*sic*]. The binding principle in this integration is the daydream. Past, present and future give the house different dynamisms which often interfere at times opposing, at others, stimulating one another.[3]

What daydreams do Plath reader-fans bring to Plath sites? How does time, once again, become playful?

On the one hand, we could argue that places are tangible. They are simply there, something or somewhere physical that can be seen and touched and visited. Although places may be tangible and real to our senses, they are in no way fixed or transparent. Indeed the play of temporality, change, and perspective on place leaves one wondering whether it is possible to 'know' anywhere at all. In *Ghostly Matters*, Avery Gordon explores how the past can control the present by highlighting the social effects of ghosts on place—the way in which a seemingly ordinary space can be rendered spectral, the ways in which silence and invisibility can be accessed. For us, we need to consider ways in which the dead may return and inhabit places.

In the above quotation, taken from Plath's poem 'Finisterre' written in 1961, the speaker describes a visit to the French coast and the sight of a statue situated looking out to sea. I took the accompanying image of this statue thirty-seven years later. Here, at this place and time, I actively conjured up the ghost of Plath; her phantom escapes from the text of the poem and begins to haunt space and place. Time passes. 'The past is everywhere', claims David Lowenthal, yet it is a past shaped by the present, an 'artifact' of the present, 'a foreign country shaped by today's predilections'.[4,5] I see Plath's past with my present eyes. It is done and undone. As Gillian Tindall suggests, a 'living, diachronic sense of the past demands a dynamic tension between what you see and what you know to have existed once'.[6]

At Finisterre, on the Pointe du Raz, the statue of Our Lady of the Shipwrecked stands looking out across the 'beautiful formlessness of the sea'. There is a strange friction between what I am seeing with my own eyes, what the speaker of Plath's poem describes, and what my daydreaming allows me to think Plath herself saw all those years ago. Time passes, but it shrinks and folds in upon itself. Indeed 'space contains suppressed time—that is what space is for'.[7] There is space here, in the stony path to the statue, to the headland and the curve of the Bay of the Dead to the right. The flowers bob and sway in space, their faces turned to the wind and the sun. But time passes and is contained in every molecule of the statue, in every flattened piece of sea grass. 'Save in imaginative reconstruction, yesterday is forever barred to us; we have only attenuated memories and fragmented chronicles of prior experience and can only dream of escaping the present'.[8] I dream of escaping the present, dreaming myself back thirty-seven years earlier to the ghost of Plath haunting this French headland.

Gordon discusses how haunting troubles our ability to distinguish between reality and fiction.[9] Is there no way other than to fictionalise this experience—this daydream? In my journal, I wrote:

Where are your peasants now with their windblown stalls and conch shells?
Out on the headland, where a bus runs the short distance from the visitor

centre to the cliffs, I can see your stripy tent sides flapping, trinkets being sold that are too bright and shiny to come from the Bay of the Dead but "From another place tropical and blue/We have never been to". Yet in the rubble of all this change, the one immoveable object. Our Lady stands looking at the sea and the sailor pleads with her, but she does not listen, she has never listened. Her eyes are still fixed on the same spot that she was looking at when you looked at her, when I looked at her almost forty years later. The infant reaches out, one leg dangling. I imagine you looking, then writing. The poem like a snapshot that led me here. My future was as vivid there and then as your past is for me, all you lacked was hindsight and time. I constantly miss you like this. An age, an era disjointed, and even when I travel back, you have already gone.

Possibilities open up here for past and future. There is an imaginative shimmying between and beyond time. The dead, in places, are not entirely gone and out of reach.

> Their place is not simply back there, in a separate and foreign country; it is assimilated in ourselves, and resurrected into an ever-changing present.[10]

Lowenthal's study of the past aims to show how the past is 'virtually indistinguishable from the present' and the past is one 'increasingly suffused by the present'.[11] Plath inhabits this space and her traces from the past transformed my visit because I had read about her past and made it part of my memory too. This visit to the French coast was more than simply the having-been-there-ness of Plath, it was about the conjuring of her ghost. And yet, even as she is so powerfully conjured, she is also out of reach. The separateness of the past seems to remerge as her traces leave both presence and loss. 'I constantly miss you like this'. The pilgrimage gets me closer, but I am still not there; I can never be there.

There is undoubtedly deliberateness to this haunting. Visiting a place and consciously seeking a connection, as a pilgrim, is carried out according to Ian Reader and Tony Walter to create a bond.[12] In other words, places can become meeting points—a site of accessibility for aspects of someone who is now lost. What Reader and Walter do not consider is the nature of, and reason for, this bond. If places become sites of engagement, what occurs in them and how are they used? As we have explored in the previous chapters, the level of Freudian identification and mourning which occurs for our Plath reader-fans is such that seeking significant places in which to revivify her ghost is not so surprising. However, what happens in these places may be. Moreover what does it mean for our reader-fans who do not mourn Plath? Why do they make pilgrimages?

Monica Degen and Kevin Hetherington claim that, 'any space does not just exist in the present. Its ghosts problematise the issue of time as well as space'.[13] The past leaves its imprint; sites that once held one function can become haunted by what is no longer there. This is an area explored by a relatively new movement called Urban Exploration, sometimes referred to as 'space hacking'. The exploration involves breaking into disused asylums, hospitals, factories, and schools to take pictures of what is left. The results are striking. Place is all important, as are traces, residues, and hauntings. But what is equally striking is the strong sense of what is no longer there.

Picture a factory production line stilled, equipment still rusting on the conveyor belt; a disused hospital ward with peeling wallpaper and a half-set of dentures beneath a decaying bed; a lone wheelchair in the centre of a yellow room; an asylum mortuary, the vast bay window painted red and the old stone autopsy table full of concrete and dirt and spiders; schools with empty corridors and half-open cupboards that spew out children's drawings of rainbows and animals and sunshine. But there are no people, no life, no bustle or purpose.

For people revisiting a disused asylum, the pointers of its previous incarnation as a psychiatric hospital are all around, not just in the padded cells and bars on the windows, but also in a less tangible way. The grand and decaying ballroom, where patients would meet once a month for a dance, leaves a happier trace than the therapy room with the broken and sinister ECT machine. Graffiti from the present day leaves its traces as strongly as the vaulted ceiling and carved woodwork. The spray paint graffiti may be the latest writing upon the place, but the traces of what were cannot help but be visible.

Intangible residues and hauntings are like air motes and, while undoubtedly certain places can breed a particular atmosphere, the role of fantasy in the observer must not be overlooked.

> Haunting is a constituent element of modern social life. It is neither pre-modern superstition nor individual psychosis; it is a generalizable social phenomenon of great import. To study social life one must confront the ghostly aspects of it.[14]

In other words, in order to know ourselves and why we respond in the way we do to certain places, we need to explore not only what is visible and there, but what is invisible and gone. While Gordon's claim perfectly describes the elements of contemporary haunting and how, in the present, we can never quite be free from the past, her model—for me—does not quite describe the two-way dynamic to haunting. If there are ruptures in linear temporality, then haunting must surely be able to speak to the present and the future as well as the past. We may be haunted by the ghosts of the past, but we may equally be haunted by futurities—that which has not yet happened, or possibilities that may happen in the future. If this is the case, then visiting Plath sites arguably becomes an active process for her followers. Perhaps reader-fans can speculate how visiting the site might help them change their future?

Yet surely this seems an impossible task. The future is unknown. The past has been and gone; it is irretrievable. Yet it is often the past that we return to—those places, events and emotions that have already occurred either to us or other people—that we use to create some sense of stability for the here and now and the future. 'All awareness of the past is founded on memory' claims Lowenthal; our identity formation and sense of self do not appear to exist in a vacuum but rely on other people, other places, and other times.[15] Although the past is irretrievable in a literal sense, it does not mean that we cannot access it through our fantasies, desires, and memories; it does not mean that we cannot playfully engage with time—past, present, and future. We may mourn and grieve for people and places that are no longer there, or have changed, and, through this very mourning, retain and reanimate that which we have lost.

Perhaps it is because these 'space-hacked' environments are neglected that they become more powerful. Lowenthal believes things which are forgotten or abandoned become more precious, more evocative because of this: 'like memories, relics once abandoned or forgotten may become more treasured than those in continued use'.[16] Never is loss more potent, or more poignant, than when we are faced with its many emptinesses.

A poem written by Plath in 1959, 'Point Shirley', describes the speaker encountering this type of haunting by revisiting the old house of her deceased grandmother—a house holding traces of the past, of her childhood growing up by the sea and the shingle. Writing about her grandmother's yard, the speaker reflects:

> *....She is dead,*
> *Whose laundry snapped and froze here, who,*
> *Kept house against*
> *What the sluttish, rutted sea could do.*[17]

Memories, like relics, rear up from the past. There are echoes but, as Edensor claims, there are no 'coherent, solid entities'; perhaps they are a feeling, imagination or maybe even something more elusive.[18] Plath's speaker could not define it. 'People need houses to dream, in order to imagine' states Bachelard.[19] For him, the poetic imagination is not an echo of the past, but a past that resounds with echoes. What we do not know is at what depth these echoes will reverberate and then die away.[20] The speaker of Plath's poem phrases it as a question:

> *Nobody wintering now behind*

> *The planked-up windows where she set*
> *Her wheat loaves*

> *And apple cakes to cool. What is it*
> *Survives, grieves*
> *So, over this battered, obstinate spit*
> *Of gravel?*[21]

'What is it?' The speaker is aware that something is occurring. By revisiting her grandmother's house, Plath's narrator is deliberately revisiting the past; although the 'planked up windows' bear no relation to the vibrant house of her childhood, filled with a neat kitchen and apple cakes, there is still 'something' surviving this change. This perfectly expresses Gordon's 'paradox of tracking through time and across all those forces that which makes its mark by being there and not there at the same time'.[22]

For Bachelard, it is the reverberations—*retentir*—through time, of the home, 'always container, sometimes contained'.[23] It is the poetics of space and the lingering presence of a long gone grandmother. The home becomes a site of mourning, 'what is it survives, grieves so'; it is also a site of forgetting, 'Nobody wintering now behind/ The planked up windows'. Gordon and Bachelard's statements poetically capture that elusive non-presence and the way in which traces of a former inhabitant may cling to the very cells of the walls. What they do not engage with perhaps, is the emotional aspects of such an encounter—the feeling of loss and emptiness that can overwhelm the pilgrim at the duality of this present non-presence. Plath's speaker ends her poem with 'And I come by/Bones, bones only, pawed and tossed,/A dog-faced sea'.[24] These lines, I feel, engage the reader in the poignancy of a pilgrimage to a place where the traces are still there, yet in many ways unreachable.

Whatever it is, these traces, hauntings, or reverberations, are the very things which mess up the tidy and chronological view of people's lives. It is this temporal instability that questions the usefulness of an ordered life. What if, far from organised and neat, our lives and selves are a jumble of people, places, and times that cannot be stacked and ordered, that do not occur and then pass, that do not remain irretrievable? What if, in fact as we have already discussed, time is so unstable that we are even haunted by what might be?

Degen and Hetherington claim that haunting 'can also be from the future, an anxiety of what we are creating—a haunting that already awaits us in advance of our arrival at some point in time'.[25] We are given the option of precipitating a haunting; deliberately visiting spaces that we know will offer us 'something'. It could be that, as subjects, we are haunted by the desire that places, traces, and residues may help us form a more coherent sense of our self. Robinson and Anderson believe that visiting places is about 'self-making'; the search for sites and symbols and places is irretrievably connected to identity formation.[26] If people do develop a sense of identity via mourning, doubling, and identification, then how might visiting sites associated with a lost loved object add to this development?

The importance of place is not a new phenomenon. The individual and social significance of pilgrimage is evident in Chaucer's *Canterbury Tales*, which captures the excitement of a journey to venerate a saint—'Thanne longen folk to goon on pilgrimages'.

Reader and Walter state that a traditional pilgrimage is very much about a pilgrim leaving their normal world and seeking something that will enrich them outside of 'normal' life.[27] The sites visited often have some form of tragedy, disruption or images of death associated with them; Chris Rojek discusses this in relation to what he calls 'black spots'—areas of sudden and violent death or the commercial development of grave sites.[28] For Sellars and Walter, visiting death sites can be seen by some as ghoulish, but that does not mean it is not an attempt to somehow make sense of the meaninglessness of death or to simply stand awhile and remember.[29] As such, the key elements of pilgrimage involve journeying beyond the parameters of 'normal' life and searching for something new in a different world. Pilgrimages seem 'to offer the experience of momentary escape from the encumbrances and pressures of everyday life'.[30] While these studies offer us rather abstracted and generalised notions for the possible occurrences of pilgrimage, what I am interested in exploring are more specific reasons for visiting certain sites.

As we shall discuss later, pilgrims of Plath may certainly be concerned with their own creative potential, and a synergy that may exist between them and Plath. Lindy Stiebal claims that homes and objects have particular power in any sort of pilgrimage because they confirm for us the physicality of an author and provide a link to their material lives, notwithstanding their temporal distance. Homes are especially attractive:

> [They] provide a focus for the pilgrimage because it is assumed to have been a central influence on the generation of the writer's creative works, almost as a reflection or extension of their character.[31]

Certainly, the homes of Plath are of particular significance to reader-fans and, in some cases, do seem to offer a physical link despite the passing of time; they allow us to 'daydream'.[32] What is interesting is whether the inability to (re) capture the place as it was in Plath's time is at the very centre of the ephemeral nature of pilgrimage. Do we need this elusiveness to retain the fascination of both place and Plath as enigma?

Approaching our respondents involves exploring some of the themes mentioned above, as well as returning to our central questions—can the dead return, and if so, does place play an important role in this process? Further, do pilgrims use haunted spaces and places to help them negotiate a sense of self? When 'pilgrimages' are made to significant Plath sites, we clearly need to be aware of the purpose of the visit. Is it being used for mourning purposes?

Is the pilgrim experiencing some form of personal communication with, or mourning for, Plath? Or is there a more communal experience occurring?

There are a number of sites visited by Plath reader-fans; it will be interesting to see whether the varying accessibility of these sites has any impact on their effect. Exactly where do Plath pilgrims go, why do they go and what happens to them when they arrive?

Peter

For Peter, places do lead to some sort of certainty—'seeing a physical place leaves nothing, in my view, for interpretation. It is what it is.' This is an apparent contradiction of Mimi Sheller and John Urry who claim that 'places are not fixed and unchanging but depend upon what gets bodily performed in them'.[33] Yet as we shall see in the later chapter on objects, there is something more tangible about that which you can see and feel right there in front of you. Even if this transparency is an illusion, there is still something there and, in some cases that can be comforting.

Despite this notion of solidity, there is a sense of Peter being disturbed by his experiences. His first visits relating to Plath were to her grave and her flat in London where she died.[34] He describes these visits as 'eerie' and yet 'starting with her death flat and grave site only got me so close, as it were, as that is where her life stopped.'

> It was a dark evening. We approached from Princess Road and Chalcot Road, turned left onto Fitzroy and stopped. There was the blue plaque for W. B. Yeats, the same one that held so much promise for Plath. Several pictures were taken of the building, from different angles. I remember feeling relief at finding it, but I also felt strange; something felt eerie about being there. That day changed me.

One of Peter's main aims in his pilgrimages to Plath was to 'in a sense get closer to her'. There is a sense of yearning here, of mourning—a wish to lessen the distance of time and space; to rediscover, reconstruct and understand the lost loved object. Places where Plath lived, visited, and wrote about hold some sort of significance, some sort of ghostly remains. As Edensor rightly claims 'Hauntings rupture linear temporality, inconveniently bringing forth energies, which have supposedly been extinguished and forgotten. Intruding into the present, ghosts repeat events and effects, reinstating a cyclical temporality'.[35] Could it be this phantasmal energy that people carrying out Plath pilgrimages tap into, aligned to the fact that she was once there?

With regard to his pilgrimages in America, Peter's account does seem to reflect this urge to lessen the distance of time and space and bring about some sort of merging:

Her father's grave in Winthrop, the house she lived in at Beacon Hill jump out of her biography and into my own. Plath's presence very absent, but somehow guides me, reassures me that the journey was worth it ... It isn't only the biography that steps into my life, but the creative works. ... Plath's New England familiar to me as my own life; my history inseparable from hers. But a clear picture (despite demolition, construction, time) of Plath emerges. All of her writing informed by the places I visited that she visited. ... I do always get a thrill in a way from seeing some place or being where she was. Even though I am seeing these places with my eyes, I do often think: Plath walked through that door. Plath saw this building. Like a graffiti artist: Plath was here.

A graffiti artist leaves traces of themselves behind, or at least traces of how they would like to be remembered, so Peter's use of this imagery is revealing. In the earlier discussion of urban exploration, present-day graffiti in a setting of the past only acts to further complicate the messiness of time. Yet here, the sense of following in Plath's footsteps is strong; the search to find something that is constantly just out of grasp creates both the yearning and the thrill—knowing that Plath has been there but is now gone, leaving only tantalising traces highlights the impenetrability of the lost loved object, which appears to be the very thing that creates the desire. Unlike the graffiti artist, we can perhaps speculate that some of the traces left by Plath were not deliberate. While we may assume her written texts are her form of 'graffiti' for future readers, there are most likely other areas in which she could not have foreseen that people would search for her—her old homes, her holiday destinations, for example. It is perhaps these less obvious traces that require the most imaginative work from the pilgrim.

Secular pilgrimage appears to have many complex layers ranging from the relatively straightforward wish to pay homage to a person, through to the desire to reanimate the past in some way. Reader and Walter argue that, by its very nature, pilgrimage is ambiguous because it crosses so many boundaries—time, space, place—and because it concerns being out of place oneself.[36] Whether this is an attempt to transcend ordinary life, to affirm a sense of identity or to seek some sort of meaning, visiting a place associated with a personal icon involves a journey that disrupts the usual accepted boundaries of time and space; it opens an eerie doorway into another time. As Peter highlights, 'seeing these places put Plath's life in some perspective. It is a doorway into either her works or her life, or both.'

Time becomes a little like a dream—unpredictable—and, in some cases, dreams and fantasies collide with our understanding or experience of the here and now. When that occurs it can be unnerving. Peter writes about his first visit to Plath's grave in West Yorkshire:

The bus follows a river and a windy road through hills and towns for eight miles. The fields are way off and lush green, with brown brick walls marking the territory. Dark clouds came and went quick and steady. As we approached Hebden Bridge I saw, atop a massive hill, a huge old church tower. I asked the lady behind me 'Is that Heptonstall?' (I had several dreams that summer about being on the bus, in bright, bright sun light travelling through land just like that of what we were seeing. And in the dream, atop a huge hill sat a church just like the one we could see. I got goose bumps on my neck and arms.)

What occurs at this meeting point appears to be confirmation—'What a light! What a sign!'—and a need to feel closer to Plath. The place becomes a focus for emotions, desires, and dreams:

At the graveside from memory I recited 'Lady Lazarus.' There were two black cats a few rows to the west. Birds flew overhead out from the bell tower, and more birds flew into the flock. The wind picked up almost instantly and I began to think that by reciting the poem that Sylvia Plath was rising from her grave. The eerie elements in place I said again 'Out of the ash/I rise with my red hair/And I eat men like air.' I asked into the wind 'Are you coming?' and it started to rain.

In her discussion of the seduced reader, Wilson explores the notion of a literary seduction, in which it is the pattern of certain letters, the flow and rhythm of certain words, that entrances the reader.[37] As Pearce suggests, 'reading was something texts could "do" to us whenever we took the leap into their uncharted territories'.[38] Here we see how a text has directly impacted on Peter emotionally.

Pearce argues that the disregard for the emotional impact of a text came about through the dominance of the structuralist revolution and, in *Feminism and the Politics of Reading*, Pearce reclaims the emotional reaction, presenting the 'reader as a lover, whose object is not to understand the text but to engage (with) it'.[39] Peter is the captivated reader whose recitation of a poem at the grave side of Plath has a ritualistic, invocatory element to it—a wish to call up the lost object of his desire like a medium during a séance. There is a wish to connect, to create a meeting point by intoning Plath's own written words. As Wilson suggests, 'by reading the books of our loved ones we are thinking our way into their very beings'.[40] Or, as John Urry claims, 'It is as though the visits of tourists, as pilgrims to sacred sites of death can produce an immortality of those that died in that place'.[41]

Although Plath did not die in this place, yet it has to be significant that one of Peter's first visits was to her 'death flat', it is nevertheless the site of her burial. The mourning process which Peter engages in perhaps not only freezes Plath's death to that moment of 'infinite deferral' but the revivification of her ghost at this site possibly ensures her some form of immortality. [47]

Also interesting is the claim that reading can lead to the ultimate meeting and merging of minds, particularly in light of our earlier discussions on the nature of the author. The interesting twist to Peter's scenario is far from being a solitary and personal pilgrimage, although on one level it is both of these things; the second purpose for Peter is to share his experiences with like-minded people:

> It's absolutely about sharing the experience with those that cannot easily see them. When I was at the first Plath Symposium at Indiana University in 2002, this man from China came up to me and recognized me from the picture of me on my Plath web site... He was so appreciative of the pictures on the web site. For him it would be financially impossible (and maybe irresponsible) to travel to Boston or London or wherever. That single comment gave me the drive to continue building the site, going to see places, and travelling farther than ever to make the information available.

The formation of a *communitas* is a space where the intensely personal and emotional can be shared, where information can be disseminated and used by others. Peter, as a reader-fan, has become an active producer—a creator of meaning—situating virtual spectators in closer proximity to the object of their desire. Furthermore, Peter has seemingly blurred boundaries between the past and the present and opened, as Samuel claims, a 'two-way traffic' between them. [43] This is the opening that allows ghosts to drift in and out—'a wandering figure that flits in and out of presence both in time and space'. [44] There is an uncanny parallel here between a ghostly figure that moves freely in time and space, and a virtual community that exists 'out there', neither material nor confined by space and time. Everything, it seems, is moving.

It is this movement and activity which is important, for rather than seeing the pilgrim as a blank page absorbing Plath, it seems more likely that the pilgrim plays an active role in imposing themselves on the scene visited. Perhaps part of this is the desire to take part in the authorial process—'Plath saw this building'—and take part in the creative transformation that saw Plath turn place into poem. [45] Certainly, this type of relationship between reader and text addresses the limitations of existing literature, dealing with this subject. As Pearce argues, most theorists are reluctant to deal with details of this type of relationship, or how this type of identification can 'shift, change, mutate and perish'. [46] But to shy away from the details of this affective relationship between reader-fan, text, and place is to potentially miss the dynamics of the relationship occurring here. Surrogate authorship seems a likely explanation for both attempting to recapture Plath and the creative process that saw her transform place into text.

Pearce discusses the notion whereby, through a 'readerly reflex', the reader 'becomes' the author.[47] She argues that once a *ravissement* has taken place, and a reader is captivated by a text, fulfilment of the textual experience can then be gained by the reader engaging in some sort of 'autobiographical (re) scripting'.[48] Discussing her own *ravissement* after viewing the Jane Campion film *The Piano*, Pearce describes how:

> By making Campion's characters the 'actors' of my own narrative, I feel the film to function as a romanticized fictionalisation of my own emotional history: a representation which is at once cathartic (it helps me 'process' the pain of my own experience) and 'fulfilling'.[49]

For Pearce, the fulfilment appears to derive from how and where she positions herself within the textual experience. The surrogacy of authorship vis-à-vis Campion's characters allows Pearce to 'process the pain' of her own experiences. We could argue that this desire to share in the 'authoring' of the texts is certainly happening with Plath reader-fans, but my data suggests that mostly it is with the purpose of understanding how she created her poems rather than a desire to usurp the authorship of the text(s) (as in Pearce's scenario).

Peter explains that his first pilgrimage to a Plath location changed him:

> Remember in 'Ocean 1212-W', when Plath's Mum read to her that poem by Matthew Arnold and Plath said that she found a new way of being happy? That's how I felt seeing my first Plath sites. I don't know if happy is the right word, but it made me feel good. As I started to see more places, I got more and more the feeling that I was accomplishing something.

The 'accomplishments', like the motivations for such visits, are complex and multi-layered. Even if their 'destination' is ultimately a fiction, Peter's account suggests that the past is not irretrievable; in some elusive and intangible way, the traces of the past life remain accessible.

For Peter, making pilgrimages to Plath sites appears to operate on a number of levels. On a personal level, it is a search or quest to become closer to the lost, loved object, not merely in the search for Plath herself, but equally to absorb some of the physicality of places that influenced Plath. By (re)capturing significant places, Peter appears to not only engage with traces left of Plath, but to take part in some sort of surrogate authorship that enables him to see how Plath herself transformed that place into a literary text.

It is important to note that Peter's activities are not strictly solitary either. The creation of a *communitas* in which to share his experiences and visits transforms Peter into an active producer of meaning—one willing to help bring other reader-fans closer to their loved object.

> Learning the finest details of her life by trekking through fields, flying over oceans, and walking across cities and time ... the ability to read between the lines (literary criticism) lost on me but the ability to *read the lines* very much in my faculties. It is a literal literary voyage. Plath is everywhere I have been and everywhere I go.

Morney

> *I have been here before*
> *although I do not think it*
> *was during this lifetime.*
>
> *Those streetlights are familiar shadows*
> *beckoning me over*
> *to whisper an intimacy—*
> *to tell me a truth about my life*
> *I have known once already and*
> *the battle to forget was rather bloody*
>
> *I won by sacrificing her life.*
>
> 'Chalcot Square'

In this poem, written for Sylvia Plath and named after one of the places she lived in London, Morney manages to merge both the issue of place and the level of identification that can occur during a pilgrimage. The speaker appears to be playing around with who she is, as well as addressing and disrupting the notion of chronological time—'to tell me a truth about my life/I have known once already'. The poem begins by suggesting the house in Chalcot Square is a place that the speaker has visited before; it is a place of familiarity, yet it also seems to be a place where the speaker of the poem has gained something by visiting at the expense of someone else. Since we know this poem to be directly addressed to Plath, we can assume that somehow the narrator is saying a struggle has taken place and she, the speaker, has won the battle—'I won by sacrificing her life'. As we discussed in Chapter One, Freud tells us that often in cases of identification with another, feelings towards the idealised loved object can be ambivalent, incorporating anger, dislike, and guilt as well as love. Whereas for Peter a pilgrimage to significant Plath sites was an attempt to 'get closer' to Plath, to reanimate the lost object of desire, Morney's visit to Chalcot Square seems to add an extra dimension to this.

Not only does the speaker appear to consume ego traits of Plath into herself so that strange places become familiar—'I have been here before/although I do not think it/was in this lifetime'—but her identity apparently merges, or doubles with, that of her idealised other. However, with classic Freudian ambivalence, Morney's speaker continues:

> *I do not wish to know again*
> *(nor do I wish to bring her back)*
> *So I turn the other way.*

Here is a puzzling statement. Does the speaker mean she does not want to resurrect Plath? Who is the 'her' she does not want to bring back? Could it be Plath, or perhaps that sense of her own self, which was happy to sacrifice someone on her behalf? Moreover, whoever the speaker is rejecting, she turns away from the place that may bring this about. Through reanimating Plath, Morney's speaker may well believe that she will be reanimating the self she has battled to lose, by sacrificing that self, she has 'won':

> *I will not stay long.*
> *A primrose grew here on this hill—*
> *bloomed briefly—and was gone.*

Once again it is the place that holds the importance in Morney's poem. The speaker does not want to linger in the place that, perhaps both geographically and psychologically, she associates with identity struggle and an unstable sense of self. Her love for the idealised other reveals dislike and guilt over the sacrifice of one self for another. There is, however, resolution at the end of the poem: 'I have no fear of this place now'. The ambivalence that is often involved in identity formation is also usefully explained, in this case, by Freud's notion of the uncanny, or *unheimlich*. For Freud, two words with the opposite meanings can often merge to mean the same thing—*heimlich/unheimlich*—'the uncanny is that class of the frightening which leads back to what is known of old and long familiar'.[50] Morney's speaker also highlights how something can be both strange and familiar at the same time: 'Those streetlights are familiar shadows…I have no fear of this place now'.

It is not only place that creates the sensation of *unheimlich*, but the unnerving threat of reanimating that which is dead. For Freud, this manifests itself as doubts over whether an inanimate being is alive. While Freud is referring specifically to waxwork figures and dolls, we can nevertheless see how this can also be applied to the haunting presence of another; it is not just the uncanny familiarity of a strange place, but the unnerving doubling of an identity and the potential return of the dead.

Perhaps it is the literary nature of Morney's textual engagement with place that makes it seem somehow more 'interior' than Peter's account, which is very much set 'out there'—exterior to himself. In contrast, Morney seems to purposefully use a Plath-place to directly explore identity and ego struggle or formation. What is curious about Morney's account is that it does not appear to draw on an actual experience; she is not referring to a specific visit to a place, in this case Chalcot Square; in fact, we do not know for sure that Morney herself has ever been to Chalcot Square. Rather, her speaker hints she has been to this place before in the guise of Plath herself: 'although I do not think it/was during this lifetime.' There is a dreamless, timeless quality to Morney's account which echoes Bachelard's notion of spaces and places allowing us room for daydreaming. It is fantasy that creates the significant experience as much as the place.

> *Those streetlights are familiar shadows*
> *beckoning me over*
> *to whisper an intimacy –*
> *to tell me a truth about my life*
> *I have known once already.*

Sonia

Whereas Morney clearly never felt wholly comfortable about her 'identification' with Plath, Sonia, believing herself to be Plath reincarnated, puts great importance on the notion of place. Sonia believes that when visiting or making pilgrimages to various Plath related sites, she is in effect revisiting places in which she herself once lived—and died—in a different lifetime. Whereas for Peter visiting Plath's death flat was 'eerie', for Sonia it was 'magical'.

The significance of time and place figures rather differently in Sonia's case; rather than the two-way haunting we have been discussing, between the mourner and the lost loved object, here we have an utter assimilation of identity. Rather than being haunted by the lost loved object, Sonia is seemingly being haunted by herself, or more precisely a former self. This connects the previous chapter on the double with the significance of place. If physical and psychic doubling can occur within the ego, then it seems this doubling can also leak out into exterior space. Her partner Florian writes, 'I think the trip was very important for S, it was a healing process for her to visit Primrose Hill, to re-experience it.' Sonia is not paying homage to a venerated writer; she believes she is reliving and re-experiencing the site of her own death. While on one level we may regard this as potentially distressing, Florian claims that for Sonia it was both 'magical' and 'healing', with some unexpected reactions. In many ways, it was an escape; Florian comments that 'S could see the results of her suicide and that it does not solve any problems'.

We see how Sonia's partner uses her and Plath's identity interchangeably. A pilgrimage to Plath's (or, perhaps, Sonia's own) death site, Florian claims, was some kind of personal liberation for Sonia. In mythology, this would be the moment the two doubles meet; one either destroys the other or offers protection. Admittedly this meeting for Sonia occurs via place, and not face to face; she is meeting her double from another time, accessing this figure via space.

Although Florian describes this as liberating, Sonia herself has a slightly different account of the day:

> We arrived in London in the afternoon and the first thing we did in London was to walk to Primrose Hill. We arrived there by dusk, and the park was covered with a soft mist. The park lighting was slowly starting to glow and I felt like floating over the meadows. It was a kind of magical and spiritual atmosphere in the park, such a contrast to the stressful journey we had. I could clearly imagine how Sylvia had lived there with the children, and had a lot of inspiration there, I guess. I fell in love with Primrose Hill, and I really long to go there again.

At first, Sonia does not merge her sense of self with that of Sylvia. In fact, there is a clear boundary of differentiation—'I could clearly imagine how Sylvia had lived there.' But desire and imagination are at play. There is an 'otherworldliness' to Sonia's account: the soft mist, the glowing park, her feeling of floating. She encounters something spiritual as a pilgrim might. It is as if something is occurring in this place but, like Plath's speaker with her grandmother's house, she cannot name it—it is beyond words. Equally Sonia yearns for a return to the place—'I really long to go there again'—although significantly, at this stage, her desire is connected directly to place and not to Plath. What occurs next, when Sonia arrives at the house where Plath committed suicide is totally unexpected:

> We continued to Fitzroy Road. It's really hard to describe the feelings when getting closer to the house where Sylvia ended her life. I had thought a lot of going there, that I would have very strong feelings coming to this place. But finally standing there, it just felt very strange. It was unreal to actually be in the place where such a drama took place with so many people being wounded for a lifetime. And even stranger; there seemed to be no trace of the event. For me it was like walking along any street in London.

The 'otherworldliness' of Sonia's experience continues. To be standing outside Fitzroy Road becomes 'unreal', and the shocking discovery for Sonia is not what she feels, but what she fails to feel; she remains unmoved by the experience. The street and the house are a neutral space 'like walking along any street in London.' Interestingly at this site, identification fails to occur fully between Sonia and Plath and the social space fails to haunt. The notion of the double slips and a space appears between the two identities. Although Sonia is able to imagine Sylvia and her children living here, a more intimate 'doubling' fails to occur. Speculation as to why some pilgrimages 'fail' is discussed later in this chapter, but Sonia also offers another explanation:

> Yes, it's strange about the empty feeling at Fitzroy Rd. If it really was me who died there, then it might be that the soul chose to remember the good things. Or that the trauma is very suppressed.

Here, Sonia changes her narrative, lessening the distance created in the above comments and instead revealing her assimilated identity with Sylvia ('If it really was me who died there ... '). Her ego has consumed the lost loved object and mourning is now taking place for both her own sense of self and the loss of Plath, the two often being linked and interchangeable for Sonia; it is doubling in the most literal sense. It is also an example where we may consider the possibility that a pilgrimage is carried out not only in memory of the lost other, but as a confirmation of the existing self. If places can remain haunted by those who have lived there, then perhaps for Sonia, this lingering presence offers some form of immortality for herself. This is a place in which she died, yet is still here able to (re)visit, however traumatic that (re)visiting may be.

In her study of the Vietnam Memorial Wall in Washington, Jill Dubisch explores other responses to trauma and mourning.[51] In an annual pilgrimage carried out across America, motorcyclists make a ten day journey travelling to the Washington Memorial Wall, called 'The Run for the Wall'. This whole journey is not only about commemorating but creating space to remember and heal. Often people on the pilgrimage are war veterans themselves, who travel to respect their dead friends and heal themselves. Yet even within this remembering, there is forgetting and a silence around the Vietnamese dead, and the US foreign policy that created the war in the first place. Clearly to remember too much in times of trauma becomes unsafe and therefore remains invisible, untouched. For Sonia, this silence becomes a sort of emotional safety net.

While at Fitzroy Road, Peter feels close to Plath; Sonia, however, creates distance:

> I stood for a long time just gazing up in those windows. I was trying to figure out in which room it happened. Imagining how the street and buildings must have looked quite the same at that time.

Sonia is aware of time, and yet it is this dimension that she diminishes above all others. Like Peter, Sonia sees places through Plath's eyes—or perhaps her own eyes in a different time. Again, place and temporality become linked; Sonia spends much time trying to figure out the actual site of death. Time has passed but has not caused much change; Sonia and Plath perceive place through different eyes and different times, but with the connection of the *heimlich*.[52]

It is a different story when Sonia visits the next Plath site, merely metres around the corner from Fitzroy Road:

> I had a feeling of sadness and emptiness as we continued walking towards Chalcot Square. When we arrived there I quickly changed mood. I felt very happy seeing the purple house with the blue plaque on it. I think Sylvia had her happiest years here. Even though she had a lot of mood swings, as always, she felt full of hope. She started to feel that she could live a quite normal life, in spite of her problems. She felt that she could have a happy family life, combined with her artistic work after all.

Earlier, we saw how urban exploration suggested that frightening and unpleasant residues left in deserted buildings seemed to have more power than happy ones. Here, it seems the opposite is true; mere metres away from an unhappy Plath site that leaves Sonia unmoved, she is blasted by traces from a much happier time in Plath's life—'I felt very happy seeing the purple house … I felt Sylvia had her happiest years here'. Interestingly, in subtle self-narration, Sonia slips and distinguishes her own sense of self as separate from Plath's identity: 'She felt full of hope…she felt that she could have a happy life'. Like the narrator of a novel who has special and omnipotent access to a character's thoughts and feelings, Sonia knows how Sylvia felt and what she thought; for Sonia, this is because she remembers this time.

In his discussion 'Facts, Insights and Hypotheses on Reincarnation', Timothy Conway discusses where our awareness of reincarnation comes from, such as Hindu and Buddhist texts, the spontaneous recall of past lives and the work of mental health professionals. He also examines why we are inclined to reject it in our culture, for example, reductionists arguing consciousness cannot function beyond the limits of the body and brain. He offers statistics, such as how one out of a thousand children spontaneously remember a past life; this he argues is not evidence for reincarnation. It could point to other factors such as deception, fantasy or obsession. But past life memories do appear to have two forms of entry: either similar to our normal day to day memory, or fragmentary memories 'associated with a name, or impressions of a landscape or house.'

Regardless of whether reincarnation is a scientifically proven phenomenon or not, it would seem that Sonia's experience comes close to this account of 'fragmentary memory'. Conway argues that traumas from past lives can be remembered in 'chains' rather than as a complete memory; if reincarnation does occur, then this seems reasonable. While offering no evidence, Conway also argues that the psychoanalyst Carl Jung believed in reincarnation, a fact that the Jungian Institute has suppressed. According to Richard Noll, the only public statement that exists from Jung on reincarnation is that he 'keeps a free and open mind' and is 'not in a position to assert a definite opinion.'[53] The resistance that psychoanalysis has shown towards the experience of reincarnation is clearly to be regretted as far as this book is concerned—remember that a similar blank was drawn when trying to find links between Freud and reincarnation.

While we may draw on Rank's notion of the double to explain Sonia's sense of possessing an identity identical with Plath, this is not so satisfactory when used to draw on existing memories of place. If Sonia does have memories from a place she has never been to before, where do these memories come from, and how might psychoanalysis explain them? It is perhaps one of the great frustrations that, while researching for this book, I have been unable to find any literature discussing this. If I were to offer a tentative hypothesis based on the psychoanalytic theory encountered so far, I would probably wish to draw upon the role that the existing discourses around Plath—as well as Plath's own work—may play in these memories. If as a reader, we discover where and when Plath killed herself via, for example, a biography, then we have the beginnings of a collective, historical memory. It may well be for Sonia that this features in a 'reincarnation flashback' as opposed to a literal memory from that time.[54]

Whether these memories are collective, historical, or personal we may never know. But, the distinctive features of Sonia's pilgrimages are much more clearly directed than those of Peter and Morney. While Peter may be attempting to regain some form of closeness to Plath, Sonia is actually (re)becoming Plath; where Morney struggles against identification with another, Sonia assumes she is rediscovering her own, previous self. There appears to be a more obvious use of places and spaces for Sonia in her identity formation, in that she uses certain sites to explain reasons for why she may feel and act like she does.

While Rank's ideas on the double can be of some help here, particularly in the sense that Sonia believes in both an ego and a physical double, it does not quite fully describe her belief in reincarnation; neither does existing literature on psychoanalysis. This, it seems, is a space that we will have to leave open:

> If it really was me who died there, then it might be that the soul chose to remember the good things. Or that the trauma is very suppressed.

Megan

In contrast to all the above respondents, Megan is one reader-fan who actively avoids Plath pilgrimages. Before beginning this analysis, it is important to recap that, although identification has taken place on one level with the emotions expressed in Plath's texts echoing some of Megan's own feelings, it seems that Megan has resisted the urge to use Plath in her own identity formation. At most, Megan states her studies have 'given me a respect for her astonishing work' but she is absolutely clear that this is where the readerly relationship ends:

> Despite this new found respect and continuing relationship with her work, I have never felt the need to visit any Plath sites (even though I was only down the road in Exeter!). I try to remain at a respectful distance from Plath's life, although like every Plath reader I feel the draw of her intense and tragic life.

On first reading, Megan appears to establish clear boundaries citing Plath as an object of scholarly interest. She has never carried out any pilgrimages to Plath-related sites despite her proximity and ease of access to the very location where the *Ariel* poems were composed. Furthermore, there are ethical issues at stake. The 'respectful distance' implies there is something unsavoury or intrusive about blurring the boundaries between the textual voice of Plath and the 'real' historical Sylvia Plath. It brings to mind the speaker of Plath's poem 'Lady Lazarus':

> *The peanut-crunching crowd*
> *Shoves in to see*
>
> *Them unwrap me hand and foot—*
> *The big strip tease.*[55]

It seems Megan does not want to become part of the 'peanut-crunching crowd', but would rather focus on the work and the words; it is Plath's texts alone that appear to feed and satisfy this relationship. Compared to the determined pilgrimage of Peter, Megan creates a distance and a boundary which she does not allow her imagination or fantasy to cross. She is neither haunted by, nor haunting, Plath.

There is still some ambiguity. Megan says she 'tries' to keep a respectful distance but despite this, she does feel the draw of Plath's 'intense and tragic life'; it is as if Megan is not quite sure or convinced that the draw of the writer's life will not suck her in at some point. In this case, it seems, Megan is resistant to discover a version of herself in Plath. Ultimately she fears that she may lose that 'respectful distance' and intrude into areas that as yet, remain unexplored: 'For me, *at the moment*, her words are enough' [My italics].

Placing distance between herself and significant Plath places, Megan's focus remains on the text. This reader-author relationship, discussed in Chapter Two, is highlighted by Foucault when he claims that writing—in particular, fiction—should not be limited by the figure of the author. Although Megan is aware of the historical writer 'Sylvia Plath', she keeps her focus on the 'implied author' in the texts, the disembodied voice that, for Foucault, acts in 'an absolutely free state'.[56]

Although she does deliberately keep this information to a minimum, Megan is aware of Plath's life history and does have some knowledge of her life and death, so we must qualify and adapt Foucault's theory. More importantly, time does not appear to intrude into this relationship; the ghosts are not recalled and returned. No mourning is taking place. As the reader, Megan also seems to acknowledge that the power may well lie within her to resurrect the dead, should she allow herself to go down this path. The active process of reading beyond, even 'behind', a text is within her grasp but would involve exercising fantasies and desires that are currently dormant. Megan does sympathise with those who have been drawn in; she acknowledges this draw herself, which she has, as yet, remained resistant to.

Anna

Anna has made two separate pilgrimages to the same Plath site—Fitzroy Road—and experienced slightly different encounters each time:

> I have visited Plath sites on two occasions. The first was in 2004, when I was in London with my mother. We looked for Fitzroy Road forever, and then finally found it. I think she took a picture of me in front of the house, but I don't remember. I don't really remember anything at all from that visit, so I guess it wasn't a life-changing moment exactly. I think I was bothered by the fact that my mother was with me—not by her in any way, but just by the presence of somebody else. I couldn't relax and take it in, because I was stressed that she'd get bored.

Like Sonia visiting this house, Anna remains unmoved, so has little memory of the visit. The fact that she is perhaps captured in a photograph appears to be the one potential element that might it 'real' or memorable.

> The type of consciousness the photograph involves is indeed truly unprecedented since it establishes not a consciousness of the *being-there* of the thing but an awareness of the *having-been-there*. What we have is a new space-time category: spatial immediacy and temporal anteriority; the photograph being an illogical conjunction between the *here-now* and the *there-then*.[57]

However, Anna half remembers a photograph being taken that will confirm for her the having-been-there, since she has little memory of the event itself. However, as we will discuss later, pilgrimages can fail to be fulfilling due to a number of reasons. In this case, Anna suggests the context of the visit affected the mood. Being with her mother, worrying that her mother would be bored, distracted from Anna's ability to relax and 'enjoy' the experience. Perhaps it is the presence of another that diminishes Anna's ability to fully exercise her imagination and fantasy. On the second visit to this site, she went alone:

> So the second time, last November, I went on my own. I went by bus up to Chalk Farm, and then walked around on the streets, thinking about Plath pulling a perambulator around there, shopping in little markets, etc.

Like Sonia, Anna actually conjures up the presence of Plath walking in the streets with her children. As the loved object, Plath leaves her haunting traces for those following in her footsteps; this haunting tells us something about her readers' identificatory process. As we have seen with Sonia and Morney, the figure of Plath becomes symbolic of their own, potentially lost, sense of self. However, the imaginary resurrection, or daydreaming, of Plath and her perambulator on Primrose Hill fails to invoke a sense of identification in Anna:

> I stood a very long time outside of her home on 23 Fitzroy Road. I felt a bit stupid, people passing me knowing why I was there etc. I felt a bit uncomfortable about that, (and about taking photos). I stood there thinking about what happened there, but I just couldn't feel that it was real.

We see that Anna as the 'looking-at' subject, both in the sense of observing the house and capturing this observation in photographs, is self-conscious and embarrassed by her actions. She tries to identify with the history and significance of the place as a Plath reader, but exactly like Sonia, remains unmoved—'I just couldn't feel that it was real'.

This distancing from reality is not so unusual in haunting; Gordon suggests that often experiences can cross boundaries that only fiction can comprehend. Rather than experiencing a transparent like reality, we are faced with a fictional sense of reality; 'Fiction is getting pretty close to sociology. Social reality seems made up and real at the same time'.[58] If we consider Gordon's claim, in light of reading Anna's own narratives of this pilgrimage, we have another instant where something is both 'real' and constructed at the same time.

The slippery nature of both time and experiences of 'reality' can have a profound effect on the pilgrim. Even something as solid as a house can lose its density when faced with the passing of time and space. For Bachelard, a 'house that has been experienced is not an inert box'—people leave traces, things become performed in the spaces.[59] It is time, for Bachelard, that once again creates the most complex confusion:

> Past, present and future give the house different dynamisms which often interfere, at times opposing, at others, stimulating one another.[60]

Perhaps it is this level of confusion that gives Anna the sense of unreality—the inability to grasp something despite standing there 'for a very long time'. Rather than feeling a connection to Plath, Anna feels 'stupid' and 'uncomfortable' and a little shameful that other people passing would know why she was there. The pilgrimage has failed to move Anna; the house is neither a site of mourning, nor a tool to resurrect the dead. The house is just another house in a London street and the traces are too 'unreal' for Anna to detect them.

This is an important response because it clearly reveals the imaginative labour required to bring a site to life. Reading Peter and Sonia's accounts, a reader would not be mistaken in thinking that the experience of the pilgrim is there at the place, waiting to be found. What Anna's response reveals is the degree of fantasy the pilgrim may need to give themself up to, in order to evoke an emotional response to a place. However hard she tries, Anna cannot bring these Plath sites to life; they do not seem 'real' to her. Rather self-consciously and a little awkwardly, Anna perhaps feels the expectations of a pilgrimage to be somehow forced, to the extent that she is unable to 'feel' Plath at all.

Unfulfilling pilgrimages

This chapter has mainly discussed how place, which is subject to time and change, can contain residues and hauntings of those that have gone before us. Revisiting these places can help us fill the lack left by the loss of a loved object, by the yearning involved in identity formation. For mourning to take place, the pilgrim necessarily needs to have identified on some level with Plath; as we have seen, this can range from identifying solely with the emotions expressed in her texts through to a belief in being the reincarnation of Plath. For Megan, pilgrimages to Plath-related places have not occurred as she actively avoids carrying them out. For other respondents, such as Peter and Sonia, we can see how travelling to significant Plath sites can be a powerful, and in some cases, magical experience.

We have also briefly considered circumstances in which identification with Plath occurred and yet pilgrims leave the pilgrimage unfulfilled, as with Anna. Why can hauntings be so strong and evident in some places and yet untraceable in others? What is it that allows us to communicate with the past and feel the presence of those long gone? It is possible that even when all the elements of a pilgrimage are in place, the pilgrim remains unmoved. Let us further explore this by looking in more detail at a 'failed' or unfulfilling pilgrimage that I carried out to Ireland.

Cleggan, Connemara, Ireland

It was here you came with only five months left to live. You stayed for five days, your holiday cut short by a cruel series of events and you returned to Devon alone. You sat one night around the table by the Connemara marble fireplace with an Ouija board and three other poets. You grew bored and went to bed early. Your bed, made from Spanish walnut. I came when I saw The Old Forge was for rent. I had never stayed in the same place as you and I wondered how it would feel to sleep in the room you slept in and eat and talk in the room you ate and talked in.

Given the dimensions for a successful and emotional pilgrimage then, it would appear that all of the elements are in place. One would assume that, for example, in the case of sleeping in the same room as the idealised other, some kind of residue or trace would be psychologically detected. The haunting of the cottage by the pilgrim, we expect, would be reciprocated by the presence of Plath:

How odd then, that almost immediately there was nothing of you there. No

The Old Forge, Cleggan, Connemara, Ireland. (*Gail Crowther*)

trace, no ghost rearing from the past. For a moment I doubted myself—had I got the wrong place? How could you be so absent?

Suddenly, it seems the pilgrimage has 'failed'. The lack of a haunting, the lack of a ghost, leaves a place neutral, ordinary ('there was nothing of you there'). This visit appears to confirm the role that fantasy plays in pilgrimage. Since we have suggested pilgrims project their own fantasies and desires onto a place, it is interesting to explore why I felt this pilgrimage failed:

> Why could I not feel you here? I had read a detailed account of your stay written by your host. And then it dawned on me. I had read nothing that you had written. Your journals from this time were 'lost', your letters possibly sealed away in trunks in university archives not to be opened until 2023. When you have been silenced, I feel nothing. When I cannot hear your voice, you are invisible, as if you had never existed at all. Other people cannot conjure you up for me and other people cannot conjure up how places looked for you. Time is no longer playful, but a slamming door. There is no way through, no way back. My voyeuristic tourism was empty because I had nothing to be voyeuristic about. My textual tourism hit an empty page. If I do not know your thoughts, how can I know anything at all about this place, about you? The year is simply 2003 and I am staying in a modernised old forge by the sea in Ireland. It is remote and there is a pier, the same pier you walked along, the same pier we both sailed from to Inishboffin and drank beer in Day's Hotel. I cannot slip between times, but remain stuck in the present.
> There is no haunting in these ruins. Just an amputation, a silence.

Seemingly, the lack of texts by Plath herself creates an obstacle to my ability to impose any fantasies and desires onto the pilgrimage site. Since I do not know what Plath—or Plath's implied author—thought of the place, and have only gained knowledge of Plath's visit through a second-hand account, I am unable to identify with Plath's experiences. The lack of Plath's voice shuts down the role of fantasy; after all, how can we play around with time and location when the very reason for being there is silent?[61] There are no 'reverberations', and 'like a beetle that has been stepped on, you flow from yourself and your lack of hardness or elasticity means nothing any more'.[62]

Conclusion

This chapter has explored the role of place and pilgrimage in the relationship between Sylvia Plath and her reader-fans. In addressing the question—how may the dead return—I attempted to establish the importance of place as having the potential to be haunted by traces of what has gone before. I discussed the possibility that ghosts appear both as spectral presences from the past and as social figures of the present.

I also explored what happens to reader-fans when they visit significant places associated with Plath, and what they might gain from doing this. Respondents who make Plath pilgrimages have spoken about a number of different experiences and offer some explanation for why they carry them out, including a desire to feel closer to their loved object, to explore or recreate the authorial process, or to pay homage to significant places associated with Plath. Drawing on a psychoanalytic framework, I argued that Plath pilgrims have the strongest reaction to Plath sites when there is some form of identification or doubling taking place—Peter and Sonia. When identification or mourning failed to take place between the reader and Plath, then pilgrimage was actively avoided and regarded as an unnecessary intrusion, as with Megan.

We also considered what was occurring when no sense of haunting or emotional connection was made in certain pilgrimages. It was concluded that, in this instance, fantasy has been asked to play such a vital role in the pilgrimage experience, and my belated recognition that there were no primary Plath texts associated with Cleggan proved an insurmountable obstacle to my connection with it. For pilgrimages to fully work, fantasy must be facilitated and not frustrated.

What can be concluded with some certainty though is the transformative power of place to impact upon the pilgrim and the pilgrim's identity formation across time and across space. Gordon perceptively observes:

Being haunted draws us affectively, sometimes against our will and always a bit magically, into the structure of feeling a reality we come to experience, not as cold knowledge, but as a transformative recognition.[63]

4

Images

Stopped and awful as a photograph of someone laughing,
But ten years dead.[1]

If places can evoke strong reactions and create a sort of rupture in linear temporality, then photographs are also poignant and material traces of what once was. In fact, photographs are creepy snatchers of time. With one click of a shutter, a moment or a second becomes immortalised and then flattened. What is it that a two-dimensional image can capture of a person or a place? A likeness? A certain look in the eye? The vastness of a landscape? None of these things are graspable, as the photographic image is hemmed in by four sides—by the viewfinder and by the edges of the picture. Often looking at a photograph, one may wonder, what is behind the person taking the picture? What is the person in the picture actually looking at? Often, it is their gaze— that we sometimes falsely believe to be looking at us—that in effect is seeing a totally different world, a totally different field of vision. We can haul a certain person or place out of time and capture a moment, but surely it is such a small moment, such a fragmented image, that it conceals far more than it reveals.

This chapter will explore ways in which photographs are connected to loss and death. In light of our two main questions, we must first ask: how do the dead return via the photographic image? Also secondly, how do people use images as part of their identity formation? Drawing upon work by Roland Barthes and Susan Sontag, the nature of the image and its many connections to temporality and death will be considered.[2,3]

However, exploring how the image may be used in identity formation also involves exploring how pictures can tell stories and draw on memories. For this we will explore the ideas of Marianne Hirsch, Soniaa Sturken, and Annette Kuhn to discuss how a personal or familial image can transform into a collective or historical image and how discourses are created around certain photographs.[4, 5, 6, 7] Equally, the work of Liz Heron highlights how the image is not only political but the starting point for innumerable narratives.[8] Do photographs help the dead return? What do Plath reader-fans do with their images of Plath?

There are fundamental differences in the viewing experience offered by photographs. Were we present when the photograph was taken? Were we the photographer, the photographed or merely attendant? In *Camera Lucida*, Barthes claims the photograph can be the object of three distinct practices: to do, to undergo, and to look. This links to the varying roles of the people involved. He calls the photographer, the operator; the spectator is all of those who look at the photograph; and the target, the referent, is the person—or thing—being photographed. Nevertheless, for Barthes, the photograph fails to capture that elusive something of a person; he delightfully describes how his self remains 'like a bottle-imp' that refuses to hold still 'giggling in my jar'.[9]

Photography, for Barthes is quite simply about death:

> Whether or not the subject is already dead, every photograph is this catastrophe. The defeat of time in them:—*that* is dead, and *that* is going to die.[10]

There is a curious paradox at play in the photograph. It is something that both (re)animates and returns while at the same time, necessarily reminds us of loss. What is seemingly gone, suddenly becomes frozen in time. In fact Sontag claims that 'after the event has ended, the picture will still exist, conferring on the event a kind of immortality (and importance) it would never otherwise have enjoyed'.[11] While Barthes and Sontag accurately describe the poignancy and melancholia of time and the photograph, it will be interesting for this book to explore whether the photograph is always '*that* [which] is dead, *that* is going to die'; I wonder whether it will be useful to highlight the possibilities of revivification that the image can bring about.[12] On the one hand, images of Plath are about death, but, as Sontag suggests, they are also about the defeat of death in some sense since they confer a type of immortality on the photographed subject. In this sense, the image in some ways continues a life; the same person is repeatedly revived and retained. The fact that the intention behind the picture may have been different further conveys the retrospective power of the image.

In relation to photographs of Sylvia Plath, Georgiana Banita expands this point and claims that most of the photographs of Plath in the public domain were not intended for the public.[13] They are private snapshots taken by her family. The importance given to them has been retroactively inscribed. For Hirsch, discussing the familial image, there is a unique encounter between private images and public meaning:

Removed from its immediately personal and more broadly cultural context, this private image acquires a very different set of personal and cultural meanings than it had in its original familial setting.[14]

In other words, the meaning behind personal images can shift and the people represented within them can become almost allegorical or representative of certain cultural groups. We need only think of contexts in which images of Sylvia Plath have been used to represent some sort of cultural ideal of the martyred woman, the doomed writer, or depressive suicide.

Soniaa Sturken deals with this dichotomy of private and public in her essay 'Personal Photographs in Cultural Memory.' She begins by discussing the nature of the photograph as being 'perceived as a container for memory, it is not inhabited by memory so much as it produces it'.[15] However, this production of memory can occur on both a personal and a social level. There is, so to speak, movement across these boundaries.

Sturken argues that a personal memory from a photograph can be shared and exchanged in public, allowing a sort of collective memory to form. This collective memory can then become transformed into a cultural memory, or even a historical memory, one which Sturken defines as 'a form of sanctioned narrative of the past'.[16] However, images do not belong to one or the other of these categories; they can belong to multiple categories or even shift about. The potential for the creation of memories and narratives from one single image becomes immeasurable. Sturken describes how a historical photograph can have the capacity to affect a personal memory, for example, a historical survivor of a war. Likewise a personal image can often acquire cultural or historical meaning.[17] The relevance of Sturken's theory for this book is immense; it explains how reader-fans may engage with familial images of Plath which have transformed themselves into holding cultural meaning.

At this point, I would like to extend Sturken's ideas about the photograph to suggest that the process of transformation from personal to collective to historical memory could well happen in reverse. In other words, once a personal image becomes public property, leading to the formation of a collective memory, the viewer may then use the collective memory to form their own personal memory. Hirsch hints at this idea when she suggests that a personal image acquires a very different set of personal and cultural meanings than it had in its original familial setting. In his letter to *The Independent*, Ronald Hayman argues that readers of Plath feel as though they are 'part of her family'.[18] If this is the case, then how reader-fans use photographs of Plath may have a distinctly familial aspect to it after all. In fact, they may create their own 'family snaps' of Sylvia Plath, as we will see later in the respondents' stories.

A photograph speaks to the viewer's imagination—certainly some more than other—and from this image, the viewer can create a discourse, or a narrative that could be personal, cultural or historical. Sontag claims photographs are 'clouds of fantasy and pellets of information'.[19] Time once again becomes unstable as we visually slip between years, between eras, between people's lives. Our playful picture-hopping holds something the subjects of the photographs do not have—knowledge of what is to come and what became. It is this knowledge that we bring to the viewing, retrospectively reading the image in light of what we know. If we view a portrait of a person unrelated to us and utterly unknown, if our eyes flicker and register the image at all, we create our own story.

Imagine yellowing, curled photographs of long-gone Victorians, stiff and formal in their studio portraits; we know they are now dead. Even though we may know nothing else about these people, we view with the knowledge of their death. Sepia soldiers of the First World War become poignant; all gone and yet somehow returned, reanimated as we view the picture. These images say this person once lived, this person once looked into the lens of a camera and a moment was captured—immortalised.

For Sontag, and Barthes, this in a way is the pathos of photography. Although photographs show people so irrefutably there, this only serves to highlight their vulnerability as they head towards their own destruction. In fact, Sontag argues, photos come unstuck over time and open themselves up to any kind of reading; our neat belief in a linear chronology becomes disrupted when we look at such images.

> The type of consciousness the photograph involves is indeed truly unprecedented since it establishes not a consciousness of the *being-there* of the thing but an awareness of the *having-been-there*. What we have is a new space-time category: spatial immediacy and temporal anteriority, the photograph being an illogical conjunction between the *here-now* and the *there-then*.[20]

This distinction can bring both relief and terror. The comfort of past generations who lived their lives, they are the '*having-been-there*'. We know this through the relief of being the '*here-now*'. However, every photograph that is taken of us, every time our image is captured makes us more aware that soon we ourselves will be the '*there-then*'.

So photography is about mourning and melancholia on many levels; it is also about loss—the loss of something that has already gone or the loss that will come in time. Both create yearning and sadness. To reanimate or resurrect from an image is like grasping a shadow—you can never hold it and, as Barthes claims, you can exhaust yourself realising that nothing can undo the '*this-has-been*'. So a photograph presents us with the crippling frustration of something both being there and not being there at the same time. It presents us with a reminder that the only way we can travel back to the person in the image is through fantasy and imagination. What exactly is it that the photograph captures and how do we read meaning into

Catherine King claims there are no such things as visual facts, there are no innocent images, and no innocent eyes viewing these images.[21] As viewers, we are led by values; these values help the eye to construct meaning. Furthermore, the image being presented has been made in this way too, resulting in layer upon layer of meaning and construction. Photographs, we could conclude, are not about authenticity; they are about storytelling. They offer us codes, signs, and signifiers, but most of all, they are not about truth. Janet Wolff is certain that photographs are circulated and surrounded by political discourses.[22] We could take this argument further and claim that the actual creation of the photograph itself, as well as reading, is surrounded by political discourse. For Barthes, the posing of objects within a photograph is an accepted inducer of ideas.[23] In other words, they are not neutral as they possess meaning.

We can see this at play in a portrait taken of Sylvia Plath and Ted Hughes in 1961 by David Bailey. The pair are seated next to each other in their sitting room in London. Behind them is a bookcase—'intellectual indicator', Barthes would say. Hughes is sitting in an armchair, relaxed, face forward but gaze to the right of the camera. His legs are crossed and resting on his knees is an open book. He looks, I conclude with my discourse, as though he was stopped reading mid-sentence. This is the writer surrounded by the things which he creates: books. Plath, on the other hand, is sitting next to him. She is not on an easy armchair, but an upright dining chair. Have the guests and photographer taken up all the available chairs? Is this an extra she has brought in herself to sit upon? She is perched on the edge, nervous and intent. Although there is half a bookcase behind her, there is also a fireplace and the hearth. Half writer, half angel in the house? Dangling from her hands is a teddy bear—no intellectual prop for her, but a signifier of childhood, children, and her role as mother. How do we read a photograph? I cannot undo the knowledge that I have about the end of their story—it is this that I bring to my viewing; as King affirms, I do not have innocent eyes. I bring my own fantasy and imagination to the photographs and it is impossible for me to look at them in any other way. Like this, discourses and stories are made, and in some cases presented as fact. Often something that we have read can inform our reading to the extent that we are sure we know the truth when in fact we are far from it.

Heron discusses how the photograph can be the major protagonist for subsequent narratives—a 'genuinely fertile novel of ideas'.[24] As we have seen above in my discussion of a photograph, it is possible to construct a narrative, often political, around the photograph. Heron also explains how one single photograph can be compelling enough to 'prompt an infinity of stories' and that 'within the same image different eyes will reveal different truths. We edit and build our own meanings, we extend them beyond the frame'.[25] This is a useful idea if we consider we are dealing with a cultural figure constructed from differing and competing narratives.

However, for Heron, the image is the starting point. In this sense, we can see how the photograph of someone we never knew could be the starting point for the creation of narratives and stories. For Sturken, who we discussed earlier, it is the 'malleability of the personal image' that allows the range of memories to shift from personal to cultural to historical stories.[26] Time and place and space are of course relevant, but not restrictive categories. We are still able to read and create meaning from photographs that were taken long before we were born.

If we extend Heron's thinking, we realise that perhaps in some cases Plath's reader-fans already have existing ideas which they bring to the image, and which will presumably influence how they read the image. It seems there may be two possible effects of this. Either their ideas, combined with the image, may confirm their reading of Plath and the photograph, or the image may cause them to adapt or alter their preconceptions. In many ways, this reflects a visual version of the author-reader relationship. In the same way, it seems impossible to access an 'authentic' historical figure via the written text, so too, the image does not allow us a transparent reading of the subject captured within its frame.

What a photograph can offer us is a much longed-for image of a lost, loved person and 'adds to it that rather terrible thing which is there in every photograph: the return of the dead'.[27] Various images of Plath are referred to as 'ghostly', 'white', 'washed out', or 'spooky'; she is a spectre that haunts the frame. We know she does not see her suicide, but we do. The image both haunts and is haunting. While this Plath we see may be trapped in a flattened black and white world, we know that she did not stay there; we know that we always give the story the same ending, even if getting to that ending differs. Does the image bring the haunting Plath back, and if so, how do her reader-fans interact with this presence? Why do some photographs move us so?

Peter

What it comes down to is that those black and white photographs reproduced in the biographies shaped—and colored—my vision of Sylvia Plath. The subject of 'images' of Plath is two-fold: there are the actual photographic images of the physical Sylvia Plath. And, in addition, there are the biographical interpretations of Plath by friends, critics, scholars, etc. that really, in a way, distort the image of Sylvia Plath. And, I say distort intentionally—especially where the biofiction genre comes into play. Those kinds of images really get one further and further from the actual Sylvia Plath.

Peter raises many of the issues from the earlier discussion in his response to Plath photographs. However, the main difference here is that Peter seemingly believes in an authentic (or an 'actual') Sylvia Plath, a person who can be accessed and known. He realises that this will not be achieved through the use of photographs. On the one hand, they are merely images of the now gone physical Plath. On the other hand, they are vehicles for interpretation and distortion; images that are used to create a political discourse to support the beliefs of friends, critics, and scholars.

In particular, it is the bio-representations of Plath which he feels are 'tossed in with actual images' to create distorted narratives. This sentence works on a number of levels. It is best understood as Peter's own image, or version, of Plath which becomes altered once other people attach their discourse to an image. However, it also points to his investment in a 'real Sylvia' that can be captured in these photographs which is then reworked with subsequent discourses. One of his fears is that 'as time moves on, who I think Plath is, is getting lost.'

This is also an example of how a personal image can take on the form of cultural status, once this memory is publicly shared.[28] A photographic image, claims Annette Kuhn, should tell a story that absorbs the viewer, but also satisfies as well, 'for the moment at least'.[29] What Peter is clear about is the power of the image and the subsequent narratives created from them: 'those black and white photos shaped—and colored—my vision of Sylvia Plath.' The use of language here is interesting, something black and white being able to colour at the same time; as we shall see below, Peter's response upon finding colour photos of Plath is striking. What we see here is Peter creating his own Sylvia Plath, moving from her texts to his extensive pilgrimages and a further intertextual reading via photographs. The images, literally and metaphorically, help shape Plath for Peter.

Peter carried out extensive work in the Plath archives and, as a consequence, was able to view many unpublished photographs of Plath. However, one shock did await him. 'I had never thought of Sylvia Plath as being "in color".' Earlier in this chapter, we discussed the role of temporality in photography and how certain images can be evocative of certain times. Sepia photographs speak of years and people long gone. The black and white image captures, freezes, flattens. For Peter, traditionally Plath had always been in black and white—'the black and white images were all I knew'. Yet the archives revealed rare images of Plath in colour which had a profound effect upon Peter:

But, upon seeing her in color, I think it just opened up dimensions of her appearance I hadn't noticed or considered. I remember being captivated, vividly, by the red lipstick and huge smile as she was holding Nicholas. Her clothing—I think she had on a red shirt and a black sweater. Her hair color too, was striking, especially considering the locks of hair that Indiana also has. It's kind of like those color pictures re-shaped my image of Plath. I think the black and white photographs somewhat and somehow 'date' her—but seeing her in color made her instantly more modern.

We see Peter becoming further dazzled by Plath; his language itself becomes colourful—'vivid', 'red', and 'striking'. He is captivated by her physical appearance and presence, which suddenly re-shapes his previous idea of Plath. Rather than the flat, dated black and white photograph, Plath appears to literally leap alive from the image. The colour photographs bring her closer both in time—she was 'instantly more modern'—and closer to Peter's understanding of her, as he unlocks 'dimensions of her appearance I had never noticed or considered'.

Despite this deepening creation of Plath, and perhaps because of gender difference, Peter does not directly identify with Plath via her photographic image. There is a viewing space in which his gaze hits something that is very separate to himself: 'I cannot think of any connection between those photographs and myself.' Plath's image is that of an attractive, young woman and an image that Peter finds noticeably attractive—'she looks good in black and white but in the color shots she's a knock out!'

We could argue that it is this beauty that creates the iconic image of Plath— the beautiful, doomed young writer who kills herself. Perhaps for many people with only a cursory knowledge of Plath, the suicide of a gifted young writer does embody all the frustration of the loss of promise and could have been. However, I would argue that for those who know more about Plath, her beauty is a happy accident. As we have seen from the first chapter, all the respondents in this research, with the exception of one, encountered Plath firstly through her writing. Therefore, it was the written word that drew them in and dazzled them, not the visual image. This is not to undermine the subsequent effects that her physical appearance may have had, but rather to highlight that it was not, in most cases, the primary attraction.

Furthermore, Plath was a notoriously tricky subject to photograph. At the Sylvia Plath 75th Year Symposium in Oxford, a panel was held discussing just how different she looks in each image. Friends claimed she did not resemble her photographs. It is this chameleon-like quality that strikes Peter:

I've always found Plath in some ways to look very, very different from photograph to photograph. I think of Plath & Mrs. Cantor on the beach in Cape Cod, and the photograph of Plath studying in school. Same person, but they look nothing alike—to me. I know that from year to year and decade to decade I look differently, but with Plath I think her appearance in photographs likely, probably, can be connected to the writing she was doing at the time.

Peter captures the frustration of never quite knowing what Plath looked like. Although Peter acknowledges 'the natural' changes over time, Plath's difference in images is so strong that for him they 'look nothing alike.' One explanation he offers for this draws a direct link between the woman and the work; he speculates that the outer appearance somehow reflects her interiority and her writing subject. This belief in correlation between writing and appearance is not an uncommon view, as we shall discuss further with subsequent respondents. It also leads to the creation of interesting, and often conflicting, discourses around images.

Peter acknowledges that although he never initially thought of Plath visually 'in color... I now know that that's not true, and clearly Plath used color in wonderful ways in her writings'. Both in photographs and in poems, the colour red stands out; it is perhaps this colour more than any that allows an intertextual reading between the poems and the pictures. Peter writes, 'in "Stings", the end of the poem is red all over':

> *Where has she been,*
> *With her lion-red body, her wings of glass?*
>
> *Now she is flying*
> *More terrible than she ever was, red*
> *Scar in the sky, red comet*
> *Over the engine that killed her ----*
> *The mausoleum, the wax house.*[30]

This is an interesting response from Peter; although Plath clearly returns to him via the photographic image, he fails to be able to identify with her through the pictures. This could partly be a gender issue, but it also seems to be connected to the chameleon-like quality of Plath to look very different; the fact that she rarely looks the same is a source of frustration. He is aware of how this shaping of Plath can be connected to the creation of discourses around certain images, and he begins to draw links between the exterior visual images of Plath, her internal thoughts, and writing production.

Ultimately though, for Peter, the images of Plath do not create the same degree of identification he achieves from her texts. There is more of a one-way feeling of haunting occurring here; Peter does not engage with the images in the same way he does with poems or with places. Perhaps, it is the Barthesian 'flat death' that limits his relationship with the photograph; although these images 'shape and color' Plath, for Peter they do not appear to have any impact on his sense of self. Indeed, it could be argued that, in this visual form, she is manifestly his gendered 'other', and more explicitly an object of desire.

Anna

In her discussion of Plath photographs, Anna raises a pertinent question considered by Barthes in *Camera Lucida*—what is it about certain pictures that 'sets us off'? Why do some photos leave you so unmoved that you do not even bother to see them as an image, whereas another photo can animate and engage?

> I've looked at many of the photographs a lot. I have two up on the wall—one is a postcard, I guess it's the most common one, the one where she is leaning against a wall, with a kind of flowery dress on and a big heavy necklace. She looks very serious. It's so familiar by now that it's lost some of its initial lure.

Anna is suggesting there is an initial flare of interest upon seeing an unseen image of Plath. Sontag suggests as much—too much viewing of certain images can dull their potency.[31] The photographs 'lure', and yet familiarity brings a flatness, a lack of excitement and adventure. In fact, Anna goes further: 'I think that is true of several of the photographs—you look at them so much that they begin to fade.' The beautiful use of language here is evocative; we know that, in a literal sense, photographs do fade, but Anna also refers to the images losing their power—fading in meaning and expression. For Barthes, with many images, we 'enter flat death'; for Anna, as a viewer, that flat death can also occur the other side of the photographic paper.[32]

However, the opposite can also occur: 'I can feel startled by new photographs, because she looks so different, so real somehow.' Plath can flare back into life and jolt the viewer:

> At the conference [Sylvia Plath 75th Year Symposium], I remember having gotten the then-new Hughes letter collection and looking through it, there were several new photographs of Plath. One where she had her hair in braids, kind of laughing, looking to her left or something. She looked very different than from other pictures, more real, that kind of startled me.

What is it about a new image that can change the perception of a person, and make them more real? On the one hand, Peter seems frustrated to be unable to locate a 'real' Plath through photographs; in a subtle difference, Anna becomes excited by the presence of different Plaths to those she has become used to. She sees this almost as gathering further knowledge to build up a more accurate picture: 'When you see a photograph you've never seen before, it's a new angle, a new face to add to the other ones.' This viewing shows that identification is not taking place with Plath; in fact Anna is not even mourning the loss of Plath. Instead, she considers her favourite photograph:

My favourite photograph is the one from Cambridge, when she is sitting in a chair, kind of staring baldly, somewhat challenging, into the camera. Because she doesn't look like a sweet little girl, she looks like an intelligent woman who is very sure of herself, and it matches her late poetry, I think. She looks interesting. I've looked at that photograph a lot.

As with Peter, Anna draws links between Plath's appearance and her interiority, almost as if the voice of those late poems stares out in visual form. There is a blurring of Plath's identities taking place with Anna and Peter, between the interior and exterior.

Anna, however, introduces temporality into the equation; she mistakes the person in the image for the actual voice of the late poems. In fact, this photograph of Plath was taken in 1956, some six years before those late poems were written. Anna's reading of this image is not transparent for two reasons. First, the photograph is posed. Plath, in front of a book case, is looking directly at the camera. She must have held that gaze, that pose, for a few seconds while the photograph was taken. It is not a spontaneous shot. Second, the narrative of a time that had not yet occurred is transposed onto the image; at that stage, the voice of those late poems did not exist. What we see, then, is what we retroactively impose with our prior knowledge; time swirls and eddies and we no longer follow a chronological line.

Again, we entertain the notion of temporality in photographs. Barthes claims the photograph does not call up the past, but attests to what has once existed. Nevertheless, 'photography has something to do with resurrection', a reality one can no longer touch.[33] In the search for the lost loved object, reader-fans need to assuage their sense of loss—their desire to regain that which they never had. Even though Anna does not personally experience this loss, she recognises that others do:

I guess that's always what fans are looking for, and why there is such an industry around her—everyone always wants something new, something that makes her come alive if only for one second. Because she does, in a way, doesn't she?

For Sontag, images are not just about death and resurrection, but preservation and usurping the real. Photos are open to multiple meanings; Sontag argues that a photograph is not only an interpretation of the real, 'it is also a trace, something directly stencilled off the real, like a footprint or a death mask'.[34] Plath is both there and not there.

As in her discussion on place, Anna has awareness about the actual practice of fandom, how it works, and the commercial interest surrounding it. Her reference to the Plath 'industry' highlights her belief that reader-fans yearn for Plath: 'everyone always wants something new, something that makes her come alive if only for one second'. It is perhaps this discussion in which Anna reveals a hint of longing in her own rhetorical question—'she does in a way, doesn't she?'—as though she is seeking some sort of poignant affirmation.

Unlike Peter, Anna enjoys the differing aspects of Plath. Whereas, for Peter, the lack of a 'true' image is a frustration, for Anna, this allows her to gather more knowledge—to know more fully the differing faces of Plath. Like Peter, Anna has a tendency to read the photographs through the life discourses, thereby imposing her knowledge of Plath's life onto the images. This is not necessarily a conscious imposition, in fact it seems more likely that there are unconscious processes at work, especially in Anna's reading of the Cambridge photograph. It is perhaps more likely that Anna cannot simply unlearn what she knows.

Anna shares with Peter an interesting separation of her own self and Plath via the image, as if the glossy film of the photograph prevents identification blurring and bleeding. The image is not really internalised in the same way as the poems and journals, and her imagination is not as fully captivated or engaged.

Kiki

> My thoughts on images of Sylvia? I remember having read *The Bell Jar*
> and *Ariel*, wanting to know what she looked like, although I am not sure
> why this should be terribly important. I guess I wanted to see if there was
> anything extra-ordinary about her face, some kind of mark of being gifted
> or a seer, perhaps.

Kiki draws comparisons between the woman and the work. Whereas Anna felt Plath's intelligence showed in her face, Kiki is curious to know whether there is anything unusual or 'extraordinary' about Plath's face, while at the same time feeling slightly puzzled about 'why this should be terribly important'.

As with most readers, Kiki first encountered Plath through her writing and it was the written text that had the initial impact, so maybe for Kiki there was a natural curiosity about what the writer looked like, even if this did not necessarily have an impact on the work itself. However, there is also a slight yearning in Kiki's desire to see Plath; she admits, 'since I so identified with her, or at least with her words, I think perhaps I wanted to see if there was anything of "me" in her face, which is perhaps a curious idea.' In light of Freud's theory of identification, that 'the ego assumes the characteristics of the object', there is nothing curious about Kiki wishing to see something of herself in Plath; it is also interesting to note that Kiki makes the clear distinction between identifying with Plath as a woman and identifying with the textual Plath. [35]

There was one photo in particular, a candid shot of Sylvia in her platinum blonde phase, with her current boyfriend taken on the beach. In it, she is in profile, gazing at him in adoration, and I swear, it could have been a picture of me when I was her age, even though I really look nothing like her. But in that one photo, I think I saw a little of what I wanted to see—a little of myself in Sylvia.

Kiki is self-aware enough to realise that, perhaps objectively, she does not look like Sylvia Plath—'even though I really look nothing like her'. However, there is something in the characteristics of Plath that she feels captures what she wants to be. Kiki experiences yearning—'I saw what I wanted to see'—and achieves some level of assimilation with Plath: 'a little of myself in Sylvia'. A slippage occurs between Kiki's earlier claim of identifying only with the texts of Plath and her subsequent admission of wanting, in some way, to be like 'Sylvia'. Does the subject want to be the other or does the subject want the other to be them?

As we can see, though, total assimilation of the loved object has not taken place, for Kiki is still able to acknowledge the space between herself and the photographic image. In fact she actively creates her own discourses around them. In an interesting coincidence, Kiki also chooses to discuss the image of Sylvia taken in Cambridge that Anna, above, says is her favourite photograph of Plath. For Kiki, this image tells a different story:

I think when I first saw her face—was it the photo of her with the long hair in front of the book case? I can't quite remember. I was taken aback at her All American, nice girl, 1950s persona. I remember thinking how in the world could this normal looking, cookie cutter, cheerleader type of person possibly know the dark contents of my heart? ... So, I suppose it was a lesson in image and how an image does not always reflect the real person.

Whereas for Anna, this photograph allows her to construct a discourse around the intelligent and bold voice of the later poems, for Kiki there is a disappointment in the banality of the photo. In wondering how someone who looked like that could possibly write as she did, Kiki experiences a strange mismatch between the written text and the image. This is a fine example of a viewer's fantasy creating storytelling around images, and highlights the complex reading processes that may take place when the photograph does not support an existing discourse. Suddenly, the photo fails to emotionally move us. Since this was a photograph taken by Olwyn Hughes—Plath's then sister-in-law—we are looking at a classic family shot, which has moved its status, as Sturken claims, from the familial to the historical. Plath is no longer just Plath but 'an all American nice girl 1950s persona.'

Yet identification with a loved object can also have a flip side; 'it can turn into an expression of tenderness as easily as a wish for someone's removal'.[36] While the ambivalence does not have to be this extreme, there can be a rejection of certain values and traits of the idealised other. Kiki, initially disappointed with the Cambridge image of the 'ordinary' Plath, reasons that:

> I learned in time that this was her façade, or maybe a reflection of what she wanted to be and never at bottom really was. I never wanted to be the kind of girl or woman that she seemed so desperately trying to be. Quite the opposite.

For Kiki, the identificatory ambivalence is perfectly summed up in her simultaneous desire to see something of herself in Plath, while equally rejecting certain values that she perceives Plath to be aspiring to. Here, Freud's model of identification seems to reach its limits. The narratives Kiki creates around certain images—Plath on the beach—reveal a level of yearning and desire to be like Plath, whereas other images inspire outright rejection.

Sonia

As we have seen in the first chapter, Sonia is the one respondent in this research who did not initially encounter Plath through her writing. In fact, her first encounters were visual images after a psychic friend told Sonia she was a reincarnation of Plath. Although sceptical, Sonia did eventually look at some photographs:

> I looked at the pictures she showed me and I agreed that she looked just like me, so I started to look at the web for more pictures. And in a very scary way almost all photos looked like me.

Sonia begins to experience the Freudian *unheimlich*, something that is familiar (Sonia herself) and unfamiliar (Sylvia Plath). Moreover, as we have seen in Chapter Two, this uncanniness takes the form of the doppelgänger or double: 'characters who are considered identical because they look alike. This relation is accentuated by mental processes leaping from one of these characters to another'.[37] Sonia quickly realised that the photographs she saw of Plath resembled photographs of herself that had been taken over the years, even down to similar poses and facial expressions. She collected some of the photographs side by side to unearth something very uncanny.

In a fascinating series of images Sonia sent to me (but requested that they not be published), Sonia is not claiming to merely look like Sylvia Plath, but is actually claiming to be her. Freud would argue that identification here has taken its most extreme form, and the ego has utterly consumed the loved object. There are no spaces or boundaries between the two. Here we are dealing in a very literal and material form with the return of the dead; Freud believes this is one of the most common causes of the uncanny. Things which create that feeling of *unheimlich*, such as ghosts of the dead or daemonic spirits, we regard as primitive thoughts and beliefs held by our 'forefathers'. We no longer, with our modern mind set, believe in them; yet at the same time we have not discarded these beliefs either. This, according to Freud, is because we are not yet totally sure of our new beliefs and so the old ones lurk within us, ready to seize any opportunity to reassert themselves. It is also, once again, evidence of Rank's notion of the double in a very literal sense.

Sonia herself is somewhat unsure about her feelings: 'I completely understand if you think I am nuts.' Yet, analysing the photographs that Sonia sent to me, I can be persuaded that much of the feeling of uncanniness comes not only from the repetition of the poses—'this inner compulsion to repeat is uncanny' says Freud—but the fear that can arise when an inanimate object becomes too much like an animate object, in this case Plath's photo becoming like Sonia.[38] Like the Freudian dolls and waxwork models, we both fear and desire that something dead will come to life.

For Sonia, as we saw in Chapter Two, the existence of a double could highlight Freud and Rank's original belief that a doppelgänger serves as an insurance against the destruction of the ego. 'Her psyche seemed to be just like mine. I have since early childhood been struggling with mental problems of different kinds, and the thought of suicide came early as well.' So the role of Plath may be to offer support to Sonia during troubled times or may, as Freud claims, come to symbolise a harbinger of death, or the fear of ego-destruction through suicide. Either way, there is a doubling of the self that becomes interchangeable with another.

On a spectrum of identification via the photographic image, we could perhaps see Peter and Anna to be opposite to Sonia. Whereas Kiki 'wants' to see something of herself in Plath, she still regains the space to realise that she does not in any way resemble her; in this sense Plath remains the 'other', outside of Kiki. For Sonia, a doubling is taking place with identity, ego, and physical appearance. The physical similarity for Sonia directly impacts upon her identity and is further, unnerving evidence that she is Sylvia Plath. Despite this extreme identification, Sonia still expresses some awareness of a separate identity—'she looked just like me' and the uncanniness seems to come from the repetition of similar poses in photographs. This compulsion to repeat is the element that unsettles Sonia.

Megan

Megan, despite her introduction to Plath via *The Bell Jar* and the poems, did not encounter images of Plath until much later:

> I don't recall seeing any images of Plath before I began researching my
> dissertation. Even as I started I only had a very vague image of a pretty,
> blonde and quite pale young woman in my head—but I'm not even really
> sure where this came from.

This vagueness relating to the historical figure of Plath can be seen throughout
Megan's accounts, in which she attempts to keep what she called 'a respectful
distance' from the author. This differs greatly to the inquisitiveness of say, Peter,
who is keen to see exactly what Plath looks like immediately after reading her
texts. It does, however, share similarities with Kiki, who sees Plath as being a
typical 1950s woman of her time. Megan's impressions of a visual Plath are
hazy and 'pale' in more than one sense; there is a very misty, generic construction
of an image taking place. Furthermore, she does not even know where these
impressions came from. Do we assume then, with Jacqueline Rose, that Plath is
simply there as a ghostly figure in our culture, whose image or persona circulates
widely, but imprecisely, as part of our recent cultural past?[39]

> The first memorable and meaningful encounter I had with images of Plath
> came when I began reading the *Journals* and *Letters Home*. Whenever I read
> anything biographical or autobiographical I am always keen to look at the
> pictures, as I feel that you can make more sense of the person and the history
> you are reading. I remember that I found any images of Plath particularly
> fascinating, as I felt the need to try and read her through these images, and I
> even sat staring at them trying to understand her, explain her work, her end.

It is interesting that Megan draws an immediate distinction between the
'implied author' of the texts she reads and the historical object of biographical
studies. As we have seen in previous chapters, it appears to be this distinction
that prevents Megan from either identifying with, or mourning Plath, as a
loved object. It is not until Megan encounters the biography that her interest
is piqued as to what Plath actually looks like. For Megan, gaining this visual
knowledge helps to further make sense of the person. Furthermore, she feels
that through these images she will be able to 'understand' or 'explain' Plath.
    Barthes asks in *Camera Lucida* if it is actually possible for a photographer to
capture the essence of someone; or rather does the viewer necessarily have to bring
prior knowledge and fantasy to the viewing?[40] In a self-aware piece of analysis,
Megan describes how she seems to read the images through her prior knowledge:

> I felt in one sense that she looked like any normal pretty woman embodying
> an age gone by, but then again I couldn't help seeing loneliness, or a ghost-
> like, ethereal quality which I guess was because I was trying to explain what
> little I knew of her life. Overall I felt a complex sadness and awe, because the

emotions that I read in her work and autobiography became real through her image.[41]

Megan raises the issue of temporality, 'a woman embodying an age gone by' and a need to untangle her complex range of emotions, such as 'sadness' and 'awe'. In other words, in the same way that some readers confuse the implied authorial voice of Plath with the historical figure, Megan is attempting to merge the visual Plath with the historical person. She shows an awareness of the construction of discourses and how we necessarily view these images through the frame of what we already know.

Barthes claims photographs are not transparent conveyors of truth or meaning. In fact, the reading of a photograph is always historical: 'it depends on the reader's knowledge just as though it were a matter of real language'. Knowing that Plath was to die young and by her own hand is perhaps what informed Megan's reading of Plath as 'lonely' and 'ghost-like'.[41] In so much as images can be about stasis (Barthes' claim of entering 'flat death'), they are equally about movement and change—a fluidity that appears to be informed by prior knowledge of the photographic subject.

Ultimately, though, it is Plath's cultural presence that informs Megan's reactions to the images; she simply cannot unlearn what it is that she already knows:

> It seems that Plath's image is imbued with so many connotations to do with her life, and now her cultural presence, that it is hard to look at them without all this in mind.

Megan's views on images of Plath appear to be more knowing and reflective than other respondents. As with her views on pilgrimage, Megan appears to be maintaining the 'respectful' distance' from Plath; this is in contrast to, for example, Kiki, who engages in playful identity formations. Yet, at the same time, Megan is aware of the powerful discourses that can surround the photograph, and knows she herself is not immune to this power. Whereas Peter and Anna feel photographs may reveal the writerly voice that emerged from Plath, Megan believes we impose these ideas onto the image, retrospectively armed with biographical knowledge. So much that we cannot, according to Megan, look at images of Plath 'without all this in mind'.

If, as Sontag claims, photographs are 'pellets of information', then perhaps, we sense the sadness more than ever in images of Plath, or the melancholia of photography.[42]

> Photography is an elegiac art, a twilight art. Most subjects photographed are, just by virtue of being photographed, touched with pathos.[43]

This becomes much more poignant when we know the end of Plath's life story.

Conclusion

This chapter has gone some way to exploring the power of the image in the lives of Plath's reader-fans. Beginning with a discussion of the intrinsic nature of the photograph, it was concluded that not only was time an issue in the power of the image, but also the attendant feelings of loss and melancholia that it had the capacity to give rise to. How some viewers responded to images of a lost loved object, such as Plath, was considered, as well as how it is possible for the dead to return via the photograph. Barthes and Sontag formed a useful model for this, but I also speculated that in so much as photographs are about time and death, they are also about revivification and the defeat of time.

It seems that there is still something elusive about the photograph. Even after all the theorising and analysis, there is a difficulty in saying why we prefer one image over another, or why we are simply not moved by some images at all. As brief visual snatches of temporality, photographs are powerful, but retain their secrets and refuse to reveal all. We find ourselves again left with questions.

'How does meaning get into the image? Where does it end? And if it ends, what is there beyond?'[44]

5

Objects

I love the thinginess of things.[1]

As we have discovered in the previous chapters, place or image are perhaps neither quite as substantial, nor material, as we first thought. The playfulness of time, traces, and memory affect both their transmission and the ways in which they are received.

This chapter will consider the role of things—of objects—and how they mediate the relationship between Sylvia Plath and her reader-fans. Can the dead return to us via objects? If so, how? Marx's notion of the mystical transformation of the commodity will be explored, to ask what it is about Sylvia Plath's things that transform them from everyday objects into something 'special' and what change occurs. By handling her things, do reader-fans of Plath attempt to conjure up her ghost?

Hallam and Hockey discuss how objects can become relics of the dead and be used as tools of mourning.[2] Attempting to preserve the dead in 'things' could be seen as an attempt to reanimate that which is lost and gone, as well as stabilise a sense of self suffering from loss.

Fandom scholars, such as Jenson and Jenkins, discuss how the emotions involved in the handling of personal artefacts can be seen to transgress the bourgeois boundaries of 'good taste' and 'rationality'.[3, 4] What meaning-making do reader-fans of Plath engage in when faced with objects connected to her? How does this impact on both their mourning of Plath, their understanding of Plath and, ultimately, themselves?

Imagine a long dead person, a dead poet, physically gone—or so it seems: a plait of hair in an archive still shiny, still lustrous and alive; handwritten manuscripts with ink blotches and fingerprint smears; spilt coffee stains; traces of skin cells, tears, blood. Laundry lists; household chore rotas; menu plans; half sewn scarlet material lying in a sewing machine; cheque stubs;

receipts; the blue eye of the turquoise swinging on its silver chain. Traces, residues. Foucault asks what constitutes a body of work; is it everything that someone has ever written, uttered, deleted? Passages, drafts, plans? He asks 'How can someone define a work amid the millions of traces left by someone after his death?'[5] For Foucault, the word 'work' is as problematic as the status of the author. Things, however, are somehow more solid, more there; the temptation is to treat them as something more reliable because of this physical presence—'the thinginess of things'. Both in conversation and in her writing, Plath discussed just how this materiality seemed important:

> *I do not trust the spirit. It escapes like steam*
> *In dreams, through mouth-hole or eye-hole. I can't stop it.*
> *One day it won't come back. Things aren't like that.*
> *They stay, their little particular lusters*
> *Warmed by much handling. They almost purr.*[6]

There is something uncontrollable and unpredictable about something that 'escapes like steam', it cannot be stopped. It is also impermanent and irretrievable: 'one day it won't come back'. In direct contrast, the speaker states clearly how 'things' are not like that. They are permanent; they stay with us, respond to handling, even enjoy being handled even, so that they 'almost purr'. The comforting solidity of these warm things explains further why, in conversation, Plath would state 'I love the thinginess of things'. Indeed, the archives confirm Plath's claim that things last and are durable; her childhood paper dolls and toys, intricate pastel drawings, and illustrated letters and locks of baby hair all survive.

In conversation, Professor Richard Larschan described how Aurelia Plath kept all of her daughter's things, everything, even down to screwed up pieces of paper she traced on.[7] When helping Mrs Plath to sort through this material years after Plath's death, he became overwhelmed by the physical mass and presence of these objects. Plath, of course, was right; her things did stay in a way that she did not. The shock of these things, the first time a reader-fan encounters something that belonged to Plath, cannot be underestimated. This occurred to me in 2007 at the Sylvia Plath 75th Year Symposium.

The Wood Carving

'Mrs Plath kept everything.'
  'Pieces of tracing paper, small scraps of material, folders, papers, cheque stubs, locks of hair, small things Sylvia made.'
  The screen flashes up an image.

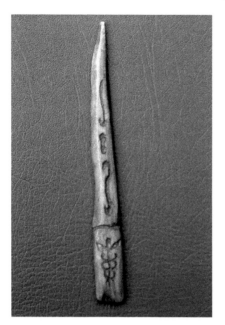 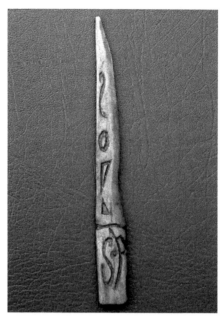

Caduceus wood carving by Sylvia Plath. (*Richard Larschan*)

It is shaped like the large incisor tooth of a great lion or tiger. Rounded and spherical, it slopes into a sharp point. The wood is light brown and smooth and looks as if it were warmed by many years of handling. Intricate carvings are visible, a snake wrapped around a knife, patterns, shapes that Sylvia first saw as an eight year old on the uniform of the nurse who took care of her dying father. These images re-emerged five years later during a summer at Camp Helen Storrow when given a small piece of wood, Sylvia chose to carve into its smooth surface the snake, the knife, the symbols.

It is this small piece of wood that now sits in the palm of my hand in the vaulted Hall in an Oxford College. The speaker, after flashing the image up on the screen, reached into his jacket pocket and produced the very wood carving he had been talking about, the wood carving that now sits in the palm of my hand.

I could not wait to hold it. A person before me was absentmindedly fingering the small object while talking to someone else and I unapologetically took it from their hands. I expected something to happen. The first time I had ever touched anything that Sylvia had made! Shouldn't something happen? I was holding something that her hands had held, something that she had made. Shouldn't there be some trace of this left, some residue like sticky fingerprints in the wood? Or would they have been erased by many years of handling by others, by travelling from America to England in the pocket of the family friend?

I felt the wood and the carved symbols with something approaching wonder and I realised I wanted to cry. Was this the closest I would get? I imagined the fourteen year old Sylvia bending over shaping and working the intricate patterns, blowing the wood shavings away and smoothing the remainder with her fingers. And suddenly a very ordinary and worthless piece of wood became transformed into something invaluable, like a saint's relic. A piece of wood that made its way back from the summer camp with Sylvia and lay in the attic of the family home for years.

'I remember/The dead smell of sun on wood cabins/The stiffness of sails, the long salt winding sheets'. The summer revisited, a person returned by a small piece of carved wood sitting in the palm of my hand. The cyclicality of time. The refusal of the dead to die; the revisiting, the revisioning, the returning. And time and years and the summer and the sea and sand and the memories of a person long dead were sitting in the palm of my hand. And I, a person who never even knew Sylvia, felt a hand reaching out across the years. The wood warmed by much handling. The wood warmed by my handling. The wood warmed by her.

The importance of the objects lies not only in their physicality but in their significance and use to the person who is no longer alive; the seemingly solid based 'reality' of these things becomes instantly undermined if we consider our fascination with them as not so much 'how-they-are-now' but 'how-they-were-then'. The relics that we invest so much meaning and value in may, for example, have been irritating clutter to Sylvia Plath. Would she have cared about a wood carving she made as a young girl? Once we have written shopping lists or menu plans, do we ever revisit them as sites of great knowledge, or are they usually thrown away and forgotten about? Moreover, if Plath herself did not invest value in these objects, why would we? How can an object be both significant and unimportant at the same time?

Marx argues that the 'mystical character of the commodity does not arise from its use-value'.[8] As Marx suggests, something a little inexplicable can occur to objects, something almost secretive. He cites the example of a piece of wood made into a table. Although the wood is altered to become a table, the table continues to be wood. For Marx, as soon as this table emerges as a commodity, something else happens, 'it transcends sensuousness', and a whole range of unthinkable transformations can occur to this piece of wood until there 'evolves out of its wooden brain grotesque ideas far more wonderful than if it were to begin dancing of its own free will'.[9]

There is a correlation here between Marx's example of the table and one object stored in the Mortimer Rare Book Room in Smith College, Northampton, Massachusetts; hanging there, on the wall, is the large six feet long elm plank that Sylvia Plath used as her writing desk.[10] In itself, this is a piece of wood—

wood made into a table and a table that is still nevertheless wood. However, what occurred on this table and the person who used it lends it a kind of mystical quality; Plath writing the *Ariel* poems on this table gives it a value that goes beyond economics. This elm plank is transformed in a way that we cannot quite define. Walter Benjamin speculates upon the 'aura' of an original object and how this aura exists simply because an object is unique; the more an object is reproduced, the more precious the original becomes.[11] In the case of Plath's desk, although it may be reproduced visually, it cannot be reproduced in any other way. There is only this one original desk upon which she wrote those *Ariel* poems; there is only this one desk that holds the ink stains and traces of that time. It is this originality that makes it so special and perhaps it is Benjamin's notion of the aura which affords it what Marx calls a 'mystical quality'.

The fascination of such objects raises some interesting questions about reader-fan's behaviour and emotions. Should I feel embarrassed by my emotional response to handling something Plath made? Should I feel ashamed that I am not having an 'academic' response? Is the desire to, for example, touch Sylvia Plath's hair 'abnormal'? In *Textual Poachers*, Henry Jenkins asks whether it can be healthy—morally, socially, ideologically, and aesthetically—to give yourself over to someone else's texts and things. He draws on Bourdieu's claim of the 'bourgeois aesthetic values' attitude that encourages detachment and an approach of distrust to strong feelings of emotion. Such emotional behaviour transgresses dominant cultural boundaries of 'good taste'.[12] Fans, he argues, are seen as 'abnormal'; as such, most existing studies treat the fan as radically other.[13] Academia shies away from this type of emotional engagement, and I have had numerous conversations with academics who are fans and describe powerful reactions to objects, then quickly add the caveat 'but I'd never publish this.'

Jenson echoes this view when she suggests that these culturally-loaded categories encourage the enlightenment-like view that rationality should be imposed and employed as a 'superior' reaction.[14] In her discussion of how fans are perceived, she argues that the enculturation of categories and hierarchies of 'good' and 'bad' taste, acceptable and unacceptable behaviour, result in the belief that emotions and emotional responses to things blur the boundaries between reality and fantasy.[15]

This focus on taste does highlight an important point for this book. It may well be that this blurring of reality and fantasy not only allows the reader-fan to receive Plath's things in a particular way, but also to manipulate and create their social meaning. The role of fantasy is surely absolutely crucial, not only in relation to the actual object itself, but also in how the reader-fan uses that object to construct a reality, a discourse or a story. Furthermore, it relates to how the object can then be used to assuage the sense of yearning and loss brought about by the lack of the loved object, Plath. The work of both Jenkins and Jenson challenge stereotypes of the obsessional, hysterical fan but also offer a way in which to begin considering the validity of fans' 'emotional' reactions to objects as being just as valid as the more measured evaluation of what Jenson refers to as 'aficionados'.[16]

The Plath archives are as much about history as they are about things. In *Theatres of Memory*, Raphael Samuel beautifully reflects upon history and memory and claims that history itself draws not only upon memory but equally myth, fantasy, and desire; 'the sense of past, at any given point in time, is quite as much a matter of history as what happened in it'.[17] As we shall see, the archives certainly inspire a sense of the past for those who view the contents of them, but myth, fantasy, and desire clearly play a crucial role in reconstructing this 'history'.

The irony here is that, faced with the durable and lasting objects of Plath's life, we encounter more than ever a move away from the cult of authenticity. If the archives are used as a way to 'get to know' Plath better, then this desire overlooks the temporal disruption that occurs when bringing history back to life. The utter unreliability of largely subjective 'interpretations', speculation, and myth-making—all themselves dependent upon the workings of fantasy and desire—abolish temporal linearity and allow what Samuel calls a 'two way traffic' between the past and the present.[18]

It is, moreover, the occurrence of this temporal rupture that causes the archives to take on a ghostly nature of their own. The past and present exchange information, and the reader-fan's fantasy and desire can leap between the two. Once again, the ghost of Plath has crept from the pages of her text and is present; 'the ghost is a nomadic figure, a wandering figure that flits in and out of presence both in space and time'.[19] It is this flitting that makes the figure ghostly and ungraspable, or, to use Plath's words from earlier, 'it escapes like steam from dreams'.

According to Gordon, to get to the ghost and the ghost's story, it is necessary to 'understand how the past, even if it is just the past that flickered by a moment before can be seized in an instant or how it might seize you first'.[20] However, I would like to argue that it is impossible to ever 'get to' the ghost or the ghost's story; it seems this ungraspable aspect is crucial, for it is the very elusive nature of not knowing that keeps the endless fascination alive in the reader. It is most likely the spaces, the gaps, the silences, and unanswered questions that create the maddening enigma. Gordon's claim that the past might 'seize you first' may aptly describe the sudden and unexpected reaction reader-fans experience when faced with Plath's things, but it does not necessarily guarantee that the past can be seized in any stable and workable way.

Although reactions may be unexpected, encountering certain objects is not; the very act of visiting an archive involves premeditation and planning. A tension exists between the conscious will of searching for relics and the unbidden conscious discovery vis-à-vis the relic. As Pearce suggests, 'I guess I am sceptical that the sensation being sought by the fans is realisable when it is being so assiduously sought out: the most powerful relics are the ones that leap out, unbidden.'[21] In their essay about material culture and death, Hallam and Hockey support this view, discussing how the sudden opening of a wardrobe, or the sight of a deceased one's coat over the back of a chair, can have a profound effect upon the viewer; it appears to be the unexpectedness of it that creates the shock.[22]

Equally, it could be the closeness in time to the death. Pearce argues that objects 'cool with time'. Relics deliberately handled and saved perhaps lose their potency, as it were. Pearce argues that, if relics suddenly occur unexpectedly, relics from long ago, they can have the same power as those associated with the recently dead.

We are faced with the tension of variable time, in the sense of the closeness to the death of the deceased; could it be relevant that Sylvia Plath is a particularly contemporary icon? There is also the question of intention, whether the relics are consciously sought after or not. However, it is worth noting that reading about the contents of an archive cannot always prepare one for the shock of the actual objects within it.

In *Dust*, Carolyn Steedman gives an honest account of the surprise and excitement to be found in archival research. She describes the nights spent in bad hotels, the huddled researchers outside the archives in a morning, eager with their pencils. Steedman captures something of this excitement:

> The archive is this kind of place that is to do with longing and appropriation. It is to do with wanting things that are put together, collected, collated, named in lists and indices, a place where a whole world, a social order, may be imagined by the recurrence of a name in a register, through a scrap of paper or some other little piece of flotsam.[23]

If archives are to do with 'flotsam', longing, and imagination, we can perhaps see why reader-fans of Plath mourning their lost loved object might deliberately seek out her relics. Whether this conscious search for an experience interferes with the power of the objects will be discussed in what follows below. Do Plath's objects help to return her from the dead? And if so, how do reader-fans use such objects?

Peter

Part of Peter's textual and scholarly productivity around Plath involves multiple visits to the Plath archives at Indiana University and Smith College. Interestingly, he begins his account with an acknowledgement of the dominant cultural hierarchy:

> When I first used the archive in May 1998, I was so nervous and I definitely felt more like a gawking peeping-tom paparazzi than anything close to a serious scholar.

Jenson deals with this deviant view of fans in her essay 'The Consequences of Characterisation'. The fact that Peter felt nervous and like a 'gawking peeping-tom' is, argues Jenson, a direct result of the literature of 'fandom' being haunted by images of deviants, or 'a peeping-tom', and fanatics, or 'gawking … paparazzi'. Moreover, she argues, 'fandom is seen as a psychological symptom of a presumed dysfunction'[24] and that fans characterised as 'them' can be distinguished from 'people like us' (i.e. professors, social critics, reputable patrons)—or in Peter's words 'a serious scholar'. Why would the habits of scholars—in this case, a visit to an archive—be deemed any less deviant than the identical actions of a 'fan'? Jenson claims this is because of 'the elitist and disrespectful beliefs about our common life'.[25] The enlightenment celebration of all that is rational and unemotional creates a hierarchical categorisation, that for Jenson is not only 'stunningly disrespectful' but dishonourable since 'little is known about the variety of ways people make meaning in everyday life'; the nature of affections and attachments and the sense of yearning or desire that these can bring about.[26]

Since Jenson wrote this in 1990s, fandom studies has sought to allow the emotional attachment of fans to be taken more seriously. However, Jenson's original account remains a powerful polemic and one this book draws upon heavily in its attempt to address the negative depiction of Plath fandom in particular. In fact, we could even go further and break down this barrier that Jenson refers to as the difference between fans and aficionados, to claim it is not the difference in knowledge and perception—I would argue, for example, Peter probably knows much 'more' in some ways than many academics who teach Plath—but the difference in enactment: how reader-fans express this relationship to Plath. There is something more 'emotional' or 'open' about their accounts. Peter stated:

> Why do I want to go there? When I first went there I wanted to see things like her journals, her handwriting, pictures of her etc. I guess I wanted in a way, to see her or **what's left of her,** things she touched and wrote on. The bulk of the archive isn't published so there are gems there too. Gems that, if read on the right day or are read a certain way, can yield a new way of reading or looking at Plath. If those things happen, then I guess, a new way of understanding her could be possible. Ultimately I think being in the archives provides information that rounds out Plath the woman, Plath the child, Plath the writer etc. It's a first-hand look at Plath's life—unadulterated. Her life without the agenda of others, like Stevenson's or Alexander's [My emphasis].

Peter is implicitly stating his sense of loss and desire to recapture or reanimate that which is gone. His realisation that she is no longer physically here, that the archives simply house 'what's left of her', reveals the lack and the loss. The remaining traces are the closest he will get to the physical Plath, (perhaps importantly) what he feels might be the 'authentic' Plath—he wanted to touch things she touched. The Freudian loss of the loved object that has echoed so resonantly throughout previous chapters is once again relevant here.

In her essay 'Remains to be Seen,' Susette Min discusses how traces constitute both presence and absence in equal measure; this idea is further reinforced by David Eng (in the same book) when he states that 'loss is inseparable from what remains, for what is lost is known only by what remains of it, by how these remains are produced, read and sustained'; it is perhaps through the handling of her things, through the touch of physical objects, that some of Plath's reader-fans attempt to resurrect her, to sustain their relationship with her in the face of loss.[27] Eng's comment perfectly captures how reader-fans use what remains of Plath in their attempts to 'know' her via her books, poems, pictures, places, and objects—what Peter calls discovering the 'unadulterated' Plath.

The durability of cultural objects, it seems, helps memory and fantasy to recreate and return the dead. We are drawn in, sucked in to what these relics can tell us. Neither dead nor alive, they contain an identity, a promise of reanimation, a promise of knowledge. As Hallam and Hockey state:

> Material culture mediates our relationship with death and the dead; objects, images and practices, as well as places and spaces, call to mind or are made to remind us of the deaths of others. Material objects invoke the dead.[28]

Objects tell us that Plath once touched this, she made this, her hands have been here, used it, created it. You can know she is still here, she will come back; she can be invoked. Her things remind us of her death and help to bring her back. As Peter observes:

> Indiana has a letter from Eddie Cohen in which he writes what it was like to be physically in her presence.[29] He writes: "I had managed, during that rather short period when I was with you, to establish a reasonable correlation between actuality and what I had created in my mind, between your physical being and the person I knew through letters. I had come to know and like the little things that make the differences in people—the sound of your voice, the way you tan, the langorous [*sic*], comfortable way you curl up in a booth, the trick you have of licking the air with your tongue when discussing an idea, almost as though you were literally tasting it, the way you double your legs under you when sitting on a couch—all these things were making you at last a three-dimensional, and desirable, person." Reading that gave me the chills, he describes the way she licks her lips; it's an incredibly intimate portrait that doesn't take much imagination to recreate.

The textual reanimation of Plath's physical presence creates a sense of the uncanny for Peter. The portrayal is so intimate that he gets 'the chills'. In this sense, the archives have fulfilled numerous purposes—keeping alive the memory and work of a dead person, giving others some kind of access to the deceased, and allowing the lost loved object to be accessed albeit in a somewhat spectral manner. Yet, ultimately, all this depends upon an appreciation of the physicality of the things there:

> I think being in the archives does give a new perspective to Plath. After reading all the published materials, it is refreshing and humbling, in a way, to go there and read unpublished materials. The biographies quote or summarize some of these materials, but it does not compare to being there and seeing the "stuff" first hand.

Peter is not claiming some sort of authentic experience but rather a realisation that the 'stuff' he can see and handle contains some kind or power or ability to invoke the imagination that a second-hand account cannot. The experience also gives rise to a spectrum of emotions:

> Emotions I remember feeling are awe (the *Ariel* papers, her dictionary, her elm writing desk and typewriter), sadness (the check stub for her oven) and absolute joy.

Plath's Royal Typewriter held in the Mortimer Rare Book Room, Smith College. (*Gail Crowther*)

This is where the malleability of time is significant; these things in the archives are viewed with knowledge and hindsight that did not exist when they were first created; history is expanded and reworked. Plath's cheque stub for her oven was, potentially for her, a mundane and necessary purchase as she moved homes from Devon to London in 1962. For us, as viewers of the archive, it invokes sadness at being the instrument of her death. Time really does create a two way flow of traffic where the past and present constantly dart around each other.

However, some items in the archives that almost seem to stop time are clippings of Plath's hair, which Peter refers to as the 'strangest, oddest thing'.

> [Hair] is reanimated as a possession capable of sustaining the deceased in close proximity to the bereaved. The physical durability of hair makes this possible as it stands in stark contrast to the instabilities of the fleshy body.[30]

So is there life in something that lasts? Does it contain even more evocative powers if the hair was separated from the person while they were still alive? Does hair that still feels soft, that still catches sunlight, that keeps colour and texture bring back the dead person? Peter writes:

> For all the Sylvia Plath places I'd travelled to... for all the times I felt 'close' to her, felt her presence pulling or guiding me down foreign, strange streets and through fields, and across so many miles; I never felt so close to her as when I held these locks of hair. The locks of hair were and are Sylvia Plath.

They were her. They were separated from the living child, the older teenager. They are her, they somehow invoke her, return her to the living, into the presence of the person holding the hair. In the archives, Peter noticed:

> The lock of hair in the baby book was so fine and light, it was almost feathery, or like what I imagine angel's hair would feel like. As Plath aged, her hair color changed as well as the texture. There was one BIG lock of hair, likely from 1945 or 1949. It was thick and heavy and I thought of the line from 'Stings' 'And dried plates with my dense hair.'

Peter draws direct parallels between the physical presence of Plath and the writerly voice of the poems, yet another example of a reader disputing Foucault's question 'what difference does it make who is speaking?'[31] There is also an element of awe when faced with such objects, describing the locks of baby hair as 'angel's hair'. We could also invoke Freud; Peter compares the solid and durable hair to something more insubstantial and wispy. Freud tells us that the deceased, often described as 'angels,' hold a dread fascination—something beautiful but inaccessible.[32]

However, the hair is not simply a tool to recall the dead. It is a social thing. It appears to be the site where the negotiation takes place between what we know and do not know. It is a particular construction of knowledge, an attempt to seize a fleeting instant, to grasp that which has already passed us by and can never be again. It is loss, and it is perhaps this loss made apparent to us, overwhelming our rationality, prolonging our feelings of mourning and our unfulfillable need to get to the ghost's story.

In fact, Hallam and Hockey demonstrate how the body and memory and time can be linked:

> We consider the body itself—a body that has passed the threshold of life, a body that is no longer a living form but through death can be reanimated as a material of memory. We can discern this transformation of the body from a living form into a dead yet socially active memory 'object' in the uses of the corpse as relic and as a substance that has been used in the mourning practices.[33]

Of course, in this case we are not dealing with a complete corpse, but part of a now dead body that was removed when the person was still alive. There is something poignant about the image of a Plath reader-fan holding her hair, feeling its texture and seeing the colour first-hand. The traces of Plath left are juxtaposed with her absence; the durability of her hair is a stark contrast to the decaying flesh of a corpse. The hair, it seems, can be used as a tool in the mourning ritual, both as a retainer of the lost object, but equally as a reminder

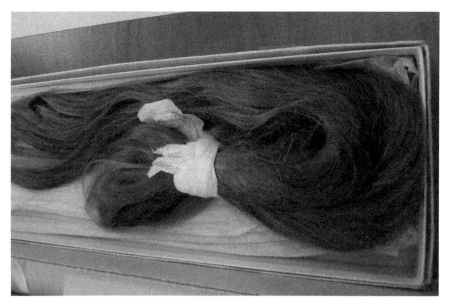

Plath's hair held in the Lilly Library Archive, Indiana University. (*Peter K. Steinberg*)

that the lost object is gone. The body is gone and can now only be transformed into a 'socially active memory' via the hair.

Hair has a long history of containing power, of magical abilities, such as the storing of a lock of a loved one's hair to bring them closer. There is something ritualistic about it. It is like an invocation:

> There are other poems of Plath's where she mentions her hair…but in 'Stings' she describes her hair as dense. I think it makes 'Stings' more powerful and provocative. As it's part of a series of poems in which Plath builds up a kind of mythic persona, it grounds the poems, or bases it in fact, bringing it back from a kind of myth into something real.

Although we could argue that Peter is merging Plath's historical voice with that of her writerly persona, it is this perceived dragging back out of myth and into reality that creates the interesting contrast; if desire and fantasy play a large part in the historical reconstruction encouraged by archival material, then the boundary between myth and reality is necessarily blurred anyway. All Peter can do is unravel his own relationship to who he perceives his 'real' Plath to be.

Derrida explored what it meant to reckon with the dead and the role— 'work'—of mourning.[34] In a Freudian manner, he claims that mourning consists of interiorising the dead, or consuming them; to give the dead anything at all now can only be through us, the living. He also claims that death appears to sever the name from the bearer of it; it is the event that 'peels the name off the body that once bore it'.[35] Peter's encounter with Plath's archival material appears to suggest the opposite—her hair and her things ground her identity firmly in her name: 'the hair is and was Sylvia Plath'. However, we cannot overlook her absence, her inaccessibility and wonder who exactly, what exactly, is 'Sylvia Plath' now for Peter?

This inevitably brings us to her grave:

> The material of the stone is effectively fused with (or closely linked to) the living bodily traces of the departed, thus establishing the headstone as a distinctive physical presence that lives.[36]

If the headstone becomes representative of the lost object, then what can we learn from the grave itself? So far, we have examined: those archival objects; those relics that spark fantasy, desire, and history; those objects that have significance because of '*what-they-have-been*'. The other type of object, however, is the tribute, the memorial that tells us something not only about the reader-fan but the loved object too. As Hallam and Hockey stated, it is material culture which can mediate our relationship with the dead.[37]

On his second visit to Sylvia Plath's grave, Peter wrote in his journal:

> I read, in order, "Sheep in Fog," "The Moon and the Yew Tree," "Kindness,"
> and "Edge." I placed two poppies at the base of the gravestone and grass was
> sprouting through the dirt. I took two small leaves of grass for my notebook
> where they remain today.

The poppies left are associated with some of the final poems Sylvia wrote—
'Poppies in July', 'Poppies in October'—and so memorialise Plath the poet, as
does the reading of her actual work. What is more interesting is not just the
leaving of a tribute, but the taking of grass from the grave. Looking back on
this, Peter appears to be slightly puzzled as to why he did this:

> I'm not sure what they mean to me now. What they meant to me at the time
> was significant. I enjoyed looking at them from time to time throughout the
> rest of that visit and periodically once I returned to the US. I felt that part
> of England, and a part of Plath, in a way, was with the words I wrote in my
> journal.

Peter is perceptive in acknowledging the fallibility of memory and action once
the intention has been and passed. However, we can again see the Freudian
mourning of the lost object, the desire to retain a part of that which is no
longer there. Furthermore, it is surely important that Peter wishes to place the
leaves of grass near his own written words. Ultimately, 'I think the archives'
existence in the first place is something to revere and to treat with much care
and respect.'

    The ordinary, mundane, and everyday objects of life become transformed.
Relics, like the relics of saints, become worthy of reverence in themselves. For
Peter, the importance of Plath's objects lies very much in their physicality, the
fact that they are what 'remains' of her. It is through these remains that she
can be most 'known'; she is the traces she has left behind. Therefore, handling
objects not only reanimates Plath for Peter—when handling her hair, this is
very evident—but allows Peter, on some level, to feel closer to his loved object.

Kiki

So far, this chapter has examined the effect of Plath's personal belongings on
the reader who physically engages with them, and how the leaving and taking
of tributes to Plath operates on different levels. However, for Kiki, the desire
to 'own' a piece of Sylvia Plath was overwhelming. In fact, she describes it as a
physical feeling:

There is a deep physical desire to possess or to at least handle her diaries, her books, to see the places she visited, etc. On a personal level, it led me to purchase two letters by Ted Hughes (on Court Green stationary) and finally to buy a book owned by her, with her book plate and name in it.

Kiki is not content with simply coming into contact with Plath's things but in a more overtly proprietary way wishes to own objects for herself. As we saw in the first chapter, Kiki felt possessive of her relationship with Sylvia Plath and felt dismay upon discovering Plath was 'lots of other people's best friend too'. With the purchase of a book from Sylvia Plath's personal library, Kiki can ensure she is the only one who handles the object. She is not unquestioning about these actions:

> It was her work—poems and stories and diaries—that drew me in, but I felt a desire to go further, to see through her eyes, or handle the things she touched. Why is it that we need this kind of 'possession' when the words should be enough?

The recurring theme of 'seeing' through Plath's eyes, which we encountered in the earlier chapter on place, once again implies an identification and a desire to somehow actively take part in an impossible task—to be present in a time that has already been and gone. If one of the results of spectral haunting, as Colin Davis claims, is to make established certainties vacillate then never more is Plath's ghost as successful as when she disturbs chronological temporality.[38]

However, the double meaning behind the word 'possession' is also interesting; does Kiki mean that the 'kind of possession' she talks about is possessing Sylvia Plath or being possessed by Sylvia Plath? The evidence from earlier chapters suggests the former; although Kiki partially identifies with Plath, it is still with a discernible distance, in that there is no blurring of identity boundaries.

Derrida in *The Work of Mourning* discusses some of the problems of dealing with and speaking about the dead.[39] One of the dangers, he says, is that we risk using the dead for some purpose of our own and Kiki's acknowledgement of this is evident by her reference to the poem 'Lady Lazarus':

> The other 'theme', continuing the proprietary line of thought, is that of owning a piece of SP. Like in Lady Lazarus when she writes of there being a charge for a bit of hair or her clothes.

We do need to ask in what sense can we 'own' a piece of Sylvia Plath? Does owning an object amount to owning a person? For Derrida, the person who is dead is no longer living in themselves to be owned; the only way they continue to be present is through us, the living. Owning a former book of Plath's as a way of feeling closer to her merges both the interior and exterior, both the past and present:

> Thus the book as one finite identity for textuality seems to keep us in the here and now by remaining with us from some past, from our past, from the past in general.[40]

As Julian Wolfreys suggests, above, the past can be reanimated or kept alive via the book. I would extend this thinking to speculate whether, for Kiki, the former owner of the book is somehow equally kept alive through her 'things'. If so, we see certain correlations occurring between Kiki and Peter, for both of these respondents somehow attempt to revivify or get closer to Plath by using objects.

For Kiki, a certain closeness is achieved by a personal possession, something owned purely by her, as opposed to the collective holdings of an archive. This need for a personal possession does puzzle Kiki; she refers to it as 'proprietary'. This seems to be an extension of Peter's desire to handle Plath objects; in this case Kiki wants to be the only one to handle Plath's things. Whereas Peter seems open to the idea that objects bring Plath closer, Kiki seems a little more resistant. She questions herself: why are the words not enough? In the same way that Kiki is a little resistant to identification with Plath (see Chapter One), she is equally wary of her own intentions and motives in what she calls 'owning' a piece of Plath.

Touching or owning things that belonged to Plath can only reanimate her so much. Keeping her present may be a way to deny the loss and yet denying the loss does not seem to lessen the yearning. This space seemingly cannot be filled with 'things'.

It seems that Kiki's relationship to Plath may operate on a number of levels of resistance, both in admitting Plath may play a role in her identity formation and in accepting that images and things can be used to bring the lost other closer. On a conscious level, we can perhaps see evidence that Kiki is haunted by the presence of Plath, yet there does not appear to be the same level of mourning and yearning that Peter displays.

Morney

It is not just Plath's objects which become treated as relics. Other people can become canonised as if by association. In an email to me, Morney reveals the extent to which an object could become almost sacred simply by being touched by someone associated with Plath:

> Alvarez and Ronald Hayman are 2 of my heroes.[41,42] So ... take a piece of paper with you to the symposium, touch Alvarez with it and SEND IT TO ME!! Haha.

Although Morney adds humour at the end of her email, the implication is that an ordinary object—in this case, a neutral piece of paper—can become imbued with some special meaning simply through the power of touch. Although the association with Plath becomes more and more removed, a transformation can still occur.

This transference of meaning and power is not unproblematic and involves disentangling idealised extensions from the loved object through a network of other people and things. What it is interesting to speculate is first, what Morney thinks will actually happen to the piece of paper once it has been touched by Alvarez (some sort of magical transference?); and second, how and why people become significant through association. Alvarez himself was aware of this tendency and, during his introductory talk at the Sylvia Plath 75th Year Symposium in Oxford, stated that he thought he might be there simply as a 'Plath exhibit or relic.'[43]

A further point to address is the possibility that canonisation by association furthers the Christ-like dimensions of Plath that we discussed in an earlier chapter. If we regard Christ-like dimensions as Baugh does, then we can see Plath embodies the enigmatic 'hero' who is never fully revealed and yet is able to attract a group of followers.[44] If, as a Christ-like figure, Plath was surrounded by those who supported her during her lifetime then, like 'disciples,' perhaps these people become important and significant in their own right? Moreover, those who do follow her, who did know her, become lucky enough to have been taught, formed or saved by her.[45]

There is something about the movement of power here. That indefinable Marxist 'thing' that occurs to objects to turn them into something special can perhaps also occur with people. How does such a shift of energy occur? Is it possible that there could ever be any theory to describe this elusive transformation? As is so often the case with Plath—both there and not there, both voiceless and vocal—there is a feeling of never quite being able to grasp that which is also slipping away.

In her stories, Morney does not discuss ever having handled any of Plath's things, or any objects relating to Plath. Therefore, comparisons between her and the other respondents is difficult. I do feel, however, that it also highlights the special nature of things and what becomes of things once a person has died. Many of Plath's possessions are now held in archives, some easier to reach than others, some only open to 'scholars'. This necessarily limits access and relates to John Fiske's essay on 'The Cultural Economy of Fandom'.

Fiske argues that like economic capital, cultural capital plays a role in the power differentials of fandom. In the same way economic capital is divided unequally, so too, argues Fiske, is cultural capital. Plath's archives, being open to 'scholars' but not 'fans', appear to be evidence of this unequal distribution of power.

> Fans are among the most discriminating and selective of all formations of the people and the cultural capital they produce is the most highly developed and visible of all.[46]

Whereas Morney may not have gained access to any Plath archives, reader-fans such as Peter have. Some of these power issues were alluded to in Peter's narrative in which he speaks of feeling like a 'peeping tom', yet the Plath research and writing conducted by Peter most likely outweighs that of most Plath academics.

Fiske's model does have its limitation for this book. Cultural capital cannot be separated from much larger issues of gender, class, race, age, and, perhaps more pertinently in this case, how all of these issues connect with access to, or provision of, education.[47] It does, however, allow us to start thinking why reader-fans who are offered no access to Plath possessions, manuscripts, or documents, may shift or filter the power of these haunting things through other objects or people.

Sonia

So far, we have discussed objects owned by Plath and objects or people associated with Plath. We will now explore objects that become significant to the reader-fan despite having no connection to Plath whatsoever.

> It was about a month or so after I discovered Sylvia. ... Yes, it was when we were going through some old clothes that had been padded away in an old suitcase. They came from a relative, who had been living in the States. This relative had worked in the US for most of her life. I don't even know exactly who she was. I don't remember her name, but I do know her name wasn't Sylvia. It was me, my mother and I believe my sister was there as well. We were at my mother's house. Right among all these dresses, from the 30's and 40's, lay a potholder, with the text 'Sylvia 1938', and it had two Swedish flags on it. I was the one who found it.
>   That was weird. It was some kind of message.

Sonia identifies a number of coincidences and associations that place great significance on the discovery of the potholder. First, the object came from America, like Plath. Second, it had the name 'Sylvia' inscribed on it. Furthermore, the presence of Swedish flags indicates to Sonia that there is some connection between this American figure named Sylvia and Sonia herself, who is Swedish. Equally, the fact that Sonia discovered this potholder amongst all of her aunt's possessions is significant; in fact, it is regarded as a 'message' of some sort. Sonia does not specify what sort of message, from where and from whom, but implicitly suggests this is some sort of confirmation of a connection between herself and Plath.

As we have seen in an earlier chapter, Judith Williamson argues that in reading a message, the individual is a creator of meaning.[48] Sonia imposes her own explanation for the discovery of the potholder. Similarly, with Morney, a person associated with Plath can become almost sacred in their own right; in

An image of the Sylvia potholder.
(*Sonia Flur*)

this instance we have an example of an object, which is not connected to Plath in the physical world, becoming imbued with significance. Again we pick up on Marx's notion of a sort of mystical transformation. By this I do not mean mystical in the supernatural sense, but in the way that meaning and value can shift and can be imposed. Behind this process is the spectral figure of Plath, sometimes closer than others, but nevertheless there.

Sonia also recounts a story of an object, a book, that became significant to her because of the message she believed came with it. The story has a supernatural quality, both drawing on ghostly happenings, coincidences, and inexplicable actions:

> Among many books about Sylvia I had bought the book 'Giving Up' by Jillian Becker. I sat and read the book in my sofa one day, and in one chapter I read that Ted had said on the funeral of Sylvia that 'everybody hated her' (Sylvia). It went to my heart and I started crying. That was a feeling I have had the whole of my life, that no one liked me. One moment later a book is falling out of my bookshelf all by itself! I look up and I see it is *Birthday Letters* by Ted Hughes! If this was a coincidence then it was a very good timing. If Ted Hughes hated Sylvia it would be rather strange of him to write this book.

For Sonia, an object becomes a more literal transmitter of messages. The book is not simply a thing, a book, but is used for some deeper purpose. It acts as a source of comfort or reassurance with regard to her self-worth, something validated by someone—or something—outside of herself. Her doubling with Plath is further confirmed by the 'performance' of things and the various ways in which something solid can communicate on behalf of someone a little more spectral and elusive.

Sonia's account of objects stands alone in comparison to our other respondents, especially since these objects were unique to her. The major difference is that there is a more magical quality to Sonia's story and an interest in what these objects can reveal about her own sense of self rather than what they have to say about Plath. Whereas Peter uses objects to feel closer to Plath, Sonia uses them to better understand herself.

The key theme connecting all the accounts so far is the ability of things to reanimate Plath. In other words, to confirm she not only once existed, but is still an active presence. For Sonia, this active presence has the ability to offer comfort and reassurance: 'It went to my heart and I started crying'. Her perception as being 'disliked' by others is seen not only to be a feature of Plath herself, but a false perception. Perhaps too, this offers some hope to Sonia, that she may also be mistaken in her self-perception: 'If this was a coincidence then it was very good timing.' Through objects, through things, Sonia is able to gain some sense of self-worth and hope of the continuing presence of Plath in her and in her life.

Florian

In the following account, Florian narrates a recent trip he made to the US with Sonia, to visit various Sylvia and Otto Plath locations and the Smith College archives. It took me some time to decide where this story belonged. Was it about place? Or images? Was it about identifications and doubling? Finally, I decided that not only was it an intersection of all of these things, but it was very much about objects too: solid, durable things.

> It was a bit hard to find Winthrop, we had no GPS and our maps were not detailed enough.[49] Therefore it was such a relief to finally get there. I remember I saw the ocean in a glimpse while driving through Winthrop and it almost made me cry. When we arrived at the hotel it was almost dark. The hotel was a pleasant surprise. Our room was very spacious, almost like a little apartment. Next morning Sunday March 15th we woke up early and went to the beach altogether. The beach was just a block away, the weather was sunny and the air was thin and clear, in other words magical. I found a very special stone, it was purple/pink with a distinct white stripe or ring. I showed it to Sonia. I didn't keep it though because I thought it would be a little heavy to bring along. Later that day Peter accidently told us about a similar stone that Sylvia describes and called a 'Lucky stone'. Those stones may be common though…

Florian merges an account of place, Winthrop, with objects, like the 'lucky stone'; paradoxically, he combines this 'magical' experience with something that he acknowledges might ultimately be 'common'. Although he discusses the coincidence of choosing an object that had meaning for Plath, he also realises this may not be significant.[50] We do have to question whether his open ended sentence ('Those stones may be common though…') leaves room for speculation.

This brings to mind the paradox Gordon discusses in relation to a spectral presence, 'I see you are not there'.[51] The person is seeing (or perhaps experiencing) something, is aware of a presence, but of a presence that is no longer there. In a similar fashion, Florian is both implicitly implying certain explanations while explicitly denying them. As a researcher, I potentially see an occasion when Florian's unconscious impulses are at work. We are allowed a glimpse into his fantasy world—perhaps he wants there to be some significance with the stone—but his conscious 'reasoning' will not allow this idea to fully form.

Florian continues his account with a mix of place and objects:

> Then we went to Johnson Ave and Otto and Aurelia's old house. My first impression I think was there was a German feeling about it (I have been many times in Germany since my mother and grandparents are from Germany), and a feeling of 'my old house'. It felt slightly familiar but that might be just my imagination. A fun detail was that Sonia said she recognised the stones on the entrance to the front door from a regression (hypnosis) she made. In the regression she told me that she had a vision of looking down on her feet, she had black shiny shoes and then there was these characteristic stones. She was about 5 or six years old in the vision. Sonia doesn't see the regression as an important event in this whole story of hers. (Another, more interesting detail from the regression is that she remembers the patterns on the floor of the kitchen where she took her life, but that's hard to check I guess…) Peter told us that Otto (probably?) planted the big tree in front of the house. It was a valuable and fascinating detail in many ways. Nimbus grabbed a chunk from the tree that we brought with us as a very special souvenir.[52]

The objects that stand out in this account are the 'stones' and 'shoes', 'tiles', and 'tree'. As was the case with Peter at the grave of Plath, Florian took a 'special souvenir'—part of the tree from the front garden of the former Plath home, which Otto himself very likely planted. In this sense, we can see how the tree itself becomes entangled with the historical figure of Otto Plath.

This is not uncommon; Hallam and Hockey state that, 'material objects can become extensions of the body and therefore of personhood'.[53] Likewise, we see a similar process occurring with Sonia and the stones and tiles she recognised from her regressions. Both Sonia and Florian identify and double with Sylvia and Otto Plath to the extent that there is identity slippage. Otto's house becomes Florian's 'old house'; Sonia sees the tiles on the kitchen floor where 'she took her own life'. Yet as with other accounts, this level of identity merging is not maintained. When Florian discusses the tree planting, it is

'Otto' who planted the tree, not 'me'. There is distance between the self and other, a Freudian feature of both mourning and identification.

In the archives, however, Florian experiences quite an intense reaction to Otto's objects. Like Peter, he is unprepared for the shock of 'things' and begins to question himself:

> I got one hour in the archive and it was a really intense experience. The photos resolutions was tremendously good, so even the photos that I had seen before was a sensation with all its shades and details. I got a much clearer image of Otto's personality. Above all my main impression was the differences between him and me I saw. It wasn't until we got home that I had time to see that we fundamentally are still quite alike. When I was sitting in the archive I got uncertain that I actually had been him.

What is interesting here is that out of all of the 'things' in the archives, Florian chooses to focus on his experience handling the—largely unseen— photographs of Otto Plath. I cannot help but feel it is at this moment when Florian neatly captures the essence of the whole discussion within this book.

He identifies with Otto, he even doubles with Otto, seeing them as 'still quite alike'. However, he is also ambivalent about this connection to his loved object and finds himself focusing on their 'differences'. He has travelled to a significant place to view images and objects. The 'flat death' of the photograph nevertheless brings Otto Plath back, and Florian gains 'a much clearer image of Otto's personality'. [54] The construction of discourses around an image, the creation of a cultural memory that Hirsch and Sturken talk about so eloquently is here, happening and in practice.[55, 56] It brings to mind Plath's own attempts to resurrect her father; in the poem 'Daddy', the speaker states:

> *At twenty I tried to die*
> *And get back, back, back to you*
> *I thought even the bones would do.*[57]

For Florian, Raphael Samuel's 'two-way traffic' is at play again as he not only tries to (re)capture Otto but sustain him in the 'infinite deferral' of death.[58, 59] After all, what can be more of an infinite deferral than reincarnation, in which one never dies but returns again and again?

How strange that rather than confirming Florian's belief, this 'meeting' results in his doubt: 'when I was sitting in the archive I got uncertain that I actually had been him'. It is not until he gets home and reflects upon the experience that his belief returns and he realises the similarities between himself and Otto remain. It may be worth thinking about Benjamin's claim that distance is required for an 'auratic presence' to be felt as Florian seems to reverse this process.[60] Although, for Benjamin, distance is necessary to retain the aura, it is when one is closest to the original object that the auratic presence is most strongly felt. Faced with Otto's images and things there in front of him seems to make Florian somehow feel more removed from his lost loved object, as though the closeness itself creates an emotional distance and a dissolution of the auratic presence. It is only with geographical and temporal distance that Florian is able to rebuild his belief system around his identity formation. This is in direct contrast to Peter, who feels closer to Plath handling her things, and Kiki, who wishes to own a piece of Plath within a proprietary relationship.

Florian's uncertainty faced with Otto's objects appears to highlight the different types of distance and the ways in which they can impact upon the reader-fan's relationship to his or her loved object. Perhaps, we might argue, it is easier to employ imagination when geographical distance is involved; being positioned face to face with objects that belonged to Otto Plath appears to interfere with Florian's ability to psychically connect with his alter-ego. Perhaps, there is no space for it. However, when I held an object belonging to Plath, it was then that my daydreaming was at its most vivid and my connection with Plath most successful. Therefore, it is worth considering how distance—and different types of distance—are as productive, and elusive, as the lost object itself.

For Gordon, encountering a ghost involves 'blasting' through the rational, through linear temporality and conventional notions of conscious and unconscious, past and present.[61] Most of all, for Gordon, 'a ghost is primarily a symptom of what is missing'.[62] Florian speaks of both his sadness and hopes:

> It felt very strange to see these sharp images of Otto, his eyes looking right back as if I was looking into a mirror. … Another feeling I got was sadness, and I think it was because I became more aware of my old mistakes. I saw this 'old me' and I wasn't happy about it. I have come much further, and seeing my 'old me' made me sad.

The key feature that appears to be missing is the actual physicality of Otto Plath, but there is also another sense of loss—a feeling that Florian somehow regrets past mistakes, missed opportunities. In this context, it is through the guise of Otto Plath that 'I became more aware of my old mistakes', while it is through Florian himself that he acknowledges the changes that have since taken place: 'I have come much further'. Gordon argues that this is really what ghosts represent:

> What it represents is usually a loss, sometimes of life, sometimes of a path not taken. From a certain vantage point the ghost also simultaneously represents a future possibility, a hope.[63]

For Florian, engaging with place, image, and objects allows him to somehow shed his 'old life' and turn to the future. In this sense, his hope for the future is similarly reflected in Sonia's account. Of course, the future is inescapably formed by the past but for Florian there is room for autonomy and change. In fact, Florian concludes by reflecting back on what Rose called the 'soap opera' of Plath's life.[64]

> I think that it didn't start with Sylvia. It started with Otto or earlier. It's not Otto's, Sylvia's or anybody's fault though. I think it's about how we handle our destiny. Everyone has their own responsibility for his/her destiny. But that is a longer story...

Conclusion

This chapter has attempted to explore the importance of 'things' and the meaning objects relating to Sylvia Plath may be given by her reader-fans. I considered the ways in which the handling of objects can return the dead, acting as a sort of 'spirit medium'. Through the touch of physical objects, some of Plath's reader-fans attempt to resurrect her, to sustain their relationship with her, in the face of loss. Using Hallam and Hockey's theories of the material culture of the dead, the durability of cultural objects was considered alongside how the temporality of traces helps memory and fantasy to recreate and return the dead. We are drawn in, sucked in, to what these relics can tell us. Neither dead nor alive, they contain an identity, a promise of reanimation, a promise of knowledge. Extending Hallam and Hockey's ideas allowed speculation on how different types of objects operate on different levels: objects belonging to Plath, objects associated with Plath, people who knew Plath, and even objects which had no physical connection to Plath at all.

Meaning shifts and it appears to shift all of the time. Yet within this spectrum of meaning, all the objects retain significance for the reader-fan; quite how the change in these objects occurs is still somewhat unanswerable. Why does a plank of elm wood, briefly used as a desk, take on the proportions of a saint's relic? As with identity, it is understandable that such an interior, elusive transformation would have its areas of silence and doubt. In the archives, surrounded by Plath's things, things she has left behind from another time, or at the grave where people leave (and take) tributes, reader-fans willingly conjure up her ghost. Sometimes, they search consciously, assiduously, for the sensations such objects can offer. Sometimes, the encounter with things is more unexpected, sudden, a shock. Sometimes, the traces are stronger than others. Presence and absence mix and blur. But even absence has a shape.

'The Present is Forever and Forever is Always Shifting, Flowing, Melting.'[1]

Browsing through Plath's work—her poems, journals, letters, and stories—everything indicates a vivid presence. Perhaps after all, that is the power of the textual voice, to continue its reverberations long after the life of the historical author? In discussing poetry, Plath implied as much:

> Surely the great use of poetry is its pleasure—not its influence as religious or political propaganda. Certain poems and lines of poetry seem as solid and miraculous to me as church altars or the coronation of the queen must seem to people who revere quite different images. I am not worried that poems reach relatively few people. As it is, they go surprisingly far—among strangers, around the world, even. Farther than the words of a classroom teacher or the prescriptions of a doctor; if they are very lucky, farther than a lifetime.[2]

Throughout this book, I have strived to illustrate that Sylvia Plath is still very much with us. I began by asking how and in what ways can the dead return; I hope to have established, building on the work by Jacqueline Rose, that Plath does indeed haunt our culture and that she returns to us in spaces that are created between the living and the dead—these spaces are both interior and exterior. Plath becomes the lost loved object, a spectral figure that can be identified with and mourned for. These processes ensure that she stays with us and is sustained in a protracted and pleasurable, long 'goodbye'. It is during this deferral of death that Plath appears to be able to haunt the human consciousness and through the powerful counterparts of love and loss, and the emotional components that make up who we are and what we feel, Plath appears as a spectral presence through reader-fans' various imaginations and desires.

But it is not just a haunting of interiority. Plath also returns via the exterior world, through traces she has left in places, through her images, her objects and things. The past offers up its remains; it is through these that we attempt to 'know' her. Ghosts do not need much space; when they do appear, they demonstrate a two-way haunting through time and space, a sort of two-way convergence, where they have transformative potential in our lives.

One major area of transformation is in our sense of self, and the second question this book set out to explore was to do with how a spectral presence impacts on our identity formation, once it has captured our imagination. It was through exploring this area and centring my analysis on both psychoanalytic and fandom theory that differences began to emerge. That Plath is a spectral figure did not seem to be in dispute; the extent to which she captured people's imagination was.

For some reader-fans in this book, such as Megan, they did not identify with Plath at all, or indeed, mourn her; Plath's textual voice stays contained within the boundaries of the page. The reader is not haunted and does not create a space for the ghost of Plath to seep out. For other respondents, their identity formation appeared to fashion itself after the loved object Plath to varying degrees. Peter, Anna, and Kiki recognised emotional similarities between themselves and Plath. Morney felt a strong connection or empathy with a distinctive redemptive element. Sonia and Florian were at the furthest end of the spectrum with total assimilation frequently occurring, but not always, to the point where they claimed to actually be Sylvia and Otto Plath reincarnated.

To attempt some tidy answer as to how a spectral presence can impact on identity formation seems an impossible task. Perhaps the process of shaping and creating an identity is such an individualistic procedure that we can merely look for patterns or similarities within this difference; I do not mind that this remains messy. In dealing with an enigmatic and ghostly figure, it seems appropriate that the full impact of this figure would itself be rather inexplicable. Psychoanalytic theory (via its focus on the processes of identification, narcissism, and mourning) can offer us a framework into why a particular person may be drawn to another, seeing traits that are similar, yet different enough, to allow room for both empathy and aspiration. Scholarship on fandom can help us to understand ways in which a fan may use a love object in their lives; these explanations offer us possible pathways into answering the specific 'why Sylvia Plath' question. I truly believe there are probably other explanations, or no explanations at all, or something so inexplicably subtle about this connection between reader-fan and writer that perhaps it cannot be encapsulated.

The huge question that emerged throughout the research for this book, one which I struggled to resist all the way through, is who, what, why, or how is 'Sylvia Plath' now? All of this mourning, yearning, and searching is for whom or what? Do reader-fans of Plath engage in some form of 'becoming', or is it

Plath herself who 'becomes' in some sort of transformative way? When there is no body, what is the 'body' of Plath?

Epilogue

The last time I visited the grave of Sylvia Plath there was snow on the ground. My foot prints left a ghostly trail across the churchyard in the shadow of the bell tower and the trees. My tulips bled red against the snow. I did not know what I was doing there but I knew that it was important; that somehow over fifty years after her death, Plath meant more to me that just about anyone. Why? Perhaps I can never fully explain this; perhaps this is part of the unspoken fascination—pondering the imponderable. I am here for now, and 'Sylvia Plath' is not dead.

> Nothing is real except the present, and already, I feel the weight of centuries smothering me. Some girl a hundred years ago once lived as I do. And she is dead. I am the present, but I know I, too, will pass. The high moment, the burning flash, come and are gone, continuous quicksand. And I don't want to die.
>
> Sylvia Plath[3]

Endnotes

Introduction

1. Wilson, F., *Literary Seductions: Compulsive Writers and Diverted Readers*, (London: Faber and Faber, 1999), p. xiv.
2. One of the few studies exploring Plath's readers is Janet Badia's excellent *Sylvia Plath and the Mythology of Women Readers*. In this book, Badia explores how misogynistic narratives about women readers, specifically Plath readers, have come into being as a backlash against contemporary feminism. This book was essential in helping me think about how Plath readers are represented in popular culture.
3. Rose, J., *The Haunting of Sylvia Plath*, (London: Virago, 1991), p. 1.
4. *Ibid.* p. 5.
5. *Ibid.* p. 2.
6. *Ibid.* p. 3. Plath wrote a poem called 'The Lady and the Earthenware Head' about a clay model of her own head that haunted her. See *Collected Poems* (1988: 69). All future quotations from poems are taken from this publication.
7. *Ibid.* p. 5.
8. *Ibid.* pp. 29-64.
9. *Ibid.* p. 29.
10. *Ibid.* pp. 65-113. The central point of Rose and Hughes's dispute lay in the interpretation of Plath's poem 'The Rabbit Catcher', in which Rose suggested there were lesbian elements to certain lines. Hughes, outraged by this suggestion, wrote to Rose that in some countries her critique would be 'grounds for homicide' (p. xiii). In a fine example of how people fall prey to the complexities and contradictions of the author-function, Hughes argues on the one hand, literal interpretations of Plath's work are 'laughable' (p. 68), yet on the other, chose to omit certain poems from Plath's final collection *Ariel*, (the more 'personally aggressive' ones) which were seemingly aimed directly at him (p. 70). Rose neatly highlights these contradictions: 'Ironically by omitting these poems on the grounds that their reference is too personal, Hughes is engaging in the very form of literal interpretation of which he is so contemptuous (p. 71). Rose expresses her understanding for how distressing this situation may be for those involved or close to Plath, but she also strongly argues that literary analysis itself can often be read differently by the person who had a lived relationship with the writer, Ted Hughes, than the critic writing it, in this case Jacqueline Rose.

11. *Ibid.* p. 69.
12. *Ibid.* p. 69.
13. *Ibid.* p. 68.
14. *Ibid.* p. 6.
15. *Ibid* p. 105.
16. *Ibid.* p. xiv.
17. *Ibid.* p. xiv.
18. *Ibid.* p. xiv.
19. Lawler, S., *Mothering the Self: Mothers, Daughters, Subjects*, (London: Routledge, 2000), p. 12.
20. Jenkins, H., *Textual Poachers*, (London: Routledge, 1992), p. 5.
21. *Ibid.* p. 5.
22. Hughes, O., 'The Plath Myth and the Reviewing of *Bitter Fame*' in *Poetry Review* Volume 80 No. 3, Autumn 1990, p. 61.
23. Rose, *op. cit.* p. 5.

Chapter 1

1. Castricano, J., *Cryptomimesis: The Gothic and Jacques Derrida's Ghost Writing*, (Montreal & Kingston: McGill-Queen's University Press, 2001), p. 3.
2. Plath, S., *Collected Poems*, (London: Faber & Faber, 1988), p. 71.
3. Castricano, *op. cit.* p. 3.
4. Derrida, J., *The Work of Mourning*, (Chicago & London: University of Chicago Press, 2001), p. 9.
5. Gordon, A., *Ghostly Matters: Haunting and the Sociological Imagination* (Minneapolis: University of Minnesota, 1997)
6. Castricano, *op. cit.* p. 22.
7. *Ibid.* p. 22.
8. Pearce, L., *Romance Writing*, (Cambridge: Polity Press, 2007), p. 92.
9. Hallam, E., & Jenny Hockey, *Death, Memory and Material Culture*, (Oxford, New York: Berg, 2001), p. 2.
10. Pearce, *op. cit.* p. 106.
11. Plath, *op. cit.* p. 201.
12. From the song 'I'll Never Be Anybody's Hero Now' by Morrissey, from the album *Ringleader of the Tormentors,* 2006, Attack Records.
13. Booth, W., *The Rhetoric of Fiction*, (Chicago: University of Chicago Press. 1980), p. 20.
14. *Ibid.* p. 88.
15. *Ibid.* p. 87.
16. It is important to note here the complex relationship not only between the historical author and the implied author, but the implied author and the narrator. They are not the same thing. Booth explains that the implied author is the presence who instructs us silently through the text, while the narrator is the voice it has chosen to let us learn. See Booth (1980) Chapter 7 'Narration: Levels and Voices' for a more in depth discussion of this point.
17. Lasch, C., *The Culture of Narcissism* (London: Abacus, 1980). Lasch argues that social developments in the twentieth century such as the rise of consumer culture, the popularity of fame and celebrity, the dread of aging and rise of the culture of youth have all led to the development of the narcissistic personality type in which individuals experience a particularly fragile sense of self. This idea of the narcissistic individual will be explored in more depth later in this chapter.

18. Lasch, *op. cit.* p. 17.
19. Quote taken from a radio interview for The British Council with Peter Orr, 30 October 1962. It is interesting how I decide to treat this text, as if somehow an interview will reveal some great insight into the historical figure of Plath herself. Intellectually, I know this is not the case. The person being interviewed is still the writer Plath and I can only assume that it is my own desire for access to the enigma of Plath that encourages me to treat this text with more transparency; perhaps there is also something about hearing her voice and my relationship to this.
20. Adrienne Rich quoted in Pearce, L., *The Rhetorics of Feminism*, (London: Routledge, 2004), p. 51.
21. *Ibid.* p. 22.
22. Barthes believed that once a text was written, the author fell away, 'writing is the destruction of every voice, every point of origin' (1977b: 142), hence the expression 'death of the author.' Moreover, for Barthes to give the text an author is to limit the text, to close the writing. The important issue for Barthes is the reader, since a text's unity lies 'not in its origin but in its destination,' (p. 148) thus 'the birth of the reader must be at the cost of the death of the author' (p. 148). It is important to lay the foundations for this idea here in the first chapter since the discussion is revisited in Chapter Two.
23. Wilson, F., *Literary Seductions: Compulsive Writers and Diverted Readers* (London: Faber and Faber, 1999). Wilson's book discusses how the reader can often be captivated, or seduced, by a book and then by the writer. She argues that the words on a page can create a captivation so powerful that the reader immediately falls for the writer. Wilson explores the role of reading and where the reader may situate themselves within a text.
24. *Ibid.* p. xviii.
25. *Ibid.* p. xvi.
26. Pearce, L., *Romance Writing* (Cambridge: Polity Press, 2007)
27. Bronfen, E., *Over Her Dead Body: Death, Femininity and the Aesthetic*, (Manchester: Manchester University Press, 1992), p. 265.
28. Wilson, *op. cit.* p. xix.
29. *Ibid.* p. xxiv.
30. *Ibid.* p. xxiv.
31. Pearce, L., *Feminism and the Politics of Reading*, (London: Arnold, 1997), p. 2.
32. Wolfreys, J., *Victorian Hauntings: Spectrality, Gothic, the Uncanny & Literature*, (Basingstoke: Palgrave, 2002), p. xi.
33. *Ibid.* p. xii.
34. *Ibid.* p. xii.
35. *Ibid.* p. xii.
36. Wilson, *op. cit.* p. xix.
37. *Ibid.* p. xiv.
38. Taken from an interview for The British Council with Peter Orr, 30 October 1962.
39. Cixous quoted in Castricano, J., *Cryptomimesis: The Gothic and Jacques Derrida's Ghost Writing*, (Montreal & Kingston: McGill-Queen's University Press, 2001), p. 4.
40. As an interesting aside, the literal pitch of Plath's voice is also a key captivating factor in her reader-fans' relationship with her; recordings of Plath reading her poems have had profound emotional effects upon listeners. Little research has been carried out regarding the 'audio' Plath that exists but Kate Moses has published an essay called 'Sylvia Plath's Voice, Annotated' in *The Unraveling Archive* ed. Anita Helle (2007) and Peter K. Steinberg wrote an introduction to

The Spoken Word Sylvia Plath, an audio CD released by The British Library (2010). In her discussion on Adrienne Rich and bell hooks, Lynne Pearce (2004), raises the issue that Rich and hooks emerge from an oral/aural tradition and that their writing is in many ways 'obviously trained on a listening ear' (p. 53). There are striking similarities with Plath, who claimed in a British Council interview in 1962 that her later poems were written in a very different way:

PLATH: This is something I didn't do in my earlier poems. For example, my first book, *The Colossus*, I can't read any of the poems aloud now. I didn't write them to be read aloud. They, in fact, quite privately, bore me. These ones that I have just read, the ones that are very recent, I've got to say them, I speak them to myself, and I think that this in my own writing development is quite a new thing with me, and whatever lucidity they may have comes from the fact that I say them to myself, I say them aloud.

ORR: Do you think this is an essential ingredient of a good poem, that it should be able to be read aloud effectively?

PLATH: Well, I do feel that now and I feel that this development of recording poems, of speaking poems at readings, of having records of poets, I think this is a wonderful thing. I'm very excited by it. In a sense, there's a return, isn't there, to the old role of the poet, which was to speak to a group of people, to come across.

41. *Roland Barthes*, Roland Barthes (1977a: 56).
42. Freud, S., [1921] 'Identification' in *Complete Works of Freud* Volume XVIII (London: Hogarth Press, 1964), p. 105.
43. *Ibid.* p. 105. Freud poses certain difficulties for feminists; his focus on masculine experience is problematic. Nevertheless, I attempt here to apply a universality to his work, in order to encompass female experience.
44. *Ibid.* p. 106.
45. *Ibid.* p. 108.
46. Plath, S., *Letters Home*. Ed. Aurelia Schober Plath (London: Faber & Faber, 1988), p. 473.
47. *Collins College Dictionary*, (London: HarperCollins Publishers, 1995), p. 253.
48. The Don Paterson poem is called 'A Private Bottling' and taken from the poetry anthology *Emergency Kit Poems For Strange Times* (eds.) Jo Shapcott & Matthew Sweeney (London, Faber & Faber, 2004).
49. Freud, S., [1917] 'Mourning and Melancholia' in *The Freud Reader* ed., Peter Gay, (London: Vintage, 1995).
50. *Ibid.* p. 585.
51. Thurschwell, P., *Sigmund Freud*, (London: Routledge, 2000), p. 91.
52. Freud, 'Mourning and Melancholia', p. 584.
53. Pearce, L., *Romance Writing* (Cambridge: Polity Press, 2007)
54. *Ibid.* p. 88.
55. Barthes, R., *From A Lover's Discourse* in *Roland Barthes A Reader* ed. Susan Sontag (London: Vintage, 1977c)
56. Pearce, *Romance Writing*, p. 90.
57. *Ibid.* p. 92.
58. *Ibid.* p. 92.
59. See earlier quote from Antonio Porchia.
60. Cockayne, A., *For Sivvy* in *Plath Profiles* Vol. 6. Summer, Indiana University, 2013, p. 438.
61. *Ibid.* p. 439.
62. Freud, S., [1925] 'Notes on the "Mystic Writing Pad"' in *Collected Papers* ed., Strachey, J., Volume 5 (New York: Basic Books, 1957), p. 179.

63. Khanna, R., *Dark Continents: Psychoanalysis and Colonialism* (Durham & London: Duke University Press, 2003)

64. Eng, D. L. & Davis, K., *Loss: The Politics of Mourning* (Berkeley, Los Angeles, London: Univeristy of California Press, 2003)

65. Min quoted in Eng, D. L. & Davis, K., *Loss: The Politics of Mourning* (Berkeley, Los Angeles, London: Univeristy of California Press, 2003)

66. Eng, *op. cit.* p. 1.

67. *Ibid.* p. 4.

68. Butler in Eng, *op. cit.* p. 472.

69. *Ibid.* p. 472.

70. Freud, 'Mourning and Melancholia', p. 589.

71. Freud, S., [1914] 'On Narcissism: An Introduction' in *The Freud Reader* ed., Peter Gay, (London: Vintage, 1995), p. 545.

72. *Ibid.* p. 554.

73. Lasch, *op. cit.* p. 10.

74. Freud, 'On Narcissim', p. 555.

75. From 'Lady Lazarus' in *Collected Poems* (p. 247).

76. From 'Daddy' in *Collected Poems* (p. 224).

77. From 'Years' in *Collected Poems* (p. 255).

78. Plath, S., *Journals of Sylvia Plath* (ed.), Karen V. Kukil (London: Faber & Faber, 2000), p. 447.

79. *Ibid.* p. 98.

80. *Ibid.* p. 512.

81. *Ibid.* pp. 511-512.

82. Freud, S., [1921] 'Identification' in *Complete Works of Freud* Volume XVIII (London: Hogarth Press, 1964), p. 105.

83. Pearce, *Romance Writing*, p. 90.

84. *Ibid.* p. 15.

85. Fiske, J., 'The Cultural Economy of Fandom' in Lisa Lewis *The Adoring Audience: Fan Culture and Popular Media* (London: Routledge, 1992), p. 39.

86. Freud, 'Mourning and Melancholia', p. 584.

87. Eng, *op. cit.*

88. Freud, 'Mourning and Melancholia', p. 584.

89. It is even more interesting to consider that Plath was so concerned about the closeness between her own personal experiences and those of Esther Greenwood that she kept the book a secret from her family and published under the pen name Victoria Lucas in January 1963.

90. Barthes, *A Lover's Discourse*, p. 435.

91. Pearce, *Rhetorics of Feminism*, p. 49.

92. Freud, 'Identification', p. 105.

93. Although the first edition of *The Bell Jar* was published under the name of Victoria Lucas, it did not take long for the actual identity of the author to be revealed after Plath's death. Subsequent editions were credited to Sylvia Plath. It has to be significant that the novel became described as 'autobiography'; indeed my own copy is not only described thus, but is adorned with a smiling photograph of Plath herself on the cover.

94. Freud, 'Identification', p. 105.

95. Jenson, J., 'Fandom as Pathology' in Lisa Lewis, *The Adoring Audience: Fan Culture and Popular Media* (London: Routledge, 1992), p. 16. In fact, Jenson's whole essay discusses not only how the celebrities become mediated, but also the fans. She argues that the media create two categories of fandom (both negative)—the hysterical individual and the hysterical crowd. Both these

types of fans are regarded as excessive, unstable and in some cases deranged. Yet, Jenson argues, really when we analyse this in more detail, in what ways do fans differ from aficionados? If we replace the word fan with professor, would they still be regarded as unstable? Clearly not and Jenson argues this is entirely due to the 'value of the genteel over the rowdy' (p. 20).

96. Grossberg, L., 'Is There A Fan in the House?' in Lisa Lewis *The Adoring Audience: Fan Culture and Popular Media* (London: Routledge, 1992), p. 53.

97. *Ibid.* p. 54.

98. *Ibid.* p. 54.

99. *Ibid.* p. 65.

100. Baugh, L., *Imagining the Divine* (Kansas City: Sheed & Ward, 1997), p. 210.

101. What strikes me here is that this is not the first time Plath has inverted male religious figures or figures in religious stories—'Lady Lazarus' being an obvious example.

102. See Ted Hughes's poem 'The Dogs are Eating Your Mother'. 'That is not your mother but her body.../Those are not dogs/That seem to be dogs/ Pulling at her..../Let them/Jerk their tail-stumps, bristle and vomit/Over their symposia.' *Birthday Letters* (1998: 195-6). See also Ted Hughes's letter to *The Independent*, 22 April 1989: 'Mr Hayman observes that her readers "feel personally involved, almost as if she were a member of the family" (meaning "their family", which makes her own family a bit of a nuisance.)'

103. Fiske, *op. cit.* p. 37.

104. *Ibid.* p. 38.

105. In general, Freud's work appears disinterested in the experience of reincarnation or any form of life after death. 'The aim of Freud was necessarily confined to the present life since the idea of future lives was altogether alien to the tradition of scientific medicine which he inherited' (Thouless 1972: xi). He does, however, seem to have regarded the denial of death as connected to some form of thanatophobia as we shall discuss in the next chapter. See Chapter Three—Place—for a further discussion of psychoanalysis and reincarnation.

106. Freud, S., [1919] 'The Uncanny' [online] people.emich.edu/acoykenda/ uncanny1.html [Accessed 11 December 2008]

107. Freud, 'Identification', p. 109.

108. The Electra Complex is a term coined by Carl Jung in 1913 based on Freud's *feminine Oedipus attitude* which explores a young girl's psychosexual sense of competition with her mother for her father's affection.

109. Freud, 'Identification', p. 105.

110. From 'Nick and the Candlestick', *Collected Poems* (p. 242).

Chapter 2

1. From 'In Plaster', *Collected Poems* (p. 158).

2. Rank, O., *The Double: A Psychoanalytic Study*, (Chapel Hill: University of North Carolina Press, 1971), p. xiv.

3. Interestingly, Sylvia Plath wrote her thesis on the notion of the double. Entitled *The Magic Mirror*, it is a study of the use of the double in two novels of Dostoyevsky.

4. It is worth noting that Rank has been criticised for his somewhat limited anthropological studies. His 'othering' certainly makes for uncomfortable reading throughout *The Double*.

5. Rank, 1971, *op. cit.* p. 37.
6. *Ibid.* p. 77.
7. *Ibid.* p. 83.
8. *Ibid.* p. 12.
9. *Ibid.* p. 76.
10. Freud, S., [1920] 'Beyond the Pleasure Principle' in *The Freud Reader* ed., Peter Gay, (London: Vintage, 1995), p. 602.
11. *Ibid.* p. 612.
12. Jenson, J., 'Fandom as Pathology' in Lisa Lewis, *The Adoring Audience: Fan Culture and Popular Media* (London: Routledge, 1992)
13. Dyer, R., (1st published 1979). *Stars* (London: BFI Publishing, 1998)
14. Rojek, C., *Celebrity* (London: Reaktion Books, 2001)
15. Reece, G., *Elvis Religion: The Cult of the King* (London: I. B. Tauris, 2006)
16. Doss, E., 'Rock and Roll Pilgrims: Reflections on Ritual, Religiosity and Race at Graceland' ed., Peter Jan Margry in *Shrines and Pilgrimages in the Modern World* (Amsterdam: Amsterdam University Press, 2008)
17. Rank, 1971, *op. cit.* p. 15.
18. *Ibid.* p. 42.
19. Booth, W., *The Rhetoric of Fiction* (Chicago: University of Chicago Press. 1980)
20. *Ibid.* p. 20.
21. Pearce, L., *The Rhetorics of Feminism*, (London: Routledge, 2004), p. 24.
22. Marcia Brown Stern (1932 – 2012). Former roommate of Sylvia Plath at Smith College and life-long friend.
23. Jillian Becker (b. 1932). Friend of Plath's in London 1962/63. Plath spent her last weekend at Becker's home. An account of this weekend can be found in Becker's memoir, *Giving Up: The Last Days of Sylvia Plath* (London: Ferrington, 2003).
24. Pearce, 2004, *op. cit.* p. 57.
25. Wolfreys, J., *Victorian Hauntings: Spectrality, Gothic, the Uncanny & Literature*, (Basingstoke: Palgrave, 2002), p. xii.
26. *Ibid.* p. xii.
27. Rich quoted in Pearce, 2004, *op. cit.* p. 52.
28. *Ibid.* p. 61.
29. Rank, 1971, *op. cit.* p. 48.
30. *Ibid.* p. 6.
31. *Ibid.* p. 15.
32. *Ibid.* p. 33.
33. *Ibid.* p. 77.
34. Fuss, D., *Identification Papers*, (London, New York: Routledge, 1995), p. 2.
35. *Ibid.* p. 1.
36. Rank, 1971, *op. cit.* p. 74.
37. Assia Wevill (1927–1969) is the woman with whom Ted Hughes had an affair while married to Plath. On 25 March 1969, Assia Wevill killed herself and Shura, her four year old daughter to Ted Hughes.
38. Fiske, J., 'The Cultural Economy of Fandom' in Lisa Lewis *The Adoring Audience: Fan Culture and Popular Media* (London: Routledge, 1992)
39. Immediately, this 'on the surface' comment raises questions that relate to issues discussed in the introduction; namely how do I, as a researcher, deal with a mixture of conscious and unconscious accounts in my respondents' statements? To what extent should I question and probe beneath this surface reading? In this account, there are many places where I suspect Kiki's unconscious thought processes to be leaking through, and other places

where she appears to acknowledge them. In some places, she appears to show resistance, in others, self-awareness. I therefore have the tricky task of both negotiating and justifying my readings without removing autonomy from Kiki's account. There are only two potential ways in which I feel I can attempt this. First is to stay self-reflexive about how I am handling the narrative. Second is to be transparent about when I start probing and be explicit that this is just one reading of many that could be possible. It is not an ideal situation, but nevertheless needs to be addressed and reflected upon.

40. Foucault, M., 'What is an Author?' in Rabinow, Paul, (ed.), *The Foucault Reader* (New York: Pantheon Books, 1984), p. 119.
41. *Ibid.* p. 120.
42. Rich quoted in Pearce, 2004, *op cit.*, p. 52.
43. Rank, 1971, *op. cit.* p. xiv.
44. Jenson, 1992, *op. cit.* p. 25.
45. *Ibid.* p. 26.
46. Freud, [1920], 1995, *op. cit.* p. 602.
47. Aurelia Schober Plath (1906–1994), Sylvia Plath's mother, wife of Otto Plath. Aurelia Plath wrote a lengthy introduction to a collection of her daughter's letters called *Letters Home* (1988). In this introduction, she describes family life with her husband, Otto, and two young children, Sylvia and Warren.
48. Rank, 1971, *op. cit.* p. 33.
49. Otto Plath published a book called *Bumblebees and their Ways* (1934).

Chapter 3

1. From 'Finisterre' *Collected Poems* (p. 169-170).
2. Bachelard, G., (1st published 1958). *The Poetics of Space*, (Boston: Beacon Press, 1994), p. 1.
3. *Ibid.* p. 6.
4. David Lowenthal's book *The Past is a Foreign Country* (1985) explores three main areas: how the past enriches the present, how our recollections make us aware of the past and how we change what has been passed down to us to affect our own heritage. Lowenthal's book is especially poignant and significant for this research when he discusses the whole issue of yearning for the past and a seemingly increasing faith in reincarnation and past lives. This quote is taken from p. xv.
5. *Ibid.* p. xvii.
6. Tindall quoted in Lowenthal, 1985, *op. cit.* p. 243.
7. Bachelard, 1994, *op. cit.* p. 8.
8. Lowenthal, 1985, *op. cit.* p. 4.
9. Gordon, A., *Ghostly Matters: Haunting and the Sociological Imagination*, (Minneapolis: University of Minnesota, 1997), p. 53.
10. Lowenthal, 1985, *op. cit.* p. 412.
11. *Ibid.* p. xix.
12. Reader, I., & Tony Walter, *Pilgrimage in Popular Culture* (Basingstoke, Hampshire: Palgrave, 1993)
13. Degen, M., & Kevin Hetherington, 'Hauntings' in Hetherington, Kevin, ed., *Spacial Hauntings Space and Culture* Issue 11–12 December, 2001, p. 1.
14. Gordon, 1997, *op. cit.* p. 7.
15. Lowenthal, 1985, *op. cit.* p. 193.
16. *Ibid*, p. 240.

17. From 'Point Shirley' in *Collected Poems* p. 110.
18. Edensor, T., 'Haunting in the ruins: matter and immateriality' in Hetherington, Kevin (ed.), *Spatial Hauntings Space and Culture*. Issue 11–12 December 2001, p. 48.
19. Bachelard, 1994, *op. cit.* p. viii.
20. *Ibid.* p. xvi.
21. From 'Point Shirley' in *Collected Poems* p. 110.
22. Gordon, 1997, *op. cit.* p. 6.
23. Bachelard, 1994, *op. cit.* p. viii.
24. From 'Point Shirley' in *Collected Poems* p. 111.
25. Degan & Hetherington, 2001, *op. cit.* p. 4.
26. Robinson and Anderson quoted in Stiebal, L. (undated) Literary Tourism www.literarytourism.co.za/index.php/News/Going-on-literary-pilgrimage-developing-literary-trails-in-South-Africa.html [accessed 18/05/09].
27. Reader & Walter, 1993, *op. cit.*
28. The examples Rojek (1993) offers are the site of James Dean's death in Cholame, California, and the Grave Line Tour of Hollywood which takes in suicide sites, assassination points, and other places of death involving movie stars. This quote is taken from p. 136.
29. Sellars & Walter in Reader and Walter, 1993, *op cit.*
30. Rojek, 1993, op cit., p. 165.
31. Robinson and Anderson quoted in Stiebal, L. (undated) Literary Tourism www.literarytourism.co.za/index.php/News/Going-on-literary-pilgrimage-developing-literary-trails-in-South-Africa.html [accessed 18/05/09].
32. Bachelard, 1994, *op. cit.* p. 6.
33. Sheller, M., & John Urry, *Tourism Mobilities*, (London: Routledge, 2004), p. 205.
34. Plath is buried in the graveyard at Heptonstall, West Yorkshire. She died in her flat at 23 Fitzroy Road, Primrose Hill, London on 11 February 1963. Heptonstall was chosen as her burial site by Ted Hughes, whose family lived in the village.
35. Edensor, 2001, *op. cit.* p. 42.
36. Reader & Walter, 1993, *op. cit.* p. 244.
37. Wilson, F., *Literary Seductions: Compulsive Writers and Diverted Readers* (London: Faber and Faber, 1999)
38. Pearce, L., *Feminism and the Politics of Reading*, (London: Arnold, 1997), p. 2.
39. *Ibid.* p. 6.
40. Wilson, 1999, *op. cit.* p. xxiii.
41. Sheller & Urry, 2004, *op. cit.* p. 211.
42. Pearce, L., *Romance Writing*, (Cambridge: Polity Press, 2007), p. 92.
43. Samuel, R., *Theatres of Memory*, (London: Verso, 1994), p. 112.
44. Degan & Hetherington, 2001, *op. cit.* p. 4.
45. Gaston Bachelard also supports this view with his belief in 'a reading pride that will give us the illusion of participating in the work of the author of the book' (p. 21).
46. Pearce, 1997, *op. cit.* p. 18.
47. *Ibid.* p. 124.
48. *Ibid.* p. 124.
49. *Ibid.* p. 124.
50. Freud, S., [1919] 'The Uncanny' [online] people.emich.edu/acoykenda/uncanny1.html [Accessed 11 December 2008].
51. Dubisch, J., 'Sites of Memory, Sites of Sorrow: An American Veteran's Motorcycle Pilgrimage' ed., Peter Jan Margry in *Shrines and Pilgrimages in the Modern World* (Amsterdam: Amsterdam University Press, 2008)

52. Although Sonia here feels nothing about the place of Plath's suicide, she does recount in certain 'visions' seeing the tiles of the kitchen floor in Fitzroy Road in her earlier incarnation as Plath.

53. Noll, R., *The Aryan Christ* on line at www.dhustara.com/book/jung.archi. htm, 1997 accessed 22/08/09

54. For example, the first time I visited the town of North Tawton where Plath lived towards the end of her life, I was able to navigate the streets from her writing alone. Seeing the landmarks she wrote about was like reliving a memory, although bizarrely, a memory I never had from seeing the place with my own eyes. Avery Gordon refers to this idea as 'rememory': 'The possibility of a collectively animated worldly memory is articulated here in that extraordinary moment in which you—*who never was there* in that real place—can *bump into a rememory that belongs to somebody else*' (1997: 166).

55. From 'Lady Lazarus' in *Collected Poems*, p. 245.

56. Foucault, M., 'What is an Author?' in Rabinow, Paul, (ed.), *The Foucault Reader* (New York: Pantheon Books, 1984), p. 119.

57. Barthes, R., *Image Music Text* (London: Fontana Press, 1977b), p. 44.

58. Gordon, 1997, *op. cit.* p. 37.

59. Bachelard, 1994, *op. cit.* p. 47.

60. *Ibid.* p. 6.

61. There is an emerging body of work dealing with the notion of place, silence and literature, one which seeks to explore the notion that silence can actually open up creativity rather than shut it down. See Maeve O'Brien: 'But I think a greater part of me is able to connect with Plath in Ireland *because* of the literary silence' (2012) in 'Plath, Coole Park and the autograph tree' (www.theplathdiariesblogspot.co.uk). This is an interesting concept that further raises questions about the ways in which people use their imagination to connect with place.

62. Bachelard, 1994, *op. cit.* p. 230.

63. Gordon, 1997, *op. cit.* p. 8.

Chapter 4

1. From 'The Babysitters' in *Collected Poems* p. 175.

2. Barthes, R., (1st published 1982). *Camera Lucida* (London: Vintage, 1993)

3. Sontag, S., *On Photography* (New York: Farrar, Straus & Giroux, 1977)

4. Hirsch, M., ed., *The Familial Gaze* (Hanover and London: Dartmouth College, University Press of New England, 1999)

5. Sturken, S., 'The Image as Memorial: Personal Photographs in Cultural Memory.' in Hirsch, Marianne, ed., *The Familial Gaze* (Hanover and London: Dartmouth College, University Press of New England, 1999)

6. Kuhn, A., 'Remembrance' in *Illustrations* eds., Liz Heron & Val Williams (London, New York: I. B. Tauris, 1996)

7. I am using the term discourse in this chapter based on Foucault's understanding of the ways in which language can produce historically and culturally located meanings and knowledge.

8. Heron, L., 'Gateway to a Labyrinth' eds., Liz Heron and Val Williams in *Illustrations* (London, New York: I. B.Tauris, 1996)

9. Barthes, 1993, *op. cit.* p. 12.

10. *Ibid.* p. 96.

11. Sontag, 1977, *op. cit.* p. 11.

12. Barthes, 1993, *op. cit.* p. 96.

13. Banita, G., 'The Same, Identical Woman: Sylvia Plath in the Media.' in *The Journal of the Midwestern Modern Language Association*. Fall, Volume 40, Number 2, 2007

14. Hirsch, 1999, *op. cit.* p. xii.

15. Sturken, 1999, *op. cit.* p. 178.

16. *Ibid.* p. 178.

17. The example that Sturken uses here is that of the personal images taken from a videotape by George Holliday of the beating of Rodney King. These images soon acquired historical meaning and were one catalyst for the Los Angeles uprising.

18. Letter from Ronald Hayman to *The Independent* 19 April 1989.

19. Sontag, 1977, *op. cit.* p. 69.

20. Barthes, R., *Image Music Text*, (London: Fontana Press, 1977b), p. 44.

21. King, C., 'The Politics of Representation: A Democracy of the Gaze' in Frances Bonner et al., *Imagining Women* (Cambridge: Polity Press, 1992, pp. 131-139)

22. Wolff, J., *The Sociological Image* Talk given at Lancaster University, 2007

23. Barthes, 1977b, *op. cit.*

24. Heron, 1996, *op. cit.* p. 457.

25. *Ibid.* p. 458.

26. Sturken, 1999, *op. cit.* p. 179.

27. Barthes, 1993, *op. cit.* p. 9.

28. Sturken, 1999, *op. cit.*

29. Kuhn, 1996, *op. cit.* p. 477.

30. From 'Stings' in *Collected Poems* p. 215.

31. Sontag, 1977, *op. cit.* p. 20.

32. Barthes, 1993, *op. cit.* p. 92.

33. *Ibid.* p. 82.

34. Sontag, 1977, *op. cit.* p. 154.

35. Freud, S., [1921] 'Identification' in *Complete Works of Freud* Volume XVIII (London: Hogarth Press, 1964), p. 107.

36. *Ibid.* p. 105.

37. Freud, S., [1919] 'The Uncanny' [online] people.emich.edu/acoykenda/uncanny1.html [Accessed 11 December 2008].

38. *Ibid.*

39. Rose, J., *The Haunting of Sylvia Plath* (London: Virago, 1991).

40. Barthes, 1977b, *op. cit.* p. 28

41. Roland Barthes describes a similar experience in *Camera Lucida* when he views a photograph of Lewis Payne shortly before his hanging. He views this picture knowing that the subject is going to die: 'I observer with horror an anterior future of which death is the stake' and he 'shudders over a catastrophe which has already occurred' (p. 96).

42. Sontag, 1977, *op. cit.* p. 69.

43. *Ibid.* p. 15.

44. Barthes, 1977, *op. cit.* p. 32.

Chapter 5

1. A comment Sylvia Plath made to a student of Jillian Becker's on Saturday 9 February 1963. Taken from a conversation with Jillian Becker 29 October 2007. Also recorded in *Bitter Fame* by Anne Stevenson (1989: 295).

2. Hallam, E., & Jenny Hockey, *Death, Memory and Material Culture* (Oxford, New York: Berg, 2001)

3. Jenkins, H., *Textual Poachers* (London: Routledge, 1992)
4. Jenson, J., 'The Consequences of Characterisation' in Lisa Lewis, *The Adoring Audience: Fan Culture and Popular Media* (London: Routledge, 1992)
5. Foucault, M., 'What is an Author?' in Rabinow, Paul, (ed.), *The Foucault Reader* (New York: Pantheon Books, 1984), p. 104.
6. From 'Last Words' in *Collected Poems*, p. 172.
7. A family friend of Plath's mother, Aurelia Plath.
8. Marx, K., ed., Martyn J. Lee 'The Fetishism of the Commodity and its Secret' in *The Consumer Society Reader* (Oxford: Blackwells, 2000), p. 10.
9. *Ibid.* p. 10.
10. Interestingly, this plank of wood was originally for a coffin, but Ted Hughes bought it and turned it in to a desk for Plath with the help of her brother Warren J. Plath. Many of the poems in *Birthday Letters* by Hughes discuss this plank being like a doorway to the grave.
11. Benjamin, W., *Illuminations* (London: Fontana Press. 1973)
12. Jenkins, 1992, *op. cit.* p. 16.
13. While the academic 'othering' of fans certainly continues, the work of scholars such as Jenson and Jenkins in the 1990s did encourage new platforms for fandom scholarship and new ways of thinking about fans. Interestingly, recent years have seen further shifts as cultural industries increasingly position emotional attachment as central to media production and engagement. In this context, as Jenkins argues in his work on Convergence Culture (2006), fans and fan practices are increasingly desirable to media corporations; shifting the fan, to a certain extent, from 'abnormal' to ideal consumer subject.
14. Jenson, 1992, *op. cit.* p. 21.
15. *Ibid.* p. 21.
16. *Ibid.* p. 9.
17. Samuel, R., *Theatres of Memory*, (London: Verso, 1994), p. 15.
18. *Ibid.* p. 112.
19. Degen, M., & Kevin Hetherington, 'Hauntings' in Hetherington, Kevin, ed., *Spacial Hauntings Space and Culture* Issue 11–12 December, 2001, p. 4.
20. Gordon, A., *Ghostly Matters: Haunting and the Sociological Imagination*, (Minneapolis: University of Minnesota, 1997), p. 164.
21. A comment sent to me in written feedback from Lynne Pearce.
22. Hallam & Hockey, 2001, *op. cit.*
23. Steedman, C., *Dust* (Manchester: Manchester University Press, 2001, p. 81.
24. Jenson, 1992, *op. cit.* p. 9.
25. *Ibid.* p. 9.
26. *Ibid.* p. 25.
27. Eng, D. L. & Davis, K., *Loss: The Politics of Mourning*, (Berkeley, Los Angeles, London: Univeristy of California Press, 2003), p. 2.
28. Hallam & Hockey, 2001, *op. cit.* p. 2.
29. Eddie Cohen began a correspondence with Plath after reading one of her early published short stories in his sister's copy of *Seventeen* magazine. They subsequently met on two occasions. The letter from which Peter quotes is dated 15 December 1952 (Eddie Cohen to Sylvia Plath) held in the Lilly Library, Indiana University.
30. Hallam & Hockey, 2001, *op. cit.* p. 136.
31. Foucault, 1984, *op. cit.* p. 20.
32. Freud, S., [1919] 'The Uncanny' [online] people.emich.edu/acoykenda/ uncanny1.html [Accessed 11 December 2008].
33. Hallam & Hockey, 2001, *op. cit.* p. 129.

34. Derrida, J., *The Work of Mourning* (Chicago & London: University of Chicago Press, 2001)
35. *Ibid.* p. 9.
36. Hallam & Hockey, 2001, *op. cit.* p. 147.
37. *Ibid.* p. 2.
38. Davis, C., *Haunted Subjects: Deconstruction, Psychoanalysis and the Return of the Dead* (Basingstoke: Palgrave, 2007)
39. Derrida does draw on the difference between knowing and not knowing the deceased. In his *Memoires for Paul de Man* (1989) he claims it is overwhelming to speak on behalf of a dead friend. What can one say? Yet Derrida argues that is all the living can give to the dead now—a voice to speak on their behalf. Nevertheless we have to acknowledge that there is a different set of expectations, a different sort of contract between mourning a dead person we knew and one which we never knew. Although, as we have seen with our respondents, this still does not prevent people believing they should speak on behalf of Sylvia Plath.
40. Wolfreys, J., *Victorian Hauntings: Spectrality, Gothic, the Uncanny & Literature*, (Basingstoke: Palgrave, 2002), p. xi.
41. Al Alvarez (b. 1929) poet, novelist and critic. Was a friend of Sylvia Plath and supported her work during his time as poetry editor and critic for *The Observer*.
42. Ronald Hayman (b. 1932). Critic, dramatist and writer. Wrote a biography of Sylvia Plath called *The Death and Life of Sylvia Plath* (1991).
43. Talk given by Al Alvarez on 28 October 2007.
44. Baugh, L., *Imagining the Divine* (Kansas City: Sheed & Ward, 1997)
45. *Ibid.* p. 201.
46. Fiske, J., 'The Cultural Economy of Fandom' in Lisa Lewis *The Adoring Audience: Fan Culture and Popular Media*, (London: Routledge, 1992), p. 48.
47. It has to be of significance here that all the respondents in this study are graduates or postgraduates.
48. Williamson, J., *Decoding Advertisements: Ideology and Meaning in Advertising*, (London: Boyors, 1978), p. 30.
49. The town where Plath grew up, Winthrop, Massachusetts, USA.
50. Plath wrote a little known short story called 'The Lucky Stone' which was eventually accepted for publication by *My Weekly* in 1961, though the publication changed the name of the story to 'The Perfect Place'. See Steinberg's article '"I should be loving this:" Sylvia Plath's "The Perfect Place" and *The Bell Jar*' about the discovery of this story in *Plath Profiles*, Vol. 1, Summer 2008.
51. Gordon, 1997, *op. cit.* p. 16.
52. Florian and Sonia's son.
53. Hallam & Hockey, 2001, *op. cit.* p. 43.
54. Barthes, R., (1st published 1982). *Camera Lucida*, (London: Vintage, 1993), p. 92.
55. Hirsch, M., ed., *The Familial Gaze* (Hanover and London: Dartmouth College, University Press of New England, 1999)
56. Sturken, S., 'The Image as Memorial: Personal Photographs in Cultural Memory.' in Hirsch, Marianne, ed., *The Familial Gaze* (Hanover and London: Dartmouth College, University Press of New England, 1999)
57. From 'Daddy' in *Collected Poems*, p. 224.
58. Samuel, 1994, *op. cit.* p. 112.
59. Pearce, L., *Romance Writing*, (Cambridge: Polity Press, 2007), p. 92.
60. Benjamin, 1973, *op. cit.*

61. Gordon, 1997, *op. cit.* p. 66.
62. *Ibid.* p. 63.
63. *Ibid.* p. 63-64.
64. Rose, J., *The Haunting of Sylvia Plath* (London: Virago, 1991)

Chapter 6

1. From *The Journals of Sylvia Plath*, (2000), p. 9.
2. From *Johnny Panic and the Bible of Dreams*, (1977), p. 93.
3. From *The Journals of Sylvia Plath*, (2000), p. 9-10.

Bibliography

Primary Plath Texts

Plath, S., *Letters Home* Ed. Aurelia Schober Plath (London: Faber & Faber, 1988)
Plath, S., *Johnny Panic and the Bible of Dreams* (London: Faber & Faber, 1977)
Plath, S., *Collected Poems* (London: Faber & Faber, 1988)
Plath, S., *The Journals of Sylvia Plath* (New York: Ballatine Books, 1982)
Plath, S., (1st published 1963). *The Bell Jar* (London: Faber & Faber, 1986)
Plath, S., *Journals of Sylvia Plath* (ed.), Karen V. Kukil (London: Faber & Faber, 2000)
Plath, S., *The Restored Edition Ariel* (London: Faber & Faber, 2004)

Biographical Texts about Sylvia Plath

Alexander, P., *Rough Magic: A biography of Sylvia Plath* (London: Penguin, 1991)
Becker, J., *Giving Up: The Last Days of Sylvia Plath* (London: Ferrington, 2003)
Bronfen, E., *Sylvia Plath* (Plymouth: Northcote House, 1998)
Bundtzen, L. K., (1st published 2001). *The Other Ariel* (Stroud: Sutton Publishing, 2005)
Butscher, E., *Sylvia Plath: The Woman and the Work* (New York: Dodd, Mead and Company, 1977)
Hayman, R., *The Death and Life of Sylvia Plath* (London: Heinemann, 1991)
Hunter Steiner, N., *A Closer Look at Ariel: A Memory of Sylvia Plath* (New York: Harper's Magazine Press, 1973)
Middlebrook, D., *Her Husband: Hughes and Plath—A Marriage* (London: Viking, 2003)
Orr, P., (ed.), *The Poet Speaks: Interviews with Contemporary Poets Conducted by Hilary Morrish, Peter Orr, John Press and Ian Scott-Kilvert* (London: Routledge & K. Paul, 1966)
Rollyson, C., *American Isis: The Life and Art of Sylvia Plath* (New York: St. Martin's Press, 2013)
Steinberg, P. K., *Great Writers: Sylvia Plath* (Philadelphia: Chelsea House, 2004)
Sigmund, E. & Crowther, G., *Sylvia Plath in Devon: A Year's Turning* (Stroud: Fonthill Media, 2014)
Stevenson, A., *Bitter Fame* (London: Viking, 1989)
Thomas, T., *Last Encounters: a memoir of Sylvia Plath* (Privately published: Bedford, 1989) My own copy numbered 131 and signed.

Wagner-Martin, L., *Sylvia Plath: A Biography* (London: Chatto & Windus, 1988a)
Wilson, A., *Mad Girl's Love Song: Sylvia Plath and Life Before Ted* (London: Simon & Schuster, 2013)

General Bibliography

Abraham, N., and Maria Torok, *The Shell and the Kernal: Renewals of Psychoanalysis Volume 1* (London: University of Chicago Press, 1994)
Acland, C., 'Haunted Places: Montreal's Rue Ste Catherine and its cinema spaces.' in *Screen*. Vol. 44, No. 2, Summer, 2003
Alexandrian, S., *Surrealist Art* (London: Thames and Hudson, 1970)
Allington, D., 'How Come Most People Don't See It? Slashing *Lord of the Rings.*' in *Social Semiotics* Volume 17, Number 1, March 2007
Alvarez, A., *The Savage God: A Study of Suicide* (London: Penguin, 1971)
Anderson, B., *Imaginary Communities* (London: Verso, 1991)
Anger, K., *Hollywood Babylon* (London: Arrow Books Limited, 1975)
Asad, T., 'The Conception of Cultural Translation in British Social Anthropology.' in James Clifford & George Marcus, 1986. *Writing Culture The Poetics and Politics of Ethnography* (Berkeley: University of California Press, 1986)
Auge, M., *Oblivion* (Minneapolis: University of Minnesota Press, 2004)
Aumont, J., *The Image* (London: British Film Institute, 1997)
Babad, E., *The Social Self: Group Influences on Personal Identity* (Beverley Hills: Sage Publications, 1983)
Bachelard, G., (1st published 1958). *The Poetics of Space* (Boston: Beacon Press, 1994)
Badia, J., *Sylvia Plath and the Mythology of Women Readers* (Amherst & Boston: University of Massachusetts Press, 2011)
Banita, G., 'The Same, Identical Woman: Sylvia Plath in the Media.' in *The Journal of the Midwestern Modern Language Association*. Fall, Volume 40, Number 2, 2007
Barbas, S., *Movie Crazy: Fans, Stars and the Cult of Celebrity* (New York: Palgrave, 2001)
Barthes, R., *Roland Barthes by Roland Barthes* (Berkeley: University of California Press, 1977a)
Barthes, R., *Image Music Text* (London: Fontana Press, 1977b)
Barthes, R., *From A Lover's Discourse* in *Roland Barthes A Reader* ed. Susan Sontag (London: Vintage, 1977c)
Barthes, R., (1st published 1982). *Camera Lucida* (London: Vintage, 1993)
Barthes, R., (1st published 1973). *The Pleasure of the Text*. From *Roland Barthes A Reader*. Ed. Susan Sontag (London: Vintage, 1982)
Bate, J., *Ted Hughes The Unauthorised Life* (New York: HarperCollins, 2015)
Baugh, L., *Imagining the Divine* (Kansas City: Sheed & Ward, 1997)
Benjamin, W., *Illuminations* (London: Fontana Press. 1973)
Bishop, J., & Paul Hoggett, *Organising Around Enthusiasms* (London: Comedia Publishing Group, 1986)
Bleich, D., *Subjective Criticism* (Baltimore & London: The John Hopkins University Press, 1978)
Blumer, H., (1st published 1969). *Symbolic Interactionism* (Berkeley: University of California Press, 1998)
Booth, W., *The Rhetoric of Fiction* (Chicago: University of Chicago Press. 1980)
Bowie, M., *Proust Among the Stars* (London: Fontana Press, 1998)
Britzolakis, C., *Sylvia Plath & The Theatre of Mourning* (Oxford: Oxford University Press, 2000)
Broks, P., *Into the Silent Land* (London: Atlantic Books, 2003)

Bronfen, E., *Over Her Dead Body: Death, Femininity and the Aesthetic* (Manchester: Manchester University Press, 1992)

Bronte, E., *Wuthering Heights* (Harmondsworth: Penguin Classics, 1995)

Buse, P., *Ghosts: Deconstruction, Psychoanalysis and History* (London: Macmillan, 1990)

Butler, J., 'Afterword: After Loss, What Then?' in Eng, David L., & David Kazanjian, *Loss: The Politics of Mourning* (Berkeley, Los Angeles, London: Univeristy of California Press, 2003)

Campbell, J., & Harbord, J., eds., *Temporalities: Autobiography and Everyday Life* (Manchester: Manchester University Press, 2002)

Casetti, Francesca, *Inside the Gaze* (Bloomington & Indianapolis: Indiana University Press, 1998)

Castricano, J., *Cryptomimesis: The Gothic and Jacques Derrida's Ghost Writing* (Montreal & Kingston: McGill-Queen's University Press, 2001)

Clifford, J., 'Introduction: Partial Truths' in James Clifford & George Marcus, *Writing Culture The Poetics and Politics of Ethnography* (Berkeley: University of California Press, 1986)

Cockayne, A., *For Sivvy* in *Plath Profiles* Vol. 6. Summer, Indiana University, 2013

Code, Lorraine, 'Experience, Knowledge & Responsibility' in M. Griffiths & M. Whitford, eds., *Feminist Perspectives in Philosophy* (London: Macmillan, 1988)

Collins College Dictionary, (London: HarperCollins Publishers, 1995)

Connors, K., & Bayley, S., *Eye Rhymes Sylvia Plath's Art of the Visual* (Oxford: Oxford University Press, 2007)

Conway, T., 'Facts, Insights and Hypotheses on Reincarnation.' online at www. enlightenedspirituality.org/Reincarnation, 1997

Cowards, R., *Female Desire* (London: Paladin, 1984)

Crowther, G., *An Authentic Self? Towards an Ethics of Reading Sylvia Plath.* MA Dissertation, Lancaster University (unpublished, 1999)

Crowther, G. & Peter K. Steinberg, 'These Ghostly Archives.' in *Plath Profiles* Vol. 2. Summer, Indiana University, 2009

Davis, C., *Haunted Subjects: Deconstruction, Psychoanalysis and the Return of the Dead* (Basingstoke: Palgrave, 2007)

Degen, M., & Kevin Hetherington, 'Hauntings' in Hetherington, Kevin, ed., *Spacial Hauntings Space and Culture* Issue 11–12 December, 2001

Derrida, J., *Memoires for Paul de Man* (New York: Columbia University Press, 1989)

Derrida, J., *The Work of Mourning* (Chicago & London: University of Chicago Press, 2001)

Doss, E., 'Rock and Roll Pilgrims: Reflections on Ritual, Religiosity and Race at Graceland' ed., Peter Jan Margry in *Shrines and Pilgrimages in the Modern World* (Amsterdam: Amsterdam University Press, 2008)

Dubisch, J., 'Sites of Memory, Sites of Sorrow: An American Veteran's Motorcycle Pilgrimage' ed., Peter Jan Margry in *Shrines and Pilgrimages in the Modern World* (Amsterdam: Amsterdam University Press, 2008)

Dyer, R., (1st published 1979). *Stars* (London: BFI Publishing, 1998).

Dyer, R., (1st published 1986). *Heavenly Bodies* (London: Routledge, 2004)

Edensor, T., 'Haunting in the ruins: matter and immateriality' in Hetherington, Kevin (ed.), *Spatial Hauntings Space and Culture.* Issue 11–12 December 2001.

Eng, D. L. & Davis, K., *Loss: The Politics of Mourning* (Berkeley, Los Angeles, London: Univeristy of California Press, 2003)

Engle, J. K., 'Putting Mourning to Work' in *Theory, Culture and Society.* London: SAGE, Volume 24, 2007

Feinberg, T., *Altered Egos: How the Brain Creates the Self* (New York: Oxford University Press, 2001)

Feinstein, E. *Ted Hughes The Life of a Poet* (London: Weidenfeld and Nicolson, 2001)

Fiske, J., 'The Cultural Economy of Fandom' in Lisa Lewis *The Adoring Audience: Fan Culture and Popular Media* (London: Routledge, 1992)

Foucault, M., 'What is an Author?' in Rabinow, Paul, (ed.), *The Foucault Reader* (New York: Pantheon Books, 1984)

Fowles, J., *Starstruck* (Washington & London : Smithsonian Institution Press, 1992)

Freud, S., [1914] 'On Narcissism: An Introduction' in *The Freud Reader* ed., Peter Gay, (London: Vintage, 1995)

Freud, S., [1917] 'Mourning and Melancholia' in *The Freud Reader* ed., Peter Gay, (London: Vintage, 1995)

Freud, S., [1919] 'The Uncanny' [online] people.emich.edu/acoykenda/uncanny1.html [Accessed 11 December 2008].

Freud, S., [1920] 'Beyond the Pleasure Principle' in *The Freud Reader* ed., Peter Gay, (London: Vintage, 1995)

Freud, S., [1921] 'Identification' in *Complete Works of Freud* Volume XVIII (London: Hogarth Press, 1964)

Freud, S., [1925] 'Notes on the "Mystic Writing Pad"' in *Collected Papers* ed., Strachey, J., Volume 5 (New York: Basic Books, 1957)

Fuss, D., *Identification Papers* (London, New York: Routledge, 1995)

Gamman, L., *The Female Gaze: Women as Viewers of Popular Culture* (London: The Women's Press, 1988)

Gamson, J., *Claims to Fame* (Berkeley: University of California Press, 1994)

Gatenby, P., *Morrissey's Manchester* (Manchester: Empire Publications, 2002)

Gauntlett, D., *Media, Gender and Identity* (London: Routledge, 2002)

Goffman, E., (1st published 1959). *The Presentation of Self in Everyday Life* (London: Penguin, 1990)

Goffman, E., (1st published 1961). *Asylums* (Pelican: Middlesex, 1974)

Goffman, E., *Frame Analysis* (Penguin: Harmondsworth, 1975)

Gordon, A., *Ghostly Matters: Haunting and the Sociological Imagination* (Minneapolis: University of Minnesota, 1997)

Gray, A., 'Narratives of Video Playtime.' in Beverley Skeggs, *Feminist Cultural Theory* (Manchester: Manchester University Press, 1995)

Grossberg, L., 'Is There A Fan in the House?' in Lisa Lewis *The Adoring Audience: Fan Culture and Popular Media* (London: Routledge, 1992)

Hallam, E., & Jenny Hockey, *Death, Memory and Material Culture* (Oxford, New York: Berg, 2001)

Harris, C., *Theorizing Fandom: Fans, Subculture and Identity* (Cresskill, NJ: Hampton Press, 1998)

Hayman, R., Letter to *The Independent*, 19 April 1989

Helle, A., *The Unraveling Archive* (Ann Arbour: University of Michigan, 2007)

Heron, L., ed., *Truth, Dare or Promise* (London: Virago, 1985)

Heron, L., 'Gateway to a Labyrinth' eds., Liz Heron and Val Williams in *Illustrations* (London, New York: I. B.Tauris, 1996)

Hetherington, K., 'Phantasmagoria/Phantasm Agora: Materialities, Spatialities and Ghosts' *Spatial Hauntings Space and Culture.* Issue 11–12 December, 2001

Hillman, J., *Suicide and the Soul* (Dallas: Spring Publications Inc, 1978)

Hills, M., *Fan Cultures* (London: Routledge, 1971)

Hinerman, S., 'I'll be Here With You' in Lisa Lewis *The Adoring Audience: Fan Culture and Popular Media* (London: Routledge, 1992)

Hirsch, M., ed., *The Familial Gaze* (Hanover and London: Dartmouth College, University Press of New England, 1999)

Hockey, J., et al., *Grief, Mourning and Death Ritual* (Buckingham: Open University Press, 2001)

Hoffman, N. J., 'Reading Women's Poetry: The Meaning and Our Lives' in *College English,* Volume 34, No. 1, October 1972 pp. 48-62.

Holbrook, D., (1st published 1976). *Sylvia Plath: Poetry and Existence* (London: The Athlone Press, 1991)

Hughes, O., 'The Plath Myth and the Reviewing of *Bitter Fame*' in *Poetry Review* Volume 80 No. 3, Autumn 1990.

Hughes, T., *Birthday Letters* (London: Faber & Faber, 1998)

Hughes, T., ed., Christopher Reid *The Collected Letters of Ted Hughes* (London: Faber & Faber, 2007)

Jacoby, M., *Individuation and Narcissism* (London: Routledge, 1990)

Jaffe, A., *Modernism and the Culture of Celebrity* (Cambridge: Cambridge University Press, 2005)

Jenkins, H., *Textual Poachers* (London: Routledge, 1992)

Jenkins, R., *Social Identity Second Edition* (Abingdon, Oxon: Routledge, 2005)

Jenson, J., 'The Consequences of Characterisation' in Lisa Lewis, *The Adoring Audience: Fan Culture and Popular Media* (London: Routledge, 1992)

Jenson, J., 'Fandom as Pathology' in Lisa Lewis, *The Adoring Audience: Fan Culture and Popular Media* (London: Routledge, 1992)

Kaplan, E. A., *Feminism and Film* (Oxford: Oxford University Press, 2000)

Kendall, T., *Sylvia Plath A Critical Study* (London: Faber & Faber, 2001)

Khanna, R., *Dark Continents: Psychoanalysis and Colonialism* (Durham & London: Duke University Press, 2003)

Kieslowski, K., *Kieslowski on Kieslowski.* ed., Danusia Stok. (London: Faber & Faber, 1993)

King, C., 'The Politics of Representation: A Democracy of the Gaze' in Frances Bonner et al., *Imagining Women* (Cambridge: Polity Press, 1992, pp. 131-139)

Koch, C., 'The Movie in Your Head' *Scientific American Mind* vol. 16, no. 3, 2005, pp. 58-63.

Kuhn, A., *Women's Companion to International Film* (London: Virago, 1990)

Kuhn, A., *Family Secrets* (London: Verso, 1995)

Kuhn, A., 'Remembrance' in *Illustrations* eds., Liz Heron & Val Williams (London, New York: I. B. Tauris. 1996)

Lasch, C., *The Culture of Narcissism* (London: Abacus, 1980)

Lather, P., *Getting Smart: Feminist Research and Pedagogy with/in the Postmodern* (London: Routledge, 1991)

Lawler, S., *Mothering the Self: Mothers, Daughters, Subjects* (London: Routledge, 2000)

Laing, R. D., *Self and Others* (Middlesex: Penguin, 1987)

Lemert, C., & Branaman, A., *The Goffman Reader* (Cambridge, Mass: Blackwell, 1997)

Lepselter, S., 'Why Rachel Isn't Buried in her Grave: Ghosts, UFOs and a Place in the West' Rosenberg, D., & Harding, S., eds., from *Histories of the Future* (Durham, NC: Duke University Press, 2005)

Lewis, L., *The Adoring Audience: Fan Culture and Popular Media* (London: Routledge, 1992)

Light, A., *Forever England* (London: Routledge, 1991)

Lindholm, C., *Charisma* (Oxford: Blackwell, 1990)

Llewelyn Davis, M., *Life As We Have Known It* (London: Virago, 1982)

Lowenthal, D., *The Past is a Foreign Country* (Cambridge: Cambridge University Press, 1985)

Malcolm, J., *In the Freud Archives* (London: Jonathan Cape, 1984)

Malcolm, J., *The Silent Woman* (New York: Alfred A Knopf, 1994)

Margry, P. J., 'The Pilgrimage to Jim Morrison's Grave at Père Lachaise: The Social Construction of Sacred Space' in *Shrines and Pilgrimages in the Modern World* (Amsterdam: Amsterdam University Press, 2008)

Marx, K., ed., Martyn J Lee 'The Fetishism of the Commodity and its Secret' in *The Consumer Society Reader* (Oxford: Blackwells, 2000)

Miles, M., 'Ghostly Pasts, Spectral Futures' in Hetherington, Kevin, ed., *Spatial Hauntings Space and Culture*. Issue 11–12 December 2001.

Miller, N. K., 'Putting Ourselves in the Picture: Memoirs and Mourning' in Hirsch, Marianne, ed., *The Familial Gaze* (Hanover and London: Dartmouth College, University Press of New England, 1999)

Min, S., 'Remains to be Seen' in Eng, D. L. & Davis, K., *Loss: The Politics of Mourning* (Berkeley, Los Angeles, London: Univeristy of California Press, 2003)

Moses, K., *Wintering* (New York: St Martin's, 2003)

Mulvey, L., *Visual and Other Pleasures* (Basingstoke: Houndsmill, 1989)

Newman, C., *The Art of Sylvia Plath: A Symposium* (London: Faber & Faber, 1970)

Nickell, J., *Looking for a Miracle* (New York: Prometheus Books, 1993)

Noll, R., *The Aryan Christ* on line at www.dhustara.com/book/jung.archr.htm, 1997 accessed 22/08/09

Pearce, L., *Feminism and the Politics of Reading* (London: Arnold, 1997)

Pearce, L., *The Rhetorics of Feminism* (London: Routledge, 2004)

Pearce, L., *Romance Writing* (Cambridge: Polity Press, 2007)

Pearce, L., and Jackie Stacey, eds., *Romance Revisited* (New York & London: New York University Press, 1995)

Rabinow, P., ed., *The Foucault Reader* (New York: Pantheon Books, 1984)

Ragland, E., *Essays on the Pleasures of Death* (London, New York: Routledge, 1995)

Rank, O., *The Double: A Psychoanalytic Study* (Chapel Hill: University of North Carolina Press, 1971)

Reader, I., & Tony Walter, *Pilgrimage in Popular Culture* (Basingstoke, Hampshire: Palgrave, 1993)

Reece, G., *Elvis Religion: The Cult of the King* (London: I. B. Tauris, 2006)

Robins, K., *Into the Image* (London: Routledge, 1996)

Rojek, C., *Ways of Escape* (Basingstoke: MacMillan Press, 1993)

Rojek, C., *Celebrity* (London: Reaktion Books, 2001)

Rose, J., *Sexuality and Field of Vision* (London: Verso, 1989)

Rose, J., *The Haunting of Sylvia Plath* (London: Virago, 1991)

Samuel, R., *Theatres of Memory* (London: Verso, 1994)

Sandvoss, C., *Fans* (Cambridge: Polity Press, 2005)

Santas, G., *Plato & Freud: Two Theories of Love* (Oxford: Basil Blackwell, 1988)

Scott, J., 'Experience' in Butler, J., & Scott, J., eds., *Feminists Theorize the Political* (London: Routledge, 1992)

Secomb, L., *Philosophy and Love: From Plato to Popular Culture* (Edinburgh: Edinburgh University Press, 2007)

Shackley, M., *Managing Sacred Sites* (London: Continuum, 2001)

Sheller, M., & John Urry, *Tourism Mobilities* (London: Routledge, 2004)

Showalter, E., *Hystories* (London: Picador, 1997)

Skeggs, B., *Feminist Cultural Theory* (Manchester: Manchester University Press, 1995)

Smith, J., *Different for Girls* (London: Chatto & Windus, 1997)

Sontag, S., *On Photography* (New York: Farrar, Straus & Giroux, 1977)

Spence, J., & Holland, P., eds., *Family Snaps* (London: Virago, 1991)

Stacey, J., 'The lost audience: methodology, cinema history and feminist film criticism.' in Beverley Skeggs, *Feminist Cultural Theory* (Manchester: Manchester University Press, 1995)

Stacey, J., *Star gazing: Hollywood Cinema and Female Spectatorship* (London: Routledge, 1994)

Steedman, C., *Landscape for a Good Woman* (London: Virago, 1986)

Steedman, C., *Dust* (Manchester: Manchester University Press, 2001)

Steinberg, P. K., 'I should be loving this: Sylvia Plath's "The Perfect Place" and "The Bell Jar."' in *Plath Profiles*, Vol. 1, Summer, Indiana University, 2008.

Stewart, K., *A Space on the Side of the Road. Cultural Poetics in an "Other" America* (Princeton University Press: Princeton, New Jersey, 1996)

Stewart, S., *On Longing* (Baltimore: John Hopkins University Press, 1993)

Stiebal, L. (undated) Literary Tourism www.literarytourism.co.za/index.php/News/ Going-on-literary-pilgrimage-developing-literary-trails-in-South-Africa.html [accessed 18/05/09].

Sturken, S., 'The Image as Memorial: Personal Photographs in Cultural Memory.' in Hirsch, Marianne, ed., *The Familial Gaze* (Hanover and London: Dartmouth College, University Press of New England, 1999)

Sudjic, D., *Cult Heroes* (London: Andre Deutsch Limited, 1989)

Trinh T. M., *Framer Framed* (London: Routledge, 1992)

Thomas, L., *Fans, Feminism and 'Quality' Media* (London: Routledge, 2002)

Thouless, R., *Buddhist and Freudian Psychology* (Singapore: NUS Press, 1992)

Thurschwell, P., *Sigmund Freud* (London: Routledge, 2000)

Wagner, E., *Ariel's Gift* (London: Faber & Faber, 2000)

Wagner-Martin, L., *Sylvia Plath The Critical Heritage* (London: Routledge, 1988b)

Walkerdine, V., *Schoolgirl Fictions* (London: Verso, 1990)

Weedon, C., *Feminist Practice and Poststructuralist Theory* (Oxford: Basil Blackwell, 1987)

Williamson, J., *Decoding Advertisements: Ideology and Meaning in Advertising* (London: Boyors, 1978)

Wilson, E., *Only Halfway To Paradise* (London: Tavistock Publications, 1980)

Wilson, E., *Mirror Writing* (London: Virago, 1982)

Wilson, F., *Literary Seductions: Compulsive Writers and Diverted Readers* (London: Faber and Faber, 1999)

Winter, J., *Sites of Memory, Sites of Mourning* (Cambridge: Canto Press, 1998)

Wolff, J., *The Sociological Image* Talk given at Lancaster University, 2007

Wolfreys, J., *Victorian Hauntings: Spectrality, Gothic, the Uncanny & Literature* (Basingstoke: Palgrave, 2002)

Wright, E., *Feminism and Psychoanalysis A Critical Dictionary* (Oxford: Blackwell, 1992)

Young, R., *Untying the Text: A Post-structuralist Reader* (London & New York: Routledge, 1987)

Young-Bruehl, E., *Subject to Biography: Psychoanalysis, Feminism and Writing Women's Lives* (Cambridge and London: Harvard University Press, 1998)

Websites

www.sylviaplath.info—Peter K. Steinberg's Plath information web site.

www.sylviaplathinfo.blogspot.co.uk—Peter K. Steinberg's Plath blog.

www.sylviaplathforum.com—archives for this discussion forum were founded by Elaine Connell.

www.hollywood-underground.com—web site for graveyard tourism in Hollywood.

www.28dayslater.co.uk—urban exploration website.

www.urbexforums.co.uk—urban exploration website.

www.sickbritain.co.uk—urban exploration website.

Index